An Incredible
Journey

The lost world of the 1930s
circled by two men in one small car

MAX REISCH

Also from Veloce Publishing –

Armstrong-Siddeley (Smith)
Art Deco and British Car Design (Down)
Bluebird CN7 (Stevens)
Bonjour – Is this Italy? (Turner)
Carrera Panamericana, La (Tipler)
Daily Mirror 1970 World Cup Rally 40, The (Robson)
Dorset from the Sea – The Jurassic Coast from Lyme Regis to Old Harry Rocks photographed from its
best viewpoint (also Souvenir Edition) (Belasco)
Drive on the Wild Side, A – 20 Extreme Driving Adventures From Around the World (Weaver)
East German Motor Vehicles in Pictures (Suhr/Weinreich)
Fate of the Sleeping Beauties, The (op de Weegh/Hottendorff/op de Weegh)
France: the essential guide for car enthusiasts – 200 things for the car enthusiast to see and do (Parish)
From Crystal Palace to Red Square – A Hapless Biker's Road to Russia (Turner)
Montlhéry, The Story of the Paris Autodrome (Boddy)
Motor Racing Heroes – The Stories of 100 Greats (Newman)
Off-Road Giants! (Volume 1) – Heroes of 1960s Motorcycle Sport (Westlake)
Off-Road Giants! (Volume 2) – Heroes of 1960s Motorcycle Sport (Westlake)
Off-Road Giants! (volume 3) – Heroes of 1960s Motorcycle Sport (Westlake)
Peking to Paris (Young)
Preston Tucker & Others (Linde)
Roads with a View – England's greatest views and how to find them by road (Corfield)
Russian Motor Vehicles – Soviet Limousines 1930-2003 (Kelly)
Russian Motor Vehicles – The Czarist Period 1784 to 1917 (Kelly)
Sleeping Beauties USA – abandoned classic cars & trucks (Marek)
This Day in Automotive History (Corey)

www.veloce.co.uk

First published in 1984 by W Ennsthaler, Austria. ISBN: 978-3-850681-76-6
This edition first published in October 2017 by Veloce Publishing Limited, Veloce House, Parkway Farm
Business Park, Middle Farm Way, Poundbury, Dorchester DT1 3AR, England. Fax 01305 250479 / e-mail
info@veloce.co.uk / web www.veloce.co.uk or www.velocebooks.com.
ISBN: 978-1-787111-65-3 UPC: 6-36847-01165-9

An Incredible
Journey

The lost world of the 1930s
circled by two men in one small car

MAX REISCH

VELOCE PUBLISHING
THE PUBLISHER OF FINE AUTOMOTIVE BOOKS

Contents

Prefaces 6

Chapter 1 Bitter pills, new plans...........9
Examination pressure – A new project – The chairman
makes a proposal9

Chapter 2 Four wheels 12
Learning to drive – Finding the co-driver: Helmuth
Hahmann – Bodywork to my own design – A quantity
of luggage

Chapter 3 The oil road to Baghdad...... 23
By the Dead Sea – Guests of the Iraq Petroleum
Company – A desert party in H2

Chapter 4 The lizard hunt 30
Temptations in Baghdad – Remodelling the car –
Hunters and hunted – Stuck in the sand – A nod in the
right direction

**Chapter 5 Where the dead crowd
close to Allah** 35
A trip to An Najaf – City of the dead: wet and dry
corpses – Familiar tunes – A serious injury: my lucky star
– High roads to Persia

Chapter 6 Dust to dust....................... 41
The tomb of Omar Khayyam – Awkward guests
– Persia's poet: Firdowsi

Chapter 7 Foreign devils 46
Eastern Persia: underground villages – Mashhad: the
dangers of photography – Helmuth in jail – An unwise
jest

Chapter 8 Urlajat............................... 55
A visa for Afghanistan – At the customs post: rough
companions and a friendly host – The rules of
hospitality – Confusing coinage – Afghan transport

**Chapter 9 Hungarian Afghans,
Bavarian Afghans**............................. 60
Among the harvesters – Windmills – Six-legged donkeys
– Robbers in chains – An engineer from Budapest – No
salami – Numskull understands

Chapter 10 Closer to India 76
Along the Northwest Frontier – From Kabul to the
ruins of Bamiyan – A permit for the Khyber Pass
– In the British fort – Curfew at Peshawar – A film
location – Cholera inoculations – In the Bibi bazaar

Chapter 11 Kashmir 81
In Alexander's footsteps – A houseboat in
Srinagar – The ascent to Amarnath tent camp – The
pilgrims of Shiva

Chapter 12 End of the first stage 86
Monsoon rains – We rescue the German consul –
Return to Vaikunth – European drinking habits – The
plight of the half-caste – A lecture in the Hindu
University of Lucknow

**Chapter 13 The land of the smiling
Buddha**...100
The trouble with travellers – Land of smiles – The
Buddha of Pegu – A missionary priest – We collide with
a vulture – Benighted in the Burmese jungle

Chapter 14 The Agency comes to call..111
With the Burmah Oil Company – Temporary marriages
– No room in the car

Chapter 15 Deep in the jungle 115
Beyond Mandalay – Into the Golden triangle – Burmese
hospitality – The versatile bamboo – The Dak bungalow

Chapter 16 Folk festival at Inle lake....119
The leg-rowers of Inle – Strange adornments: Red
Kareni and Padaung women – Concepts of time

Chapter 17 Special delivery..............123
Letters for Keng-Tung – An improvised dictionary – By
cart trail to Thailand – A night by the river – Crossing
the Salween – Rescued from a torrent – Up to the axles
in mud – Fever – The 'wanted poster'

**Chapter 18 Dead prince and
living prince**....................................132
The Sawbwa of Keng-Tung – Tung oil – Hauled by an
elephant

Chapter 19 Honour the yellow robe 136
Rainy season in Keng-Tung – How to smoke opium
– Helmuth's holiday: a Buddhist monastery and a night-
time festival – Tauma Tillee and the typewriter

Chapter 20 Laughing with Simba 144
Half a bridge to Siam – Chieng-Rai – Simba's rattletrap
– A skilled driver – The differential breaks

Chapter 21 Two motorcycle fiends 161
Borrowing a BSA – A boxing match – The car is
dismantled – By boat down the Mekong – Into Laos –
The French customs officer

Chapter 22 Success at last.................166
Luang-Prabang – Unloaded by convicts – A parcel from
Austria – Modified rapture – The car is rebuilt – The
golden Buddha – Pioneers of Route Coloniale Numéro
Sept – Late for dinner – We reach Hanoi

Chapter 23 Held up in Hanoi.............180
The ball-bearing visa – A rail excursion to Yunnan-
fu – The Michelin Railcar – How to get to
China – Misleading maps – Sounds of gunfire – Back
to Hanoi – The effects of damp – Over the Red River –
Into China with the French consul

Chapter 24 Old Mr Lai Shi 187
An arms dealer in Nan-ning – A tooth extraction – The
comforts of rice wine – Presenting ourselves in
China – Hot wheels to Liu-chou – The advantages of
Latin

**Chapter 25 Motor car versus
evil spirits..193**
Life is cheap – Proper terms of address – The effects of
a full beard – Behaviour of pedestrians explained

Chapter 26 In China it's different 197
A hazardous river-crossing – An invasion of evil spirits
– Franciscans from South Tyrol – A roast dinner – The
first car in Chi-Yang

Chapter 27 A war zone......................203
Crossing the Hsiang-Kiang – Germans in Chang-sha
– The boat not taken – Encounter with an army –
Driving through road-blocks – An opium war

Chapter 28 What Marco Polo saw.......225
King-te-chen: town of porcelain – Beauties of
Hangchow

Chapter 29 Shanghai 228
Driving on the Bund – Signing chits – The international
press – The high life of Shanghai – Sacrifice of the
beard

**Chapter 30 Problems for the foreign
visitor 233**
Crossing to Japan – Customs hold-up in Nagasaki – A
traditional guest-house – Dangers of the bath – Geishas
– A driving test and a vehicle check – Permission to
travel – We break a record

**Chapter 31 'Yuku michi' in the
land of delights 243**
Landscapes of Hondo – The island of temples – An
American tourist – The year of flowers – Poor state
of the roads – Politeness of drivers – No motoring
atlas – Place names – A helpful lorry driver –
Streetlighting

Chapter 32 The long goodbye 249
The volcano Aso-san – Repeated interrogations –
View of Mount Fuji – Rucksacku rucksacku – Rained
off – Meeting with a film director – A mention in
the newspapers – An excursion by train – We sail for
America

Chapter 33 Crossing America............255
Entry formalities in Seattle – With Charlie to Mount
Rainier – A forest fire – A ski pro in Yosemite – Death
Valley

Chapter 34 The collector...................269
The Greyhound buses – On show in Dallas – A
tempting offer

**Chapter 35 Mexico to Salzburg:
disaster strikes!...............................272**
Breakdown in Mexico – The technical genius of
Mr Blair – Forty hours at the wheel – With Ford in
Detroit – Washington and New York – We sail on the
Bremen – A leathery tan – A dramatic ending

**Chapter 36 Epilogue: the story
continues 277**
The survival of the Steyr 100 and its post-war career
– A word from the author's son

Appendix 278

Index..287

Preface to the German language Centenary edition

Dr Max Reisch, pioneer long-distance traveller, writer and transport geographer, was born on 2nd October 1912. Travel was his life's passion, with a special preference for the Orient, Arabia, and East Asia.

His expeditions by motorcycle and motorcar were already legendary in his lifetime, with the success of his first trip to North Africa in 1932. Max Reisch wrote many books describing his expeditions. The two most successful ones are lavishly illustrated with photographs and have been on sale in bookshops for decades.

The account originally entitled *Transasien* has been available in German since 1939, and was revised with many illustrations under the title *Im Auto um die Erde* (upon which this translation is based). The travel book *Indien: lockende Ferne*, describing the motorcycle journey from Vienna to Bombay in 1933, has been continuously in print in German since 1949. (For details of books and English translations, see https://en.wikipedia.org/wiki/Max_Reisch. The official Max Reisch website, www.maxreisch.at, is in German, but does contain links to all editions of Reisch books.)

Max Reisch charmed his public not only as an author, but also as a skilled lecturer. Several films have been made celebrating the travels of this well-known Austrian: *Auf den Spuren von Sven Hedin* (In the Footsteps of Sven Hedin), *Bis ans Ende der Welt* (To the Ends of the Earth), *Ein Leben im Reisefieber* (A Passion for Travel), and *Max Reisch – Autopionier* (Max Reisch – Motoring Pioneer).

His life's journey ended in 1985, but his unique style still captures the imagination of new generations, who jump on board to follow his adventures.

Peter H Reisch, July 2012

Preface to this edition

As the son of Dr Max Reisch, I have great pleasure in writing the preface to this book, and in providing some of the background to the exciting story of my father's journey.

My father's passion for discovering more about unknown regions of the world through long-distance travel provided the Steyr works with a welcome opportunity to send its newly-developed motor car – the Steyr 100 Type – on a spectacular trial run, and in 1935 it offered him a car for the purpose.

The Steyr-Werke had its origins in the Österreichische Waffenfabriks-Gesellschaft, which produced high-quality rifles and pistols, exporting them all over the world. However, even before the end of the First World War, the company realised that it would be necessary to vary output with the addition of other high-quality products, and this led to the famous 'Waffenrad,' or army bicycle. These bicycles were of the highest quality, so tough as to be virtually indestructible. For nearly 100 years they remained on the production list of the Waffenfabrik and the companies which succeeded it, namely the Steyr-Werke and Steyr-Daimler-Puch AG. After the end of the First World War, motorcar production was started in the plant built at Steyr in the last years of the war, beginning with the Type II, IV, VI and VII models developed by Professor Hans Ledwinka and the successful Steyr Type XII built in the mid-1920s.

The catastrophic conditions created by the world economic crisis of the 1930s made it necessary for the Steyr-Werke to join forces with the Österreichische-Daimler-Motorenwerke and the Puch-Werke (which had already merged in 1927) in order to have any chance of surviving as a large-scale enterprise. Founded in 1934/35, Steyr-Daimler-Puch AG produced cars, heavy goods vehicles and cross country vehicles at the big motor plant in Steyr, Upper Austria, where it continued to operate successfully with a mixed output right up to the 1980s.

From 1987, Steyr-Daimler-Puch AG was sold off to nine different foreign companies active worldwide. In 1998, the remainder of the group, comprising the vehicle and drive technology divisions, was sold to Frank Stronach's Magna International, and since 2001 it has functioned as an independent subsidiary of the Magna organisation.

The Steyr 100 used by Max Reisch on this journey was a forward-looking design in the early 1930s. This completely new type of motor car was characterised by the streamlined bodywork, swing axles, thermo-siphon cooling, dynostarter, central lubrication, and much more, which, together with its succeeding models (the 120, 200 and 220 Types), allowed the Steyr-Daimler-Puch AG a particularly successful run of car production up until the Second World War.

For the purposes of the expedition, the Steyr 100 was fitted with special bodywork as requested by Max Reisch. On dirt roads, on tracks and on trails that could scarcely be called roads at all, the strengths (and weaknesses) of the Steyr 100 became evident.

Although the original journey was only planned as far as Shanghai, the success of the run led to its being extended to a round-the-world trip. After a journey of 19 months, packed with incident and not a little adventure, Max Reisch and the Steyr 100 arrived back in Austria, safe and sound, in December 1936.

1
BITTER PILLS,
NEW PLANS

So, at last I was a celebrity. I'd been to the Sahara and then, the year after that, to India in the tracks of Alexander the Great. However, I had been the first man to do this on a motorcycle. The press had hailed this as a pioneer achievement for world transport, and Bruno Dietrich, university Professor of Transport Economics at the Hochschule für Welthandel (College for World Trade) in Vienna, was well satisfied with the results of both expeditions.

The college porter greeted me warmly on my return, and took to dropping useful hints such as, "Professor X is in a good mood. Go for the viva today. You can't fail!"

Nor did I, but I scraped through that exam (and the one after) only by sheer luck. I soon realised that, in the long run, luck won't last without hard work. The janitor may drop hints, and the girls do their best to prompt their 'famous' fellow student, but all this counted for nothing when my knowledge was so sketchy that I ploughed in spite of all their help.

A couple of spectacular failures brought me back down to earth from my Indian heaven. One experience in particular showed me how hard it was to serve two masters. I couldn't ride round the world *and* keep up with my coursework – the two things were incompatible.

I had a special aversion to the Merchandise course, and I had scarcely attended a single lecture. My limited knowledge of the subject had been gathered from the crammer in the college café, but, armed with what I knew, I presented myself for the examination. In the ante-room of the Institute for Merchandise Studies stood a man wearing an overall, and stacking books on a shelf – evidently one of the college servants.

"Can I speak to the Professor, please?"

"Yes. What do you want?"

"I'd like to present myself for examination."

"Indeed. What is your name?"

I told him, rather self-consciously. After all, I was the one who had been to the Sahara and to India. I was slightly annoyed, too. As a servant it was none of his business. I wanted to speak to the Professor.

"Well, well. So you want to present yourself for examination? I'll tell you something, Mr Clever-clogs Reisch. If you are supposed to have sat through my lectures for a whole semester and still don't recognise me, the best advice I can give you is to go away and come back in six months at the very earliest."

This unhappy experience even made the university rag week magazine, and everyone found it hilarious, except me. To raise my morale I got busy with plans for a new travel project – "By motorcycle to China." It wasn't really all that far. Following the great caravan route through Asia, which runs south of the Himalaya from the Mediterranean to the China Sea, I had already covered half the distance on the land journey to India. Now it was time to do the second half, from India to China. As Professor Dietrich, who had encouraged my previous plans from the scientific angle, said: "An interesting project in transport geography! The object would be to avoid the long sea route round Singapore and to look for a road link between the Indian subcontinent and China through the top of Southeast Asia."

I was so inspired that I used the documentation available in the Institute to produce a plan, one to whet the appetites of those directors of the Steyr-Daimler-Puch company who would have to come up with the money. It was a handsomely bound brochure with maps, diagrams, estimates of time and costs, all designed to excite their interest.

I would have preferred to present and explain the project myself, but the secretariat informed me that the director was away on business. Would I be so good as to send in everything on paper? I was not at all keen on this, as it would probably mean getting just a short impersonal letter back: "We very much regret, etc." There was a real danger of this, as we were actually in the middle of a serious economic crisis.

However, I had no choice. I sent it all in on paper, but before I did so I revised the whole plan, making it sharper, more precise, more confident, with a higher estimate of the cost. Then I waited. It took a while, during which time I grew extremely impatient with all professors and directors, with God and the world in general, and with myself. My conscience began to plague me. Had I said something stupid at one of my slide-shows or in a newspaper interview? I had already been advised to be more circumspect during my impromptu lectures. For example, I had once made a cutting remark about the consular secretary in Baghdad, and the Shah of Persia had lodged a protest through his emissaries in Vienna, concerning the picture of a camel caravan outside the Persian ministry of justice in Tehran. Apparently this was an outrageous slur, seeing that Persia was now modern and that there were no camels on the streets of the Persian metropolis! Had I said something wrong concerning my trusty 'India Puch' motorcycle? The spokes had snapped, the saddle springs had broken, and I had said so. I had also, quite forcefully, presented the case for a four-speed gearbox and rear-wheel suspension. Had I said anything else to bring the work of the Austrian craftsman into disrepute?

I wasn't aware of any transgression, but the nagging doubt persisted.

At last the answer came, but not from the Managing Director. What was this? I had to read it twice before I grasped it.

"The Chairman will be expecting you for a discussion on October 2nd at 3pm."

This was an ominous missive. Should I be glad? Or was I to receive a dressing down from the highest authority? After such a long wait, my conscience nagged me even more.

3.10pm. "The Chairman will see you now." How awful it sounded!

I have read about dictators whose offices take such a long time to walk through that the whole approach amounts to a ritual humiliation. I had much the same experience. I seemed to be getting smaller and smaller. "You fool!" I said to myself, "You shouldn't have raised the cost of the trip, you should have reduced it!"

Then, as if from a great distance, I heard a voice.

"We found the results of your journey to India most gratifying."

I bowed silently.

"However, our motorcycle has now had enough publicity." The Chairman paused dramatically (causing my heart to plummet decisively to my boots), and then continued, "Does it have to be a motorcycle? Is there any reason why you should not take a car?"

The Chairman's 'any reason' made me think.

Well, was there any reason?

I pulled myself together and said, "But that would be a splendid plan. Beyond my wildest dreams!"

The Chairman smiled. "We see things from a wider perspective. We are very concerned with our new model, the Steyr 100, and we want to prove its worth to the rest of the world. Would you be capable of driving our new model through China?"

"Yes, Mr Chairman." (It was like a fairytale!)

"Shall we say double the sum you suggest in your outline?"

"Yes, Mr Chairman." (Things like this only happen in films!)

"We value the standard product, so there must be no mechanical alterations. The man in the street must feel that he could drive his Steyr 100 to China too."

"Yes, Mr Chairman."

"When will you want to leave?"

"In May," I said, off the top of my head, not wanting to appear indecisive.

"Good. Until then we shall provide you with a saloon version of our new model so that you can familiarise yourself with the car. You'll discuss everything else with Director X, Director Y and Engineer Z. Good luck!"

The interview had lasted about ten minutes. I staggered out of the conference room with my head in a whirl – by car to China, I'd raised the cost of the trip and they'd doubled it, a saloon car for my personal use!

By car from the Mediterranean to the Yellow Sea!

Easier than by motorcycle, or harder?

I couldn't say.

2
FOUR WHEELS

I was still in a daze, and didn't know whether to be happy or not. In the Ressel Park behind the Steyr-Daimler-Puch AG administration building I was assailed by conflicting ideas. Cheer up (went one of them), this time you won't get your knees skinned or burn your calves on the hot exhaust pipe, and you can take as much luggage as you want, right down to the tennis racket! You're a heel (went another), didn't that good and faithful motorcycle take you all the way to India? Wasn't it a real friend to you? And now you're leaving it in the lurch! This was a particularly painful thought, as I was in love with my motorcycle, with the many shared memories and with its powerful language. I could tell everything from the sound of its voice – whether the engine was too hot or too cold, whether it was working cheerfully or reluctantly, whether the petrol was good or bad, or whether it was beginning to suffer from some secret malaise. And now I was about to exchange my talking motorcycle for a taciturn car. This was a novelty for me, and a bit weird, quite apart from the fact that I couldn't even drive!

I could ride a motorcycle, but the car was a big question mark, and in a few months I was meant to be driving it to China.

The Chairman must have had considerable faith in me. He probably reasoned that a car and a motorcycle are basically the same thing. Many readers of this book will share this opinion, but it was never mine. I tried to adapt myself, but all the same, I made several basic mistakes that gave me trouble on the trip. The details will be evident later on.

As I wandered through the Ressel Park that autumn day, with doubt gnawing away at me, I saw in my mind's eye the expedition car in the desert, in the jungle, in China, and finally, the happy homecoming. Hadn't I been born under a lucky star, as my mother always said? Had it been only coincidence that the Chairman had summoned me today of all days, October 2nd, my birthday?

I had plenty to do in the months that followed. As for my studies, by some miracle the penny dropped and I passed one exam after another. Soon I had taken my driving test and was practising diligently. It really was a joke – fancy being entrusted with a motor car expedition without being able to drive!

The saloon car that the Chairman provided for me to 'practise' on was the last word in automobile engineering: a robust engine (four-cylinder, 1360cc, 32hp) on a very sturdy frame with swing axles on all wheels, hydraulic brakes, and central

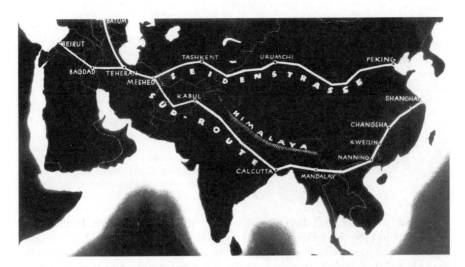

Above: In ancient and medieval times, the Silk Road and the southerly route permitted the exchange of goods and ideas between western countries and the Far East. These famous caravan roads are now open to motor traffic.

Below: 1933: The first motorcycle to cover the land route to India. The famous India Puch was shown at many exhibitions at home and abroad. The new project was designed to conquer the route from India to China, but the company Chairman saw no point in another motorcycle trip. Instead, we were to take the new Steyr car and drive across Asia by the southerly route.

Our brief was "From the Mediterranean to the Yellow Sea." We then continued right around the world. The brand new A2020, pictured here, has as yet no inkling of all the problems we would face together on the 40,000km journey. Technical data: four cylinder engine, 1385cc, 6/32 horsepower, four-speed gearbox, with swing axles to front and rear, chassis and engine both straight off the production line (as strictly required by the makers) – "The man in the street must feel that he could drive his Steyr 100 to China, too." The bodywork was a special conversion, which turned out to be too heavy, and had to be altered in Baghdad. The car had three seats with the centre one set slightly back, giving all three passengers a comfortable space. Behind each of the outside seats was a storage compartment. In the luggage space behind were stowed containers for water, petrol and oil, tinned food, camp beds and personal belongings.

lubrication. Pressure on one pedal was enough to oil all the joints simultaneously. The bodywork was the first mass-produced streamlined body in the world and the two doors on either side were not constricted by any central post. The Hunderter Steyer was a work of genius, designed at the Steyr works by the engineer Jentschke, who had trained under Porsche.

For the expedition, I had asked the works to provide the chassis only. As for the body, I wanted to build it according to my own ideas. I did away with the running boards (which were the norm in those days, and which limited the breadth of the passenger space) and I used the whole width to install three seats in a row. Nearly in a row, it would be fairer to say, as the middle seat was set back by about a quarter of a metre. This gave more shoulder room for all three, besides allowing enough space for the legs of the passenger on the middle seat in spite of the gear-stick and brake handle. Another result of this arrangement was that behind the outer seats it was possible to fit two very useful compartments for odds and ends. I dispensed with the idea of doors altogether. Instead there were, to my eyes, two very elegant cut-outs in the sides of the vehicle on which I worked long and lovingly to design the perfect curve, making it just possible to get in and out in comfort. The whole thing rather resembled a Jeep, as people later remarked, but of course the Jeep was not invented until five years after this.

Why three seats? This was so we could take on board a companion or interpreter from time to time. We even had an American doctor along with us for a while.

In the back of the car there was plenty of room for water tanks, cans of petrol, spare parts and personal luggage. There was rather too much space available, so that after the limitations of the two motorcycle journeys, I was seduced into losing my sense of proportion and packed all sorts of luxuries that I now deemed permissible. Problems ensued, as the car was now heavily overloaded with spare parts and personal effects. This fatal error could well have scuppered the expedition.

Tel Aviv: There were more camels than automobiles on the streets of the newly-built city.

But let's return to the smart saloon and my driving practice. I did not dare turn up in front of the university in this luxury car. I parked it in a nearby side street and walked the last few hundred metres like a good boy, since I did not wish to arouse the envy or even the resentment of the lecturers and professors. At that time, the price of the car was 7000 Austrian schillings, and only high earners could afford one. A tram ride cost 12 groschen, and lunch in the university canteen cost 90 groschen. I remember quite distinctly that none of the professors owned a car. I was the only one, and (understandably) I didn't let anyone know, except of course my travelling companion Helmuth Hahmann. He was a very skilled mechanic, who had cared enough to take a special training course at the Steyr works. This proved to be absolutely indispensable later on, as the differential broke no fewer than three

Above & below: Palestine 1935 – Even in those days there was a sharp contrast between orthodox Jews and modern Arabs. Has the pendulum swung the other way today?

times – once when we were only in Arabia, then in the jungle in Thailand, and for the third time in Mexico. Helmuth mastered these repairs – which on a swing-axle car are very difficult – and also the ongoing maintenance of the vehicle in an exemplary fashion. For that I thank him, and for conscientiously keeping the log and for lending me his diaries, which have clarified many details and enriched the present account. He also lent me his films, so that eventually, in 1983, the ÖAMTC

LÉGATION
DE LA
RÉPUBLIQUE FRANÇAISE
EN AUTRICHE

VIENNE, LE   5 Février 1935

Le Ministre de la République Française en
Autriche a l'honneur de recommander particulièrement
au bienveillant accueil des Autorités Civiles et Militaires Françaises dans les États du Levant sous mandat
français, ainsi qu'aux Autorités dépendant du Gouvernement Général de l'Indo-Chine, M. Max Reisch, de nationali
té autrichienne, qui effectue en automobile un voyage
d'études à travers l'Asie.

M. Reisch est muni d'équipements de campe-
ment ainsi que d'appareils cinématographiques et photo-
graphiques. Il a déclaré n'être point porteur d'armes.

M. Reisch, dont l'expédition bénéficie
de l'appui du Gouvernement Fédéral d'Autriche, est per-
sonnellement et favorablement connu de la Légation./.

Aux Autorités Civiles et Militaires
Françaises dans les États du Levant
sous Mandat français.

Preparations: In response to the request of the Austrian Foreign Ministry, each of the fourteen states we traversed provided us with their highest recommendations and also informed the diplomatic representatives in the individual countries, so that they all knew we were coming. Note the specific reference to the fact that no arms were to be carried on the expedition. Further preparations included the setting up of depots for tyres, spares and fuel at particular locations.

(Austrian Automobile and Motorcycle Touring Club) was able to produce from our combined footage the new film (with soundtrack) *Auf den Spuren von Sven Hedin* (In the Tracks of Sven Hedin).

I had always looked up to Hedin, the great Swedish geographer, and we followed in his tracks on the first part of our journey. It was he, and of course my Trade and Transport Geography teacher, Professor Bruno Dietrich, who inspired my journeys and helped to get them off the ground.

So my brief, as Chairman Götzl had put it, was simply to take the new Type 100 and drive it straight across Asia, from the Mediterranean to the Yellow Sea. What the gods were not telling us was that, after Shanghai, this would turn into a journey around the world. For the 'Transasia Expedition' from Haifa to Shanghai, a distance of around 23,000km, I had counted on taking nine months. This became fourteen, and in the end the whole round-the-world trip lasted nineteen months: to be precise, from 23rd April 1935 to 7th December 1936.

Luckily there was a lot we didn't know this time, in particular that we were going to need half a year for Southeast Asia alone. However, this was in any case the very first crossing of Burma and the Shan States (Golden Triangle), Thailand, Laos and modern Vietnam.

Above: A British aerial photograph, taken in 1935, of the big oasis town of Karbala, the next greatest Shi'ite shrine in Iraq after Nadjaf.

Below: Desert people are always ready to help. They know subconsciously that they might be the next ones to need assistance. Digging out the car on the way to the holy Shi'ite desert shrine of Nadjaf.

Main image: Sandstorm in the Syrian desert between Damascus and Baghdad. The air is charged with electricity, unnerving humans and animals alike. All at once, the sinister wall of sand rolls forward at high speed. Camels huddle together, caravan drivers wrap up tightly in their burnouses and lie under blankets, sheltered by their bales of goods. If there is no oasis within reach, the car driver must turn his vehicle's nose into the storm and wait.

Right: This was the desert spiny-tail bagged by Helmuth Hahmann on the way from Baghdad to An Nadjaf. Herodotus called these creatures 'land crocodiles.'

Left: These enormous water wheels on the Tigris scoop up water in small clay jars. Aqueducts convey the water to the gardens.

Below: A summer custom in Baghdad was to travel upstream by motor boat and swim back down with the current in the relatively cool waters. This was how I had my accident, reported (with some exaggeration) in the press back home. The expedition suffered too, since our sponsors thought I had taken an unnecessary risk.

Wiener Neueste Nachrichten   Dienstag, den 18. Juni 1935

Max Reisch in Bagdad schwer verunglückt

Der bekannte österreichische Motorsportler Max Reisch, der sich auf einer österreichischen Transasien-expedition zur Autodurchquerung Asiens befindet, ist in Bagdad schwer verunglückt.

Reisch badete am 10. d. M. im Tigris und wurde von einem schwimmenden Baumstamm, mit dem er unter Wasser zusammenstieß, am Oberschenkel so schwer verletzt, daß er nach großem Blutverlust in das städtische Spital gebracht werden mußte. Ueber Veranlassung des österreichischen Konsuls wurde Reisch von den besten Bagdader Aerzten behandelt.

Reisch mußte sich einer Operation unterziehen und wird vermutlich noch einige Wochen in Spitalspflege bleiben müssen.

In den ersten Tagen war sein Zustand sehr ernst, doch ist nunmehr jede Gefahr vorbei.

Max Reisch ist einer der jüngsten Pioniere des österreichischen Sports, der seine sportlichen Reisen mit wissenschaftlichen Exkursionen verbindet.

In der ganzen Welt bekannt, wurde der junge Wiener Sportler durch seine kühne Motorradreise nach Indien, die er vor Jahresfrist mit seinem Kollegen, dem Wiener Studenten Herbert Tichy, unternahm.

Left: The horse-drawn tram from Baghdad to Kadimain, which operated up until 1946.

Right: Towers for the disposal of corpses in the Valley of Death by the desert city of Tadmor (Palmyra), where once Queen Zenobia reigned.

Main image: The old centre of Baghdad, where Haroun al Rashid once walked in disguise to eavesdrop on his subjects.

Above: The beginnings of motor transport. The small Model TT Ford 'lorries' were grossly overloaded, but room could always be found for a few passengers.

Right: Caravan guide in the Syrian desert. The desert scene was still dominated by camel caravans and their confident guides.

Below: Our gramophone in the desert. This tiny fold-up gramophone, which could play ordinary records, delighted our Arab friends.

3

THE OIL ROAD TO BAGHDAD

The expedition left Vienna in style on 20th April 1935 (Good Friday) and subsequently took the ship from Trieste to Haifa. On the motorcycle trip to India in 1933, Herbert Tichy and I had ridden all the way through Turkey. To get to Baghdad we had taken a cautious route round the edge of the desert, and then kept pretty much to the banks of the Euphrates. This time, from further south, I opted for the shortest way through the desert. The more enquiries I made, the more our plans were thrown into confusion. It needed patience and a cool head to accept all the proffered advice, both asked and unasked, and to test its validity.

"You have to lay out £170 if you intend crossing the desert alone. The money is to underwrite the cost in case they have to send out an air search for you," the Director of Customs in Haifa told us. This requirement did exist, but it was waived if a number of vehicles travelled in convoy.

The owner of a largest desert haulage company, Mr Nairn, was intent on scaring us with a variety of tales of accidents and banditry. The best solution, in his view, would be to load "this funny little car," (as he called it) on to one of his big trucks for the special low price of £35, "because he was a sportsman at heart." This offended our sensibilities. The idea of the 'Trans-Asia Expedition' being carried piggyback through the desert was deeply insulting! Mr Nairn had overstepped the mark, and so we took our leave.

We next sought advice from the Automobile Club of Palestine. An ageing English spinster received us in the elegant club quarters of the King David Hotel. No, she really couldn't say how it was done, and no, she had no maps or route guides either. However, tomorrow there was to be a gymkhana, in fact a competition for the best turned-out motor car on the Arab sports field. Would we like to take part?

And so it went on. We were astounded: vehicles drove through the desert almost every day to the city of the Thousand and One Nights, and yet nobody knew how it was done! (Except Mr Nairn, of course, and he was making a living by it.)

The fourth suggestion came from Chaim Nathaniel, and it could have been a lot worse.

"Attach yourselves to my convoy. It's a caravan of motors under military protection, leaving Damascus next Thursday. I'm prepared to take you with me, although I shall probably get into trouble about it. Only good cars are meant to drive in the desert." This last remark rankled with me, so we did not even ask him the price.

Then Helmuth had the brilliant idea of paying a visit to the Jerusalem office of the Iraq Petroleum Company. In all the worry and confusion I had quite forgotten that I was carrying a letter of recommendation to them. I need only say that this visit poured balm on the wounds inflicted by Mr Nairn, Chaim Nathaniel and the old sourpuss at the Automobile Club.

"What took you so long? We've been waiting weeks for you!"

We were speechless.

Mr MacPherson, top dog at the IPC, leafed through a folder clean and clearly marked with the legend "Austrian Transasian Expedition," containing letters from Vienna and London and newspaper cuttings about the planned trip, all neatly filed. I sensed that the fortunes of our journey were now interwoven with those of a worldwide organisation, and that fate would smile on us.

"So what can I do for you?"

"How do we get to Baghdad?"

"Oh, we've got that all in hand. As guests of the IPC you will receive permission to use our private road through the desert. This road is only for IPC official vehicles, and our patrols turn back any other traffic. Now, here are your permits."

This opened up a completely new perspective on the desert crossing, since we would not be taking the ordinary route via Damascus and the oasis of Rutbah Wells, but following the oil pipeline to Haditha on the Euphrates before joining the familiar road to Baghdad.

Five telegrams were immediately dispatched to the relevant pumping stations in the desert, and Mr MacPherson bade us a kind farewell.

"We British have got living in the desert down to a fine art. You'll be amazed!"

We set off on our desert journey the following day in good spirits, and full of high expectations. The car glided down through the gorges of Judea over bubbling-hot asphalt until a sign-board in Arabic, Hebrew and English proclaimed the words 'Sea Level.' The way descended another 400 metres and it is a peculiar feeling to know that all the water in all the oceans of the world is towering above you like mountains.

In front of us stretched the leaden expanse of the Dead Sea. Was it true that it was impossible to sink in it? We tried it for ourselves. You lie on top of the water, motionless, like a cork. Swimming in the conventional sense is not really possible, since hands and feet flail around in the air more than the water. According to the brochures, one could "smoke a cigarette, read a newspaper undisturbed or hold up a sunshade." You could buy postcards, or have your picture taken in these positions. A Jewish photographer lurked constantly on the look-out for fresh victims. Imagine Miss Liddledale in Nashville, Tennessee, marvelling at the picture of Mrs Tucker, "Myself in the Dead Sea, in the beautiful Holy Land!"

However, reading a newspaper in comfort is just a publicity stunt, really. After only a few minutes the salt begins to affect you. You itch and burn in every pore and want nothing else but to get out of the hell-brew. Twenty per cent salt content should be enjoyed in moderation. Get into the Jordan double-quick and rinse the salt crust off completely.

It's just possible that this was the spot where John baptised Jesus Christ. What is certain is that, where the doughty British General Allenby crossed the river, it is now spanned by a fine bridge bearing the general's name. We were grateful to him for the bridge, less so for his exploits. However, any connection with road-building and civilisation ended here, as we left Palestine and entered the independent emirate of Transjordan.

This was where Asia really began.

The track leading up out of the Dead Sea depression along the slopes of the Jordan valley was stony and steep. We had to get over a high point of 1200 metres in the El Barka mountains on the way to Amman, the capital of Transjordan. The May sun blazed fiercely on the walls of rock, and the engine laboured its way up in first gear. The radiator thermometer was already showing over 90°C.

"This car is far too heavy!"

Helmuth nodded silently.

Out of the corner of my eye I could see the anxiety in his face. The overloaded springs were groaning on the bumpy road.

100°C. The radiator boiled and whistled. I stopped the car. Helmuth dug out a map of Asia.

"Here's Palestine and there's China. We've come about 400km so far and there are about 23,000 still to go."

We sat there for a long time brooding, side by side, with the big map of Asia on our knees. We were both very depressed and I thought back rather wistfully to my trip to India on the motorcycle. No boiling radiator then, but no means of carrying these mountains of luggage either.

Our weight was at the root of the whole problem, and, recognising this, I finally said, "We'll have to downsize. The back section of the body must be radically trimmed and we'll throw out some of the luggage."

But would this be guaranteed to stop the engine overheating in such a climate? Our log reads, "Why has the engine no water pump?" When you thought about it, the mass-produced thermosyphon cooling system was perfectly adequate for Europe. But what about this expedition? Why had the factory not built in a water pump? I was trying to shift part of the blame, but on the other hand it had probably been my responsibility to make the factory aware of the climate problems. Then again, the management had insisted on no changes being made. A mass-produced car, such as any customer could buy, was to drive across Asia! This was certainly a great idea as regards advertising, but we were the ones suffering the consequences.

Helmuth smiled but said nothing. We agreed that the first thing to be done in Baghdad was to rebuild the body.

Easier in our minds, at least, we drove on again as darkness fell. Night journeys are beautiful in the East. Over the landscape arched a sky sparkling with a plethora of stars that seemed almost within our grasp. Among the rocks of the gorge huddled flocks of storks, shining like patches of snow as the light fell on their plumage. They were not alarmed, being tired from their long journey. They had come from the Sudan, and the next day they would fly on towards their northern kingdom and the European spring. A few of them raised their heads sleepily from their feathers and followed us with the long, serious gaze of philosophers. Perhaps one was thinking, 'Funny, these humans, going south just now!'

At eleven o'clock at night we pitched our tent, the expedition's first overnight camp in the open. Sleeping on camp beds was wonderful, and I thought back to the many long, long nights I had spent on the bare earth during earlier motorcycle journeys. However, I could not really enjoy my soft bed, knowing the price we were paying for comfort. We had scarcely fallen asleep when we were awakened by a dazzling light. Figures sprang unceremoniously out of a car and hurried towards us. We also leapt out of bed, to be accosted by a stream of voices in Arabic until we agreed on English. No, we were not brigands or thieves. No, we felt quite safe here and needed no protection, thank you very much! Emir Abdullah's military patrol saluted, got back into their car and soon vanished into the darkness.

Sixty kilometres north of Amman, the oil pipeline runs pretty well straight from west to east. We wanted to join up with it as soon as possible. The sandy track frequently crossed the rails of the famous Hejaz railway, on which only one train a week now ran, to Maan in southern Transjordan. Originally this railway operated regularly over 1300km to Medina, but today it is not much more than a line on the map. Sleepers, rails, signal equipment, and even the station buildings were carried off piecemeal by the Bedouin, so I wouldn't have wanted shares in the Hejaz railway; I would have preferred the Iraq Petroleum Company, whose pipeline lay up ahead in the glistening desert. You cannot actually see it. Only an endless embankment of earth indicates the presence of the strong steel tube, 30 centimetres in diameter, through which the 'liquid gold' pulsates. From where we stood it was 800km to Kirkuk where the petroleum gushed out of the ground. In the other direction it was 150km to the Mediterranean.

We turned our eyes eastward, where the poles carrying the telegraph wire grew ever smaller, fading away on the shimmering horizon. There was another 600km of desert between us and Baghdad. Would we get lost? Did we need a compass? Was a desert journey a high-risk undertaking? The answer to all these questions was, "No!"

We had three good friends along the way: the telegraph wires above us, the oil pipeline beneath us, and in our pocket the letter from the IPC. A desert journey like that was child's play. We had only to tie a wire to a stone and throw it over the telegraph line and a team would be out to check on the interference within half a day.

There was not much evidence of the built road that MacPherson had talked about. The desert surface was hard and rocky, and we had to follow the tracks of the IPC company vehicles. Often the route veered far away from the telegraph line, but always returned to it.

On the evening of May 30th two slender towers emerged from the haze enveloping the wide plain. Soon we could also make out the aerial stretched between them. Walls and houses took shape. The first pumping station, H5, lay ahead. The site was extensive, perhaps several hundred metres square, and enclosed by a high fence that resembled barbed wire. The sentry let us in, reasoning that no white men could be robbers.

Even this late in the evening it was still oppressively hot. The manager of H5, Mr Meadows, was sitting in his bungalow in his shirt sleeves. Whisky and soda was brought, and the revolving ceiling fan drove a refreshing blast of air into our wide-open shirts.

"Did you have a good journey?" asked the manager, before handing us a telegram:

"Hope you arrived safely H5. Good luck on rest of journey. MacPherson."

The care lavished on us was most touching, and all in the British sporting spirit as we discovered, luxuriating in the bath-tub and washing the dust of the desert from our bodies. Our bath water was crystal-clear, pumped up from a considerable depth. Don't imagine that an oil company station such as this is nothing but a lonely little house in the wilderness. There are five of these desert towns, all alike as peas in a pod. Around the machine rooms, power plants and pumps are grouped the repair shops, the garages for lorries, cars and armoured vehicles, the sheds, the telegraph and wireless stations and the tents of the native workers. There is even a fairly green garden area with a few stunted trees separating the technical installations from the bungalows of the engineers, the communal dining-room, the recreation room and the guest-house. The bungalows are built low and flat so as to present the minimum of vulnerable surfaces to the desert storms. Double-glazed windows set in steel frames are carefully insulated with felt strips. There is a fine-meshed net for protection against mosquitoes. It's a mystery how these insects have found their way on to the isolated station. They apparently make their journey across the desert by stowing away on caravans, or on parts of vehicles protected from the wind. At night you have the choice either of sleeping under the turning ceiling fan and so developing rheumatism, or being bitten to death. Choosing between these two evils at least provides variety.

With all these details I'm forgetting the centre point of the pumping station, namely the fort. This lay right in the middle of the desert town, and its massive tower was the only multi-storey building. It was amazing how strongly fortified the station was, and Mr Meadows seemed to think me rather naïve when I asked whether such a fortification was really necessary.

"The pipeline has been attacked quite frequently," he explained to me. "In times of unrest, the entire station staff, European and native, can retreat into the fort which has supplies of food and water for three months."

The cosy picture of desert life that Mr MacPherson had painted for me in the safety of his office in Jerusalem seemed actually a little misleading.

Ibn Saud, ruler of nearly the whole of Arabia, was becoming harder to please. We were told that only recently two British planes had been driven off course by a storm into his territory. They had been shot down, and Ibn Saud had sent the two bodies to the Palestine High Commissioner.

With its world-wide powers, IPC was not to be deterred. Security was provided by armoured vehicles and trucks armed with machine-guns. Of course, we didn't notice any of this as we sat down to dinner in the evening with the engineers. If there hadn't been a storm raging outside, with fine sand trickling down the window-panes, we could almost have believed ourselves ensconced in the dining-room of the King David Hotel in Jerusalem. It felt every bit as safe. The entire proceedings made it seem even more improbable that we were actually in the middle of the desert. We were served noiselessly by an Arab boy dressed in spotless white. A menu card, produced on the station's own printing press, listed delicacies, including some flown in fresh by plane.

Such delights and a high monthly salary notwithstanding, I wouldn't care to be an IPC engineer. The boredom was totally soul-destroying. Three years in the desert is no picnic. At the next station everything was exactly the same as at H5: the bath was refreshing, the food was good, the waiter was clean and the engineers were just as gloomy. It was the same in H3 – rooms numbers 2 and 3, the same refreshing bath, and so on. All this desert comfort was becoming quite boring. How ungrateful humans are!

Mr Taylor, manager of H2, presented us with a printed invitation to his desert party. "A convivial get-together. We take turns to hold one every two months in one of the pumping stations. It's the only chance we have to unwind from the nerve-deadening routine in these godforsaken places."

"So it was a good thing we brought our dinner jackets after all," said Helmuth. (It was very kind, the way he consoled me for the ridiculous quantity of luggage which irked my conscience.)

The desert party exceeded our wildest expectations. Engineers from the other pumping stations came several hundred kilometres in cross-country vehicles, and late in the evening a plane landed too, bringing in the Chairman and six ladies from Haifa.

Our amazement knew no bounds. The ladies were in evening dress and Arab servants, magnificently garbed, distributed the most exquisite food. No expense had been spared for drinks either. If it had not been for the humming of the ceiling fans and the tight fly screens on the windows, you could have completely forgotten that you were in the desert. Then there was dancing, never mind that there were fourteen gentlemen to stand up with only six ladies. Later in the evening, we fetched our gramophone records and the Viennese waltzes excited much applause.

"So it was a good thing ..." said Helmuth.

"I know, I know," I interrupted him. "It's kind of you to be always consoling me, but it doesn't change anything."

As a farewell gift we presented Mr Taylor with all our waltz records, as a small token of gratitude for his generous hospitality.

That left us a few kilos lighter. We couldn't bring ourselves to give away the wind-up gramophone, since the engineers already had such splendid electric record-players, but we intended to dispose of it in Baghdad. Our dinner-jackets, which had enjoyed only one official outing in the desert, now had to be jettisoned. At the H2 party we had very wisely had ourselves photographed, and there we were, dinner-jacketed, with the dinner-jacketed engineers of Arabia. On the next occasion we would be able to say, "So sorry, we did have dinner-jackets with us and here is the visual proof, but unfortunately these essential (to the British mind) garments have succumbed to the rigours of the expedition." With these pictures we hoped to remain socially acceptable in British colonial circles, even without dinner-jackets. We kept our party photos constantly to hand, safely tucked into our wallets. Ridiculous as this may seem, it's the British way.

At the final station, H1 at Haditha on the Euphrates, we said goodbye to the oil pipeline and all its comforts. It was with a certain melancholy that we consumed our last English breakfast and found ourselves alone once more. This desert crossing was so safe and easy that I'm almost ashamed of it.

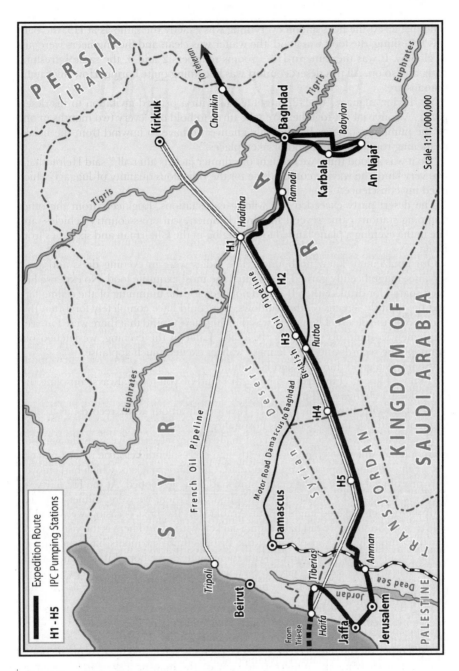

Map 1: From Haifa through the Syrian desert.

THE LIZARD HUNT

I knew from past experience that to arrive in Baghdad with visions of the enchanted orient and the splendour of the caliphs is to court disappointment. What appears over the horizon as you strain your eyes from far out in the desert? Not the crowning domes of mosques, not slender minarets, but a tall mast with a wind-sock, hangars and a modern concrete control tower: the trademarks of a world in which you can get from Baghdad to London in two days, and to Calcutta in three. In such a world it seemed faintly ridiculous still to be driving about in a car. But what would we have seen in three days of all the country that stretched tantalisingly ahead of us?

Like me, Helmuth soon overcame the shock of the unromantic approach road to Baghdad, and was enjoying the sight of the lush groves of palm trees surrounding the modern villas we drove past, and closing his ears as we turned into New Street. Lemonade sellers shouted, cars hooted, numerous horse-drawn carriages created a veritable concert of bells, but the traffic of New Street was characterised in particular by the Baghdad omnibuses. These were passenger vehicles with a body resembling a large bath-tub taking seven people, at a pinch. For a few pence, one could travel for longer than any European could bear to sit on the tiny wooden benches.

The Turks had blasted their way ruthlessly through the old alleyways of Baghdad to construct this modern high street. However, even after their intentions had been obvious for some time, houses that had been marked for destruction in the project were still being bought up in large numbers. The purchasers were banking on the well-known fact that people in the East tend to secrete valuables in the walls, ceilings and floors of their houses and, because of their customary mistrust, only alert their families as they breathe their last. If the last breath arrives unexpectedly, then the treasures remain firmly their hiding place, leaving a delicate task to the resourceful speculator when a house is demolished. It is said that such efforts are frequently rewarded.

With the onset of the hot season in Baghdad, everyone was sleeping in the open on simple iron bedsteads, even at the Tigris Palace Hotel. To European eyes it looked, on nights like these, more like a sanatorium than a hotel. The beds were ranged next to each other on the big terraces, only occasionally separated by a "wall" of potted plants, thus allowing an uninterrupted view of the man next door in his pyjamas. There were only men, since European women could not stand the heat in Baghdad and fled from the city at the beginning of summer.

We were glad to get ourselves invited as often as possible to the coolest house in Baghdad – the German consulate. It was refreshing just to see, in its entrance hall, an enormous painting of the icebound Zugspitze. Even more refreshing was the German tropical beer, sent down from Hamburg. When a fresh consignment arrived, it never failed to enhance the consulate's social life to a considerable degree, and although there were never such glittering occasions as the IPC desert party, everyone had a whale of a time.

We had also arranged for the consulate in Baghdad to receive our mail, including the legendary saddle spring with which readers of *India – The Shimmering Dream* will already be familiar. On the motorcycle trip to India, Herbert Tichy's saddle spring had broken and we went from one poste restante to the next in vain expectation of the replacement we had ordered. Now, after two years, the saddle spring had turned up and was of no value whatsoever, so I consigned it solemnly to the depths of the Tigris. In Helmuth's opinion, I would have done better to sell it in the bazaar, where a use can be found for absolutely anything. Not a mechanical use, maybe, but wouldn't those nickel-plated thingummyjigs have made a most original necklace for some Bedouin beauty? Hadn't we seen in bazaars everywhere the uses old bicycle wheels were put to, or a driving sheave instead of calibrated weights to discourage petty cheating? The Orient had not quite disappeared from Baghdad, and anyone who turned off New Street into the little byways might still glimpse much of its romance. Not always unalloyed, it must be said, since American gramophone music mingled with the harsh cries of Arab women, while the scribes (who wrote out letters and documents for the illiterate) used a typewriter with Arabic characters and a carriage running, most unusually, from left to right.

There was a strong temptation to buy odds and ends in the bazaars, but it was no good giving in to it, for this would have meant transporting a load of prayer rugs, hookahs and burnouses. No, we would use our time in Baghdad to make a radical reduction in the weight of the car. The operation proceeded in the big yard belonging to the Arab Bus Company. Once upon a time, the camel caravans camped here. Now it was a bus station, with buses departing in all directions. The arches surrounding the yard housed workshops where radiator plumbers, engine mechanics, electricians, vulcanisers and body builders patched up rickety boneshakers. We hired the tools we needed and set to work on a plan that we had spent much time discussing. The metal plates were detached from the wooden body structure, and the frame trimmed down with saw and chisel until it seemed small enough. Then the plates were fitted back on to the new shape and screwed into place, with all the surplus wood and metal being shared among the Arab boys who had come to watch. Then a tailor in the bazaar re-cut the hood to the new measurements and so, after its facelift, our rather clumsy delivery van emerged as a sleek little vehicle, a good 80kg lighter. More importantly, we had come to the realisation that we now had only half the luggage space. Anything that could not be stowed would have to be left behind. No constraint could have been more beneficial.

We sent our surplus luggage in two directions. Unnecessary luxuries were sent home, including the gramophone and the dinner jackets. A crate containing spare parts and tinned food began a sea journey via Basra to Hanoi in Indochina, so that we would find a depot there, as well as in Calcutta (optimists that we were).

It was a relief for us anyway, and also for the car, as we noticed immediately on the little excursion we made from Baghdad in the days following. On my trip to India I had already made one daring visit as an 'infidel' to a site of particular sacred significance in Shi'a Islam: the city of Karbala. This time we wanted to go further than Karbala to an even holier site, for if those who lie buried in the earth of Karbala are fortunate, then those whose last resting-place is An Najaf are even more so. The mosque there shelters the bones of Caliph Ali, a near relative of the great Prophet. Those who are interred closest to its walls have the best prospect of gaining Ali's intercession at the Last Judgement. So say the mullahs, and charge correspondingly large sums for a grave at the foot of the mosque. Rich Shi'ite merchants are perfectly willing to give up huge sums for a preferential place, and so the time-honoured association between business and religion goes on.

We drove the 120km from Karbala to Najaf through unremitting deep sand, able to advance only in first or second gear. Suddenly, something leapt up in front of us. They were lizard-like creatures, resembling small crocodiles, but with a much thicker tail, shorter and armour-plated. There were four or five of them.

"Desert spiny-tails!" shouted Helmuth, "We've got to have one of those little beasts!"

Most of them are actually quite sizeable creatures, and the largest of these measured about a metre and a half. Herodotus referred to them as "land crocodiles." Several of them had disappeared into holes or sandy hollows, but one of them found no hiding place and fled before us at extraordinary speed. We drove after it, finding to our glee that it wasn't cunning enough to dart from side to side like a hare does. However, it scuttled ahead on a swerving course, which made it difficult to keep up with, until at last it ran out of breath and came to a sudden stop. A comical scene ensued. About twenty metres ahead of us, the little beast stood rooted to the spot and goggled at the car. We could clearly see the animal's flanks quivering.

Helmuth had a revolver, but of course in his haste he couldn't lay his hand on it. Then something unexpected happened. The lizard surged forward in a last burst of strength, coming straight at us. It was a sickening moment. We sat rigid with fear in the open car which didn't even have doors, leaving our bare calves exposed to any attack. The beast was upon us – and then it dashed under the car! We looked around in all directions, but there was no lizard to be seen. It was lying under the car, motionless.

We exchanged baffled glances. Here we were, sitting right on top of our quarry, unable to get at it, hearing only the creature's wheezing breath somewhere beneath us. Helmuth rummaged around for his revolver, which then needed loading. At last he was ready.

"Tickle him with a stick."

"I haven't got one."

"Use the spade."

I unbuckled it carefully from the side of the car, leant out, and poked around underneath. The lizard dashed out on the other side. Bang! A second shot, bang! And the lizard lay dead. Helmuth was quite bowled over by his amazing success. We could now view the lizard at our leisure. The head, back and tail were armour-plated with tough horny scales. I don't think these desert lizards (Uromastyx) present a danger to humans, but their size is impressive. We strapped the animal on top of the spare wheels, intending to roast it when we got to Najaf and take home the armour-plating as a hunting trophy. What had become of our good resolutions? Here we were, overloading the car yet again!

On we went towards An Najaf which the Arabs also call Najaf-Mashhad – the city of the tomb. But how would we get there? By hunting the lizard we had lost our tracks and our orientation. Which way lay the road – right or left? Off the main Baghdad-Damascus highway, plenty of motorists had already lost their way and come to grief. One lorry crew had died of thirst a full eight miles away from the road. This only happens to Europeans. The Arabs have a quite uncanny sense of orientation, but if you are trying to make for an oasis using a map and a compass, then the first requirement for your calculation is a precise knowledge of the point you are starting from. Once you are lost, then every subsequent attempt at orientation is a lottery. You know that you must be *approximately* at such-and-such a point on the map, but it is this 'approximately' that spells danger, because an oasis is only a tiny point in the sea of sand that is the desert. In the annals of modern desert exploration there are cases on record of expeditions calculating a bearing to an oasis, but never arriving there. They passed only a few dozen kilometres to the left or right of it, and on out into the fatal emptiness of the desert.

Fortunately, things were not so tragic on the journey to An Najaf. There was motor traffic, caravans made their way towards the holy city, and somehow we were sure to stumble on the right track again. We were trying to force the car through a deep, sandy wadi using its own momentum, but it is amazing how a layer of sand only 30cm deep can slow you down. The engine gave two loud coughs and, with just enough time to throw it into neutral to avoid stalling, we stuck fast, and in a particularly nasty spot too. True, the car wasn't 'in over its axles,' in motoring parlance, but the engine simply lacked the power to overcome the massive resistance of the sand. There was only one answer – unload. In heat far exceeding our high-summer temperatures at home, we laboriously dragged the luggage forward to the edge of the wadi. We even rolled the spare wheels across too, dragging the dead lizard.

Would that do it? The engine sprang to life, and yes, the wheels turned – but only on the spot. The car would not budge an inch. We tried laying rubber mats under the rear wheels, but it was useless. The sun's burning rays fell nearly vertically upon us, we had lost two hours, and it was still a long way to An Najaf.

Without our noticing, the leader of a caravan had approached us. We only looked up when he came and stood right in front of us, and could not understand his words or what he was trying to tell us. Over and over, he gestured energetically first at the car and then along the wadi in an easterly direction. We tried sign language in our turn. 'Please help us!' With mime and hand signs we begged as persuasively as we could, and soon strong brown arms were delving in the sand and freeing the car. Unconditional comradeship and a readiness to help are part of the unwritten law of the desert, and here was the proof yet again. In a short time we were up and running, and were soon back on firm ground. The leader pointed as before in the same direction, and then at the car. Did this mean we were completely lost?

"An Najaf?" I asked, pointing in the same direction as he did.

The Arab nodded his head vehemently, which was as much as to say 'no.' Fortunately we were already acquainted with this oriental usage, or we would certainly have driven off along the wadi and ended up stranded somewhere with an empty fuel tank. We might have been found after a few days – or not. How much could depend on misinterpreting a nod of the head!

5

WHERE THE DEAD CROWD CLOSE TO ALLAH

These desert tracks were marked by an odd assortment of objects: a camel skeleton – and there were still plenty of those – but also the wreck of an old Chevrolet, gnawed bones and empty petrol cans. How long would it be before everything found along a caravan road was just mud-guards, old car bodies and wheels? There were clean areas here and there, small squares marked off by stones. Should Moslem travellers be passing at the hour of prayer, they would take their mat from their camel or their car, spread it out between the stones, and perform their devotions.

If the needs of the soul were catered for, then there was similar provision for the functions of the body. At home, we could clean ourselves with folded paper out of a wooden box, but here you would take one of the little round smooth stones that were neatly stacked in two pyramids within the enclosure, only taking care not to pick one of the stones from the top of the pile which had been exposed to the full force of the sun's rays, or uncomfortable burns would result. After use, it would be replaced on the other pyramid (the pyramid with the used stones was usually recognisable) and after a few days' thorough work by the sun and wind, it would regain its pristine smoothness and cleanliness. Once the second pyramid had reached its full height, then it could gradually be transferred back to the other side again, thus sparing these practical desert people the trouble of filling up wooden boxes with folded paper.

There was now no doubt that we were on the right road to An Najaf. We were constantly coming up with funeral caravans bringing mummified bodies embalmed in ashes to the holy city. They were often on the road for months, carrying to their longed-for destination those dead of the Shi'ite sect who had been rich enough to afford the luxury. They came from Persia, from Uzbekistan, from Ferghana, from Afghanistan. Individuals who, in death as in life, had forsworn traditional forms of transport would have their coffins loaded into a car, or even an aircraft, to be landed in the desert with its strange cargo somewhere in the region of An Najaf. The contents of these coffins, it must be said, consisted mostly of unembalmed or so-called 'wet' corpses. Transporting them was in fact completely illegal, but this didn't bother anybody. They simply made a greater effort, understandably, to get them to their destination as speedily as possible.

The dome of the mosque of An Najaf was still a far-off gleam in the afternoon sunlight when we found ourselves driving between thousands upon thousands of graves. It was a seemingly endless cemetery, a belt 2km wide encircling the city. Flat gravestones lay close together in no sort of order, interspersed with mausoleums in the shape of miniature mosques made of brick or ceramic tiles, and these resting places, some meaner, some richer, some magnificent, sheltered a veritable ocean of the dead, all united in the one hope of finding salvation in this place.

The sun, glowing red and more like a strangely flattened ball than a disc, was just sinking on the horizon when we halted at the north gate of An Najaf. It was too narrow to allow access to the car, and a policeman in a clean khaki uniform took us to the police building outside the city walls. It stood among the graves like a small fort. The young commander was proud of his English, proud of the telegraph apparatus that had already alerted him to our arrival, and proud of the banquet he was intending to give us. But he was delighted, as were his men, when we contributed our slaughtered lizard to the proceedings, as in these parts it was regarded as a great delicacy.

As we sat at table in the courtyard under the open sky, we heard the sound of marching feet and then a loud "Attention!"

Had we heard right?

A military band had marched in. The commander of the fort gave the signal and the band blared out. It was not easy to identify the tune, peppered as it was with a certain amount of Arabian dissonance, but it was *Fest steht die Wacht am Rhein* ... We were very surprised, but the bandmaster was grinning from ear to ear. Then he played *Muss i denn, muss i denn zum Städtele hinaus.*

We sang along, and the general enthusiasm knew no bounds. The maestro had served with the Turks, who in the First World War had themselves had German instructors – also apparently in music – and thus the familiar tunes had found their way to the Arabian desert. We attempted to return the favour of this greeting from home by singing the latest national hit *Wir Kameraden der Berge.* I don't know whether it was any good, but we were applauded all the same as if we had been two operatic tenors.

Night had long since fallen, one of those deep blue star-spangled Eastern nights, enfolding the dark silhouette of the dome of the mosque and its four tall, slim minarets. We lay down to rest under a tent of stars, bedded in the courtyard of the police station along with the soldiers. This was a good thing, as we would have been ill-advised to try any other place in holy An Najaf.

The next day we took a walk in the city under police guard to see the golden gate of the mosque of Caliph Ali, but our escorts were uneasy until we reached the cover of the bazaars. The facial expressions of the priests guarding the gate of the mosque were too threatening, and any attempt to get inside would undoubtedly have brought painful retribution. Europeans have been killed here just for taking photographs.

We were delighted, therefore, that a caravan that had set up camp outside the city gates had no misgivings about being immortalised on celluloid. As for the young unveiled girls, curiosity overcame their shyness. They walked with a lovely swing in their stride, and looked quite magnificent with their dark fiery eyes and finely-cut features. Gold earrings and a gold-mounted pearl in the nostril were their only ornaments. On the other hand, the old Bedouin women were repulsively ugly. They resisted with screeching any attempt to photograph them (and quite right too!).

Cooking over fires of camel dung was still going on all around, and bread was being baked on flat, heated stones. The saddles and loads were still piled up around the camp, and the camels, including valuable white racing camels, were still hobbled by the front legs. But that evening the caravan was due to depart in the direction of central Arabia, to Mecca nearly 1100km away, intending to reach its destination in 63 days.

We, however, returned to Baghdad.

It was still just as hot in the city of Haroun al Rashid, so we were only too pleased to be taken up the Tigris in the consular motor boat. We leapt into the water, and let ourselves be carried downstream with the current. Many Europeans were happily cooling off in the same manner, but not many were as unlucky as I was. While swimming along I suddenly felt a violent laceration and the water round me turned ominously red. I was just able to get to the river bank where I was pulled out with a long gaping wound in my belly. What had happened? Had a shark from the Persian Gulf lost its way and come up the Tigris? This happens sometimes, so they say, but not often. No, my injury was more 'industrial' in origin. I had swum too near the bank, where a cut-open petrol can with jagged edges had lodged, causing my ugly wound. I had to have stitches and lie on my back for ten days. Helmuth tried to comfort me with Thermos flasks full of ice-cream, but even these could not raise my spirits.

To make matters worse, the news got into the Vienna papers, and to this day I don't know how. The headline "Max Reisch – accident in Baghdad" spanned three columns in heavy type. It was all we needed to discredit the whole expedition.

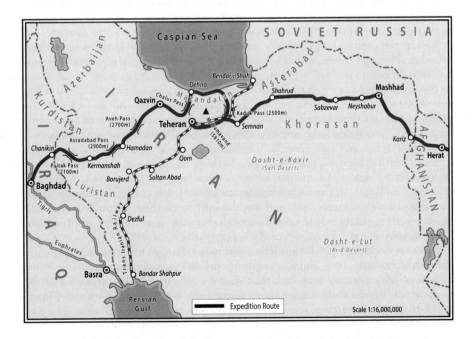

Map 2: The route through Iran.

Whether this accident in the Tigris was really so unfortunate is open to question. Because of my injury we were held up for ten days in Baghdad and this saved our lives. It was Destiny, Providence, Fate, Kismet – the predestination of all living and dying, as determined by Allah and preached by Mohammed.

I had a good friend in India, Latif Hamid, who, during our motorcycle trip (recounted in *India: the Shimmering Dream*) had taken it upon himself to hide our dynamo because he wanted us to stay in his house a few days longer. It had been understood that I would pay him another visit in Quetta. We had exchanged numerous letters, and he was awaiting our arrival. Because of the accident in Baghdad we were late arriving in Quetta, but four days previously the greatest earthquake of the century had razed the city to the ground, leaving 4000 dead. Even with help from the British soldiers, we were unable to find the street where Latif Hamid's house had once stood.

In my great sadness I began to reflect. My thoughts went back to Baghdad and how bad-tempered I had been, lying in the heat of the hospital. If I had been spared all that, then by now I would be lying under the rubble of Quetta.

I still had a heavy bandage round my middle as we left Baghdad, but it was better to accept the slight discomfort than to stay pent up any longer in that city whose walls radiated such infernal heat. Now we could make for the mountains of Persia and the cool, high altitude breezes. We breathed in great draughts of the fresh mountain air, and our lungs expanded as we looked eagerly towards the heights. The car crawled in second gear up the steep hairpin bends of the Paitak pass. The capital cities of Iraq and Iran were linked by a reasonably good road, constructed by the Russians during the First World War. Buses now managed the 980km in three to four days, whereas caravans previously took four weeks.

Nevertheless, there had already been a period, in the heyday of the great pre-Christian Persian Empire, when the 'postal service' and the speed of communication between different localities in this huge land mass was second to none. Down below in the gorges could be seen the traces of a derelict roadway, along which the post riders of Darius and Xerxes once galloped, and, without any of the technological aids on which we pride ourselves today, accomplished feats deserving of the highest respect. The mountain ranges, the deep gorges, the sand desert of Lut and the salt marshes of Kavir were no obstacle. Thousands of farsachs of post road (a farsach is about 7km) crisscrossed the land, proclaiming the power and greatness of the Achaemenid Empire. We could scarcely imagine how, with the primitive methods of those far-off days, the modest roadway we saw below had been carved out of the landscape! It was scarcely two metres wide and yet on these stones, worn smooth by hundreds of thousands of sandals, and on this rock, scored into deep grooves by innumerable wagons, the armies of Alexander the Great had marched to India and the mounted couriers of Ghengis Khan had swept through from Inner Mongolia to the Mediterranean. Interminable caravans carried trade between the two cultural centres of Mesopotamia and Turkestan, and it was here that their route joined the famous Silk Road, which for centuries formed the overland link between Europe and China. All that can be seen of the old road today – collapsed, buried by rock falls, choked by thistles – is a sad remnant of its former glory.

The old realisation that roads were vital for holding together a far-flung empire had helped in the reconstruction of modern Iran. Every day, Persia's new roads carried hundreds of motor vehicles delivering goods, people, mail and newspapers to the smallest villages. The most important thoroughfares had police protection, just like our own. The police stations were visible on hill-tops, each like a small fort with a watch-tower and armoured vehicles in the courtyard. Strenuous efforts were being made to clear the country of bandits, who were apparently still flourishing in certain parts. This was nothing new, for we passed by a cave in which 300 years ago Shah Abbas had had forty thieves walled up alive as a dreadful warning to others. Shades of Ali Baba.

Motorisation was progressing all the time, but the camel had by no means outlived its usefulness. On the contrary, it had acquired a new role, transporting mainly petrol along with other goods not requiring speedy delivery. A camel carried four cans each holding eighteen litres. Petrol caravans such as these were on the road for weeks at a time in order to replenish filling stations in the farthest villages and oases. Each can was stamped with the trademark 'BP.' To the Englishmen in the refineries of Abadan in Southern Persia it was 'British Petroleum.' The Persians called it 'Benzine Persane.' Both sides were right, as the Shah earned as much from the concession as the Anglo-Iranian Oil Company did from the petrol. Thus 'BP' suited everybody, with only the camels complaining under their burden.

Sitting in our nice car and enjoying the romantic country air of Persia, I showed Helmuth the exact spot where our tiny motorcycle tent had stood two years before, when Herbert Tichy lay inside with serious blood poisoning, delirious with fever.

What a time that was! And now we were travelling by car in comfort.

Kaswin, the town we went through on our way to Tehran, is for Persia rather what Schilda with its citizens the Schildbürger is to Germany: that is, a town of fools. Of the many hilarious stories concerning its inhabitants, I like the 'modern' legend best, about the Kaswin man faced with a factory chimney for the first time in his life. "What's that?" he asks in amazement, and since it is obvious where he comes from, they answer him by saying, "It's a well that's been taken out of the ground to dry."

In Tehran there was a joyous reunion with friends from the time of the motorcycle trip (see *India: the Shimmering Dream*, chapter 15). There was also some mail for us at the consulate, including some from our taskmasters "hoping that we should now make more rapid progress." Well, the fault wouldn't be ours!

The money transfer promised in the contract had arrived in Tehran, and at the Persian State Bank 'Melli' we changed it for a wad of brand-new toman notes. We bade a happy farewell to our friends, and to the rather colourless city of the Silver Lion, and drove out through the East Gate towards the Kavir desert, Mashhad, and, we hoped, Afghanistan.

We spent the night quite a way further on in one of the motor caravanserais on the road to Mashhad. The accommodation left something to be desired, but there was a hearty Persian meal of tea, rice, mutton, vegetables and water melon. We ate in company with Persian lorry-drivers, some of whom spoke a few words of English, Arabic or Hindustani. Many of them had ridden with camel caravans up until a few years ago and had now switched to motors. The lorry owners made heavy demands on their drivers. Every day they spent up to 16 hours behind the wheel of the heavy trucks, and quite often they used opium to help them through the crises of

Persian letter of recommendation issued by Iranian legation in Baghdad and produced on a Persian typewriter.

fatigue. This meant that they slept like dead men in the caravanserais, usually next to their vehicle. However, they never forgot to take the weight off the lorry's springs by jacking it up so that the springs were free and unburdened, and thus able to recover from a hard day's work over Persian roads. This was naturally an extremely tedious job, but in earlier times the camels had to be relieved of their loads every morning after a long night's march through the desert. The motor vehicle was now cared for in the same way. Of course, it would not have been necessary if the trucks had not been so ridiculously overloaded. Two-tonners were carrying double their weight! This depressed the springs to such an extent that they often touched the mud-guards. No wonder the tortured springs cried out for relief.

DUST TO DUST

Strange – is it not? – that of the myriads who
Before us pass'd the door of Darkness through,
Not one returns to tell us of the Road,
Which to discover we must travel too.

We were still some way off when we saw domes shimmering through the bluish haze of the desert. It was the building that bears true witness to those famous poems – the tomb of Omar Khayyam. For me, it is the most beautiful and most perfect embodiment of every flight of fancy concerning the magic of the East. Khay-yam means 'tent maker,' an epithet that must refer to a very early stage of his life, for Omar later became an astrologer, a sage, and above all the author of a profusion of vivid lyrical verses, still current amongst the people of Persia, and not only there, for they speak a language intelligible to all human beings which goes straight to the heart.

In the 14th century, about 300 years after his death, Persia raised a memorial like no other to her great son. We drove along beside an unprepossessing brick wall, made out of mud bricks. No one would suspect the jewel concealed behind it, but the wrought iron gate that allowed a first glimpse into the lovely gardens within is a work of art in itself.

When the gates opened, it was 50 metres to the main façade of the tomb. The way was lined with flower beds brilliant with the colours of roses, narcissi, cyclamen, golden ranunculus, pansies and many other species whose names were as unfamiliar to me as the flowers themselves. The beds were in ornamental shapes – Arabic letters, the Tree of Life – while in the centre goldfish played in a blue-glazed pool. This unique blue was repeated a hundred times over on the monument itself. The portal was all of blue-glazed tiles with arabesques, blossoms and flower patterns; small blue columns divided the double windows, of which there were two rows, one above the other; and over the structure hung the delicate dome, elegantly curved, also covered with glazed tiles and forming the roof of the great inner chamber, whose walls were sprinkled with every kind of decoration, inlaid with polished stones of all colours. The floor was covered with magnificent soft carpets. Stained glass windows cast lights in muted colours on the mighty sarcophagus of reddish stone, inscribed with the life-story of the great poet. A pious silence reigned in the

41

chamber. In spite of all its lavish and colourful decoration, the effect was in no way oppressive or disturbing.

In smaller side rooms one could admire books and manuscripts with sumptuous leather and metal bindings, collections of miniatures, jewellery and soapstone carvings.

Still in a daze from all we had seen, we rested under an apricot tree whose branches bent low under the weight of its fruit. Our Persian guide waved to us to come and eat, and it was surely in the spirit of the poet that we enjoyed a little of life's bounty before the enchanting vision of his tomb. He was well aware of the fleeting nature of all things, but for that very reason he strove to enjoy them to the full. Eastern ballad singers may thank his love of wine for charming lines like these:

> *You know, my Friends, how long since in my House*
> *For a new Marriage I did make Carouse:*
> *Divorced old barren Reason from my Bed,*
> *And took the Daughter of the Vine to Spouse.*

So we left the blossoming oasis and its beauty behind us, and plunged once more into the singular emptiness of the desert. The sky had been livid for days, and a heavy layer of thick fog seemed to be descending on our lungs and choking us. But was it really fog? We were reminded now not so much of the poet's lines, but of the words of the Bible. "And the sun was darkened ..." This was exactly what happened when the fog turned out to be a swirling mass of sand, whistling and singing as it tore across the open plain. The storm erupted so suddenly that we scarcely had time to pull down the hood and insert the side-panels.

In the open desert, the howling storm attacked our lone vehicle with random buffetings from every side. Gusts seized it as if trying to fling it sideways. It required a strong grip on the steering wheel. Our cockpit slowly filled with dust, which seeped in through every crack. There was no protection from that fine desert sand. We were anxious for the cameras and wondered what surprises lay in store for us. The carburettor was objecting and began to pack up in spite of the filters. By simultaneously disengaging the clutch and stepping on the gas I tried repeatedly to keep life in it. I pitied the poor engine, having to swallow all that dust, but we couldn't spend the night out here in the wilderness and so we crept forward, in spite of the fury of the elements. There was still no sign of a village or caravanserai, only the abandoned ruins of former hostelries that motor traffic had made redundant.

Spending the night in the open was out of the question. We had to find shelter as soon as possible to get protection from the sand that was stinging and whipping both us and the car, so on we drove. I have no idea what force our storm measured, but the whirlwind often seized the car and flung it several metres to one side, although my hands never turned the steering wheel at all.

Sand and salt rattled on the windows. In the beam of the headlights sparkled thousands of salt crystals, whipped towards us by the raging storm. We began to itch violently because of the salt and dust, but otherwise it was quite comfortable inside the car, filled as it was with the smoke of fragrant Persian cigarettes, which brought on a kind of cosy contentment. The storm might be raging but nothing was going to happen to us. Even if sand got into the cameras it wouldn't be as bad as all that. We'd often read about things like this happening, but what the hell ...

While the car forced its way forward through the wind and darkness, my thoughts went skipping backwards. I found that I had let go with one hand and was patting the steering wheel affectionately − my faithful travelling companion! All through Asia its tyres had run over sharp scree and hot sand with not a single flat to show for it in our scrupulously-kept log book!

"We've had the most amazing luck," I said to Helmuth.

This was a mistake, for scarcely were the words out of my mouth than there was a knocking and bumping and the car was running on a wheel-rim.

"Oh, very funny," observed Helmuth. Calmly, we finished smoking our cigarettes, since a couple of minutes wouldn't make much difference. Then we had to get out. The storm nearly blew us over. We were in the middle of total blackout. Added to this, we couldn't coax so much as a flicker out of the emergency torch. I put the jack under the axle and turned the handle for a long time, but the jack simply sank into the sand. Helmuth put a plank under it and then the car rose and freed up the wheel. The salty sand was whipping our faces and trickling down our backs under our shirts, mixed with sweat. After half an hour we managed to change the wheel and climbed back into the car with our eyes sore and streaming.

Time to go! The engine showed willing, and continued its battle with the elements with renewed vigour. Very late that night we eventually reached a place with a sheltered caravanserai.

The next day's journey brought a pleasant change. With a recommendation from the Anglo-Iranian Oil Company in Tehran we visited Abdul Hussein, the company's petroleum agent in Nishapur. A policeman took us to a nondescript house where we repeated our experience at the mausoleum of Omar Khayyam. Miraculously hidden behind the bleak, desiccated wall of mud brick was a veritable paradise, with splashing water and the colour and scent of flowers. The courtyard was lined with columns. Against all expectation, we had entered a little palace.

A servant offered us seats and we gave him our cards, which we had taken care to have printed in English, French and Arabic. Within a short time the dutiful retainer was back with Abdul Hussein's gracious invitation. We entered the inner part of the house. Our host rose from the cushions on which he had been sitting next to a low table set for smoking. He perused attentively the letter of recommendation addressed to him. It was laid out in two columns, with the English text on the left and on the right the Persian, produced likewise on a typewriter.

Abdul Hussein led us out on to the terrace where we sat in comfortable western-style chairs. Although we had been travelling for hours and were covered with dust, we dared not ask for water before we had drunk the inevitable welcoming beverage of tea, always served in tiny glasses.

We sat facing a large pool of water, a reminder of how much we wanted a bath. The temptation to dive into it and wash the dust of the desert from our bodies was almost irresistible A glorious prospect! But it was not to be.

"If I could just wash my hands!" I groaned privately to Helmuth. He looked at his own dusty hands and arms which were streaked with sweat and dirt. Our hair stuck to our foreheads, our scalps itched from the dust. Physical and mental discomfort increased as we were obliged to swallow yet more glasses of tea.

A servant brought the hookah.

"Curse the thing!" I thought as I carried the long tube to my lips. What we really wanted was a bath! That and nothing else. Should we ask for it? No, we mustn't, for it might be very bad manners. We were doomed to stay dirty and must accept it.

New guests arrived – the police commander and the doctor. The hakim spoke some German, learned from his medical books, so we let Abdul Hussein know that we were very happy in his house.

He replied with restrained satisfaction, "My house is but small and Allah was not so gracious as to give me earlier warning of your arrival." We made fulsome protestations of praise and apology. The nargileh went round, the smoke bubbled through the water in the glass container to be drawn into the lungs in deep draughts. We were still unwashed.

Several hours went by – smoking and tea drinking. Tea drinking and smoking.

Then all of a sudden a servant brought a small ewer and stood patiently before me. I understood and stretched out my hands, rubbing them expectantly, whereupon a tiny spurt of water trickled over them, and the "purification" was over. I watched as Helmuth lovingly massaged a couple of drops into the palms of his parched hands before the hakim's pointed fingers stretched out in their turn. Even he received no more than a teaspoonful as the servant scuttled round to the police officer and finally to Abdul Hussein. The ablutions for five people had taken barely a minute, yet everyone seemed perfectly satisfied, except us.

This ceremony signalled the start of dinner and bowls of fruit were brought in. Unfortunately we were not versed in Persian etiquette and could not decide whether we should begin or whether we should wait. We decided on the latter. However, everybody else waited too. I glanced secretly at the clock. The company sat for a full hour without batting an eyelid over the bowls full of tempting grapes, apricots and pomegranates. Conversation began to flag. All attention seemed to be on the fruit. The police officer had already cast several glances in that direction and the hakim was wriggling uneasily on his chair, as Helmuth and I had been doing for ages in sheer desperation. It had been so easy the day before in the 'motel,' where for the price of a few krans we could eat and do as we pleased.

Abdul Hussein was the only one who knew how to preserve his dignity. He reclined in a relaxed fashion and smoked the nargileh, whereupon the conversation dried up entirely. An air of menace hung over us, as of a gathering storm. From the meaningful glance cast in my direction by the hakim, I felt that something must happen soon.

"To hell with it!" I said, voicing my thoughts, and none too quietly. With the desperate courage of an animal at bay, I lunged forward, seized the finest of the apricots and took a great bite.

My action set everything in motion and a wave of relief seemed to run through the assembled company. In a few minutes the bowls were emptied. Rice, legs of mutton, flatbread, eggs, hashed fowl and melons were then delivered in quick succession, but Abdul Hussein ate nothing until prompted by me.

So that was the Persian way! And yet we were still unwashed in, of all places, the town that, at the express desire of the greatest Persian poet, had used the proceeds of his life's work to create a lavish water system. Even so, Firdowsi – 'the Heavenly One' – did not live to see its completion.

The 60,000 couplets of his colossal epic Shahnameh brought together all the old Persian heroic legends, and thus immortalised them in poetic form. Sultan Mahmoud the First had promised the poet a gold piece for every couplet, but jealous rivals plotted to turn the Sultan against him, and the aged poet fell from grace. Only much later did the Sultan realise his mistake, and by then it was too late, for, as the caravan carrying the 60,000 gold pieces made its way towards Nishapur, Firdowsi's home, it met with the poet's funeral procession at the entrance to the city. However, he himself had no need of public honours to ensure lasting fame, as the tailpiece to his epic states:

> *The man of wit and faith, the great of heart,*
> *Shall praise my name and glorify my art,*
> *For words like seeds I scattered far and wide.*
> *So shall I live, as though I never died.*

7
FOREIGN DEVILS

The road, which had for so long run monotonously straight, now began to bend about and to rise and fall as the desert became hilly. We were nearing Mashhad, the great place of pilgrimage, the Mecca of the Shi'ite world.

On the last rise in the ground countless little stone pyramids were silhouetted against the sky. What could they signify? It was only when we stopped on the summit that we found the explanation. This was the spot where the whole panorama of Mashhad emerged for the first time – a sea of houses interspersed with numerous trees and gardens, with the gilded dome of the great mosque towering over all. As far as the eye could see, the city was ringed with fertile cultivations, poplar woods and villages. It was no wonder that this sight greeted the pilgrims like a vision of the fields of paradise. They had journeyed maybe for many weeks on the backs of camels, toiling and suffering, with only heat, sand, dust, the monotonous yellow-brown plain and dried-up salt ponds, when all at once, this radiant city lay before them. The moment needed a memorial. Here they must thank their God that they had overcome trial and tribulation. So that was the origin of the little stone pyramids, and also, nearby, the low walls enclosing places where prayer mats might be spread.

I wonder how many of them were celebrating not only the end of a long and arduous journey, but also the moment when, for the very first time, some inkling of splendour and beauty entered their lives. We considered the poverty of many of the dwellings we had observed on our journey from Tehran to Mashhad. Villages in eastern Persia are invisible but for domes about two metres in height, built of a mixture of mud and straw. There is no street through the village, and the domes are closely packed together. Smoke rising through an opening in the centre of each one betrays the fact that village life goes on below ground. We were impatient to discover how. At first we clambered around between the domes, then down a narrow air-shaft pierced with small window openings. The dwellings (if you could call them that) which we reached in this way were dreadful – dark, stuffy and full of smoke and an indescribable stench. At first we could make out nothing at all, as our eyes were still recovering from the dazzling sunlight, but we soon saw women, children and puppies romping around on the floor. They froze immediately on seeing us, and stared in amazement as if they'd seen a ghost.

A man appeared from somewhere to guide us round this extraordinary village of caves. Each room led into another. In one, old people lay huddled in rags, in another there were tools and primitive implements, in the next a whole family lived and slept, and the fourth was a byre. In it stood a fat-tailed sheep that seemed to have injured its heavy appendage, for its tail was carried in a wooden frame tied to its back. This body-part serves as a store of food in times of hardship, and the animals present a grotesque spectacle, dragging their tightly swollen tails along behind them. All the rooms of the underground village were connected by door-openings, of which only a few were hung with a filthy piece of cloth. It was not particularly hot, indeed cool draughts of air seemed to reach some of the rooms, but it was like being in a labyrinth. Just as the feeling of suffocation was becoming intolerable, our guide opened a little door and we found ourselves suddenly standing in the open, on the roadway next to our car. Before, we'd had no idea there was an entrance here at all. Now we looked back once more and saw all the domes packed close together in an area of about 50 square metres. It was unbelievable, this sort of settlement in the hot dry steppe.

We thought of that village as we looked out over the radiant panorama of Mashhad, and wondered what its inhabitants would have felt, standing in such a place. We drove down slowly, and it did not take much effort for us to feel that we were in paradise, too. Gardens were planted everywhere, the streets were moist, free of dust and lined with huge shade-giving trees.

On one pretty, well-kept house we read the inscription 'British Consulate.' Good. In the next caravanserai we would have a shave and a change of clothes and then come back and make our formal approach to the consul. Our entry visas for India had to be checked in any case, and besides, we could scarcely evade British surveillance. I must allow that this was carried out in an exceptionally discreet and pleasant manner. Of course, Mr Humber, the consul, was already thoroughly informed about our journey, where we were going and why. Just as he had received this information, so he would pass it on to his colleagues in the towns that lay ahead, and just like his other colleagues he immediately issued us with an invitation to tea. This, as everyone knows, is the best and most relaxed way of sounding out a visitor.

We were already aware that the many official invitations we received along our way from consulates and other authorities were no reason to feel especially honoured. There were plenty of shady European characters, adventurers and even political agents knocking around Asia which made it understandable that any European would be given a thorough going-over.

It was not only representatives of the European authorities who were interested in where we were from, where we were going and why, but also the local powers-that-be. We had scarcely settled into our conversation with Mr Humber over a cup of tea than a police official appeared. We had omitted to report to the police immediately on our arrival, in flagrant defiance of very strict Persian regulations.

"You had better go along straight away," advised Mr Humber, "or you'll have nothing but trouble."

We were sorry to have to interrupt the pleasant tea-party, and promised Mrs Humber that we would return the next day to finish the story of how we struggled over Abdul Hussein's bowls of fruit. At the police station we were subjected to a long interrogation and finally released, although they kept our passports.

At the office of the Anglo-Iranian Oil Company we were provided with a guide to show us round the town. We were determined to see the famous mosque of Imam Reza, and possibly to photograph it. Crowds of people pressed around its gates, the bright costumes of Luristan and Uzbekistan mingled with those of Anatolia and Bactria, all pushing and shoving towards the entrance of the mosque.

We asked Jamshid, our guide, whether we would be allowed in.

"Out of the question! Even in disguise you would be discovered, and then ..."

What would happen then became clear when we noticed the hostile and suspicious looks we were getting from the pilgrims. They made us extremely uncomfortable. We could feel them drilling into us on either side and from behind, wondering what business we had to be there. We were completely surrounded by believers who had come from afar to pray to the great God of the desert and to His Prophet.

"Even if you got inside without being recognised, Mohammed Imam Reza, the patron saint of the mosque, would have his own way of testing you. There is a stone in the mosque. It is not heavy. Anyone can lift it, if he is a believer! Since you are not, you would not be able to lift the stone and that would give you away."

We agreed that we had better not suffer any such examination, but surely the Prophet's ire would not be kindled by our taking a picture of the great crowd of pilgrims outside the mosque?

Jamshid thought we might risk it. We withdrew a little way from the seething mass until we were under one of the trees that ringed the big square. From here we had a view of all the people and of the mosque itself. The huge main gate and the minarets towered skyward. Blue and yellow glazed tiles sparkled in the sunlight. The gateway was adorned with an electric clock of gigantic proportions, which seemed a gross insult to the timelessness of Asia.

Helmuth raised his camera, ready to press the shutter and was startled by a roar from every side of "Aks! Aks!" Everywhere rang with the shrill cries, "Picture! Picture!" The menacing crowd surged towards us, but three policemen who had been watching us the whole time, as if they had only been waiting for an incident, were on the spot at once. The first of them glowered at us and said brusquely, "Chavaz." Helmuth handed him the obligatory photographic licence, but unfortunately the good man could not read, as he was holding the paper upside down and merely pretending to study it. He grabbed Helmuth roughly by the arm and the three of them set about marching him away. The crowd roared enthusiastically and swarmed after them.

I was allowed to go with Helmuth as far as the little police house, but then the door was slammed in my face and there was no alternative but to drive out to the British consul. The consul was not in. The consul was playing golf and I found him way out in the desert. Although he had only got as far as the fourth hole he came back willingly.

Helmuth, as he told us later, had been taken into a courtyard surrounded by barred cells. He was pushed into one of the empty cages and locked in. He could then observe at his leisure all the bad characters in the rest of the lodgings. Just before this he had, in true oriental fashion, quietly slipped a couple of coins into the hand of one of the policemen, saying "Chai", whereupon he was speedily provided with tea and grapes. When he proceeded to light a cigarette as well, a hand appeared at the bars. His neighbour was begging for a cigarette. Just for fun,

Helmuth pressed a quantity of them into the man's dirty fingers and soon became aware that the "criminals" were playing fair – cigarettes and lights were passed on through the bars and soon everyone was smoking, laughing and waving to him. It was all extremely jolly.

The British consul thought so too, and could scarcely hide his amusement on seeing my poor, jailed travelling companion. The senior Persian police officers bowed profusely and stammered apologies. In the office, Helmuth's chavaz was solemnly returned to him, tea and cigarettes were proffered, and he was advised in the politest terms that he might take photographs anywhere, but no more near the mosque.

Continued on p54

Above: Shah Reza Khan Pahlevi had put his armies to work on a huge road-building project throughout the country. The Alborz mountain range was conquered by the Dehno Pass at an altitude of 3200 metres. Today, there is a tunnel under the pass at 2600 metres.

Right: The Eastern Gate of Tehran, where camels still plodded peacefully alongside the motor car. The caravan route from Tehran to Masshad on the edge of the Kavir desert was a difficult track to follow, about 1000km in length. This beautiful gate has long since disappeared, a victim of urban development.

Above: This was probably Tehran's first motor car: a Russian armoured car from the First World War.

Left: Persian fakir. Life in the numerous monasteries of southern Persia resisted all attempts at modernisation, as here at Mahum in the Dasht-i-Lut desert.

Above: Shah Abbas (16th century), justifiably called "the Great". He was the most significant ruler of the Safavid dynasty and built many roads and caravanserais. In his time the whole land was safe for travel.

Above: The northern regions of Persia were occupied for some time by the Mongols. They brought with them a way of life typified by yurts and enormous vehicles resembling a modern motor caravan.

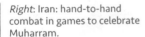

Right: Iran: hand-to-hand combat in games to celebrate Muharram.

In the desert towns of Yazd, Kerman and Bam, these wind towers, known as badgirs, were designed to ventilate the houses with cool air.

Above: In Persia Islam has almost entirely obliterated the old religion of Zoroaster. Many Zoroastrians (also called fire worshippers) fled to India and it is only in Yazd, an oasis in central Persia, that a minority survives to tend the eternal fire in this temple.

Above: The rich culture of Persia, with its famed Achaeminid and Sassanid dynasties, was an early object of research for European archaeologists. This drawing by the Frenchman Texier of the royal tombs at Nakch-i-Rostam near Persepolis dates from 1852.

Never again did a policeman in the city of Masshad ask to see Helmuth's chavaz, however many photographs he took. Every precinct seemed to have heard about the incident. All the same, our car was frequently surrounded by an inquisitive throng and we were besieged with questions, depending on the speakers' knowledge of English or French. Could the car float? Yes, of course! And fly? Well, naturally! The Persians' credulity amused us. One of them said that the vehicle resembled an armoured car, at which point I got carried away and replied, "It is one, and our machine gun is hidden in the back!"

Alas, this was a big mistake. The mullahs used the joke to whip up feeling against us. Doubtless they still bore us a grudge for venturing into the hallowed area of the mosque, and they feared for its treasured collections of gold, silver and jewels. In Masshad they had probably not forgotten that only twenty years earlier, Turkmen raiders on horseback had stormed the mosque and desecrated it.

The following afternoon we were surrounded by an excited crowd, demanding to see the machine gun. It was no use our protesting that we didn't have one, or the police lifting up the tarpaulin to prove just how harmless the contents of our luggage space really was. The people would not be reassured, whilst the mullahs kept on whispering, "But they do have one ... And they took an aks, a picture of the mosque, the foreign devils!"

In the end, the foreign devils had no choice but to beat a hasty retreat from that all-too-holy city.

Above: Evening shadow play in Persia. Stark walls such as these usually concealed flourishing gardens.

URLAJAT

It was 280km from Masshad to the Afghan border, on the best road we had found anywhere in Persia, maybe because it was strategically important and well-constructed, but little used. Traffic between the two 'brother peoples' was scarcely worth mentioning; indeed, their two empires were divided by a strip of no-man's-land about 30km wide through which we now bumped along with difficulty and very little to guide us. Our direction was indicated by the beaten caravan path, by a pair of half-obliterated vehicle tracks – evidently old ones – and by the telegraph wire. What would we find in Afghanistan, the country about which we had heard so many conflicting reports?

Included in our onboard library was the book about the Citroën expedition with caterpillar-tracked cars, *La croisière jaune* by J P Dauliac (1931-32). Concerning the Persian-Afghan border, he writes on page 22:

"In Kariz, the Persian border post, the Iranian guide to the expedition, Colonel Esfandiari, painted a gloomy picture of Afghanistan. 'No roads, no bridges over the larger rivers, no security on the caravans because of war with the Uzbeks and the nomads are constantly fighting one another. Did you know,' he continued, 'that we are still without news of five Europeans who left Persian soil two years ago in Kariz, heading for Herat and Kabul?'"

Was it really as bad as that? Certainly there had been queries in Masshad, "What? You've got an Afghan visa?" and then much head-shaking, because an Australian had been stuck in Masshad for months waiting for permission to enter the country. Indeed, I had not been able to get a visa either when, two years previously, I had badly wanted to go by this shorter and much more adventurous route on the motorcycle to India.

This time I had been successful, but you could have written a book brimming over with accounts of the Herculean effort and irritating uncertainty. It now became clear that studying at the university in Vienna had its uses. One became friendly with other students; with luck one of them might come from Afghanistan with connections to the Minister of War, and might use these connections for the benefit of his fellow students.

Even now it was not that simple. In Tehran we had still not known whether our application would be accepted. Many telegrams were exchanged between the two capitals before we could at last collect the visas. With studied indifference, I remarked casually on leaving the Afghan consulate in Tehran, "I take it that there won't be any difficulties over the car?"

We were much afraid that this elaborate 'piece of luggage' might seriously hinder the granting of permission to enter the country, so we had not mentioned it to begin with.

"Ah, so you want to take a car?" commented the consul, shaking his head thoughtfully. "I really cannot tell whether you will have difficulties. It depends entirely on the customs office at the border."

As yet we had seen no customs house, but after a journey of three hours through no-man's-land a large fort appeared on the horizon. We stopped and stowed our photo- and cine-cameras in the compartments behind the seats that held our provisions. In Afghanistan, where religious observance was so strict, it was clearly better not to advertise the 'picture machines.'

The car cast a long shadow across the plain as we neared the Afghan border fort. Dusk would soon become night. The great fortress was half-dilapidated and resembled an enormous ruin. Ghostly fires burned in the courtyard where the Afghans were roasting meat. Rifle barrels glinted, reflecting the flames, horses scuffled their hooves and strained at their traces under the walls and arches that stood out dark against the evening sky. A soldier led us into the interior of the fort.

It was the first time on this journey that I had felt any trepidation. The rough companions camped around the fire were silent, hands in the act of conveying a bloody joint of meat to the mouth stopped in mid-air and the foreign intruders became the object of hostile stares. There was a deathly hush, whilst only the horses took no notice and continued to paw the ground.

My heart was beating heavily. Yes, this was really Asia as I had imagined it in my childhood, savage and unpredictable, full of hatred of the infidel. That was the true Asia I had known as a boy, reading Karl May's adventures of Haji Halef Omar.

I plucked up all my courage and tried to speak, but the words stuck in my throat. Then I managed to cough up the one word "Salaam," which echoed hesitantly round the courtyard. Nobody answered, but the man just in front of me, dressed in baggy breeches and burnous, brought his mutton shank up to his mouth. The tension broke and they all turned back to their meal. Nobody took any more notice of the two foreigners who did not believe in Allah. The soldier led us through ranks of warriors towards the rear of the fort and disappeared inside with the letter of recommendation in Afghan, provided by our student friend Mahmudi in Vienna.

We waited. We waited a very long time. Then suddenly the door was thrown open and an Afghan officer, resplendent and immaculately dressed, hastened towards us and greeted us with the words "Glad to meet you!" We were quite taken aback at this, but on he went in good English. "What a coincidence, just imagine! Mahmudi, who gave you this letter, is a good old friend of mine!"

Leaving the savage romance of Asia behind us in the courtyard – the Afghans roasting their meat, the stacks of rifles – we were soon sitting in a comfortably furnished room where conversation came easily. We gathered from hints he dropped that this man with intelligent eyes and rather sad lines around his mouth had not spent all his time among rough-and-ready fighters like these, and that his stay at the fort was in some sense a disciplinary posting. Before receiving us as emissaries from the outside world, he must have had a quick wash and brush up, and probably spruced up his quarters, too, which was why we had to wait so long.

He now told us things about Afghanistan and its inhabitants that were to prove of great value to us in subsequent encounters. The Afghans are a freedom-loving people. Carrying weapons is a matter of course for every man, but so is their use on the very slightest provocation. Gulam Ali (our kindly host) therefore advised us most insistently to stop when we encountered Afghans on horseback. If the car should cause a horse to shy and throw his rider, then an Afghan would consider this a disgrace demanding revenge. Even better would be to offer these sons of the soil a cigarette straight away. The rules of hospitality were held so sacred that this was, in effect, a way of disarming a man who would never think of raising a hand against his host.

We slumbered peacefully that night on our camp beds which we put up in Gulam Ali's study. Outside, the savage company kept watch defending the fort, incidentally defending us as well. Whether this additional task gave them any satisfaction we did not know. The commander had given the orders, that was all. On the following morning I was impatient to see whether we would discuss the customs clearance, a topic that we had scrupulously avoided the night before. Gulam Ali had certainly behaved like a friend, but it was hard to be sure.

At breakfast (to which we contributed some of our tinned food) we asked about our passports and requested a nice clear stamp. Nearly all customs officials in Asia love this and feel flattered to be asked. However, Gulam Ali did not seem at all bothered, which didn't augur well for successful customs clearance. He gave us the passports and announced, "I'd very much like to see your car." I was assailed by uneasy forebodings, but he looked the vehicle over and demonstrated amazing technical knowledge. Then he said, "I would advise you to leave soon or you will find yourselves in the heat of the day before you get to Herat."

We didn't need telling twice, so we shook his hand and gave him our thanks, leapt into the car and started the engine.

"Goodbye, and a safe journey!" he called to us. Then we slipped into gear and were soon moving. We were in Afghanistan.

What a country! No vehicle import licence, no waybill, no bonded warehouse, no baggage check. It was as if we had walked in barefoot over the frontier.

After the trackless wastes of no-man's-land there was now a road of sorts which snaked along the Heri-Rud, now to the left, now to the right of the river. Each time the road crossed the river on a high arched stone bridge of almost biblical antiquity, we made a halt and plunged into the stream. Unless you have tried travelling through the urlajat under the scorching July sun, you will scarcely credit this pathological desire for water. Urlajat, 'the native soil,' is what the Afghans call their own land. We made a new discovery, which was to soak our shirts as well and put them back on dripping wet. This would then cool the whole body for quite a while in the air stream as we drove along.

Herat has a population of 50,000 and looks like a fortress with the many high and ancient walls that enclose the town proper. The streets were pleasantly clean and they were cleaned in a most original fashion. A man would carry on his back, in the manner of a rucksack, a goatskin tightly bulging with water. What had once been the goat's leg now served as a hosepipe which sprayed out a stream of water when waved back and forth over the street.

They were less particular when it came to keeping petrol clean. We learned that one of the caravanserais had begun to convert to motors (which at that time were not nearly as important in Afghanistan as in Persia) and they did indeed bring us several open cans. All sorts of rubbish collected in the funnel sieve – small pebbles, straw, lumps of dirt. The finer dirt bedded down in the tank. Still, at least we had petrol. Then it was time to pay for it. Sixty litres of petrol cost 748 Afghan coins. Woe to him who hesitates counting it out! He may find that he has to start counting again just as he nears the end. These coins drove us to distraction. We went into the Herat currency exchange office with four Persian 100-toman notes and came out struggling under the weight of two bags and a small box full of coins.

I never fully got the hang of the coins. There was the afghani which for practical purposes stood in relation to the kabuli at a rate of 9:10. After that, a kabuli was divided for some reason into 66 kani. Either you had to be very good at mental arithmetic or big-hearted enough to let yourself be robbed. There was as yet no paper money in Afghanistan.

If the caravanserai outwardly resembled the Persian motor halts, the vehicles we met there were totally different. There was even one make represented nowhere else in the world: 'Afghan.' On closer inspection, this proved to be a clever marketing dodge perpetrated by the efficient Americans, who had had this name put on the radiator and bonnet of a GMT (General Motors Truck). Otherwise Afghanistan imported only chassis, the rest being built on by the sons of the 'native soil' themselves, heavy wooden coachwork in the shape of an omnibus, durable but not beautiful. They used wire netting instead of window glass, and, instead of leather seats, wooden benches down the length of each side. Not comfortable, but it saved space, although it was mostly not intended for passengers, since so many goods were stacked between the floor of the vehicle and the roof that only a metre of space was left on top. Into this the people packed themselves happily like sardines. On the outside, though, the wooden coachwork was brightly painted with landscapes, mosques and decorations which we in Europe could never emulate.

That applied also to the resourcefulness of Afghan drivers. We once passed a man who was smearing a mixture of torn-up felt, honey and flour between the bars of his leaky radiator. The radiator stopped leaking! By chance we met the same vehicle again the following day and could be satisfied that it was in perfect working order.

However, all things considered, the Afghan was not much in favour of the motor car. The many camel caravans and troops of donkeys that we met as we travelled on from Herat to Kandahar had to be treated with special care. We were trespassing on their centuries-old rights, and for the time being, in complete contrast to Persia, we took second place. The proud people of the Urlajat were still highly conscious of their importance as camel drivers, and we became aware of a frank disdain of motors from both man and beast. We could overtake the caravans only with extreme caution, making every effort to show courtesy.

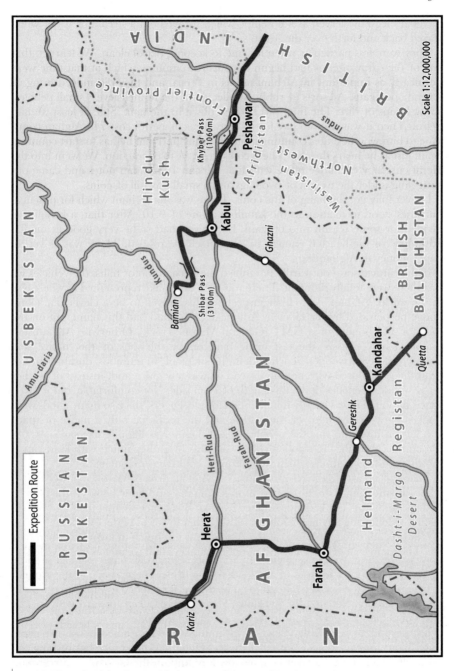

Map 3: Through Afghanistan, with detours to Quetta and Bamian.

9
HUNGARIAN AFGHANS, BAVARIAN AFGHANS

"What on earth is that?" called out Helmuth twice in quick succession, and each time I stopped the car so that we could take a closer look at curious work practices among the Afghans, which we had never seen before. The first time it was peasants cutting corn in their bare stony fields. There were even some unveiled women among them, beautiful pure-bred creatures. But for the moment we had no eyes for them, being only interested in the hands of the peasants. They were wearing a kind of glove over the left hand with the thumb and forefinger massively elongated by curved sticks of wood. As if with pincers, they were able to grasp whole sheaves at once which they then cut off with a sickle. The stalks fell bundle by bundle at incredible speed.

When Helmut started the cine camera, all work came to a standstill and, as on previous occasions, we and our diabolical machine were assailed with fierce and angry words.

The windmills had less to say for themselves. We photographed these odd structures at a safe distance from both men and animals. Revolving on a vertical axle were sails woven out of straw, designed to catch the wind on one side only. This was why the other side had a curved mud wall around it, the height of a two-storey house which looked like half of a tower. It was a curious sight. Just as strange, maybe more so, was the manner in which the sacks of corn were brought in on the backs of little donkeys. We were constantly amazed at the loads these animals were expected to carry. They were scarcely visible, except for the head and the spindly legs which seemed to stick straight out of the mountain of sacks, tittupping busily along as if powered by an unwearying engine. In addition, a long tall man would sit proudly up front on the neck in front of the load, letting his feet hang down to the ground. Whenever the little donkey refused to go further or threatened to sink into the sand, the rider simply stretched his feet down lower and marched forward with it. The effect of these six-legged man-donkeys was totally ludicrous.

Just beyond a pretty little village of gleaming-white flat-roofed houses we came upon more human subjects for our camera. These had no choice but to keep still for us. We had crossed a river by a narrow ford and on the far bank, seated round a campfire, we found the usual group of wild-looking, heavily armed Afghans. However, the Afghan badge on their turbans told us that we were dealing with

60

Above: The big question at the Persian-Afghan frontier was whether we would be allowed in with the car. There were no international documents for Afghanistan.

Left: Afghanistan is a strict Islamic country which forbids other religions to practise or to proselytise. The guardian of this tomb regards the 'white foreign devils' with suspicion.

Above: A clever dodge: harvesters wear a 'hand extension' with which they can grasp a whole sheaf of corn at one go.

Right: The largest Afghans seem to ride the smallest donkeys. When the donkey gets tired, the rider can walk along with it without getting off. These are called 'six-legged man-donkeys.'

Windmill near Herat. The axle is vertical and the sails are made of straw mats. Experts say that this is the oldest type of windmill and that it originated in Central Asia.

bona-fide policemen. Even so, we approached them rather cautiously, but they were already waving to us, chattering, laughing and pointing towards the vaulted cellar of a tumbledown house. Out of curiosity we looked inside and leapt back with a cry of alarm. The police had struck lucky and arrested half-a-dozen robbers whom they were now about to convey to the nearest police station. There they squatted, shackled together with heavy chains, leering up at us so horribly with such devilish faces that the thought of meeting any of their kind running around free quite terrified us. At our request some of these savage fellows were dragged up into the light and we were able to take as many robber photos as we wished.

We stole sideways glances at each other, wondering if we weren't beginning to show a certain similarity to them. Because of sunburn we had not been able to shave and had finally decided to let our beards grow. We had persuaded each other that this would not alarm our fellow countryman in Farrah should we turn up unexpectedly. In Herat we had learned, to our great astonishment, that there was supposed to be an Austrian living in Farrah, the most feared and the most hated town in Afghanistan. Because of its appalling climate – scorching hot in the daytime and very cold at night – this town, with its malaria and its typhus, is regarded as the Siberia of Afghanistan. Political prisoners live there, and although they are allowed to move about freely must not go beyond a boundary set at a certain distance around the town.

The object of our search was one of the few men to live here voluntarily. He was apparently employed as an engineer on the building of a bridge. On the road we met with a troop of men dressed partly in European clothing, wearing sheepskin caps. A policeman had come with us in the car and was now pointing them out. I must confess I would never have recognised the man as a European. We addressed him in German, but he was so surprised that for a moment he could scarcely utter a word. Then it all came tumbling out in three languages at once, German, Afghan and Hungarian.

"It's Budapest I come from!" he said.

Budapest, fancy that! He was overjoyed to be speaking German again after so many years and was quite beside himself. It was a while before he could give a coherent account of his experiences, which were fantastic enough.

In the First World War two German expeditions had attempted to secure Afghanistan as an ally against Britain. One of them was under the leadership of Oskar von Niedermayer, famous counterpart of Colonel Lawrence. In the face of great difficulties he forced his way from Palestine through Persia to Kabul. Our Hungarian had taken part in this venture, together with six Austrians. The expedition had ended in failure, and most of the participants had attempted to reach East Asia by way of Turkestan and Mongolia, from where they eventually returned to Europe in 1918. However, the Hungarian stayed in Afghanistan and contracted to build roads and bridges. He became naturalised to such an extent that he converted to Islam, became an Afghan citizen and married an Afghan woman, and we saw him now as an official of the Afghan government. He showed us the site of the bridge being built over the Farrah-Rud. We observed that it was going to be a beautiful bridge.

"Yes," he agreed, "but nobody knows when it will be ready. We are always lacking something vital to the construction – wood for the framework, cement, nails, clamps, and skilled workers most of all."

Above: The ark, or citadel of Herat. In the 1930s it was a virtually impregnable fortress in the centre of Herat. Later in the century, wars reduced it to rubble, but it has recently undergone extensive restoration.

Below: Giving way proves difficult on this stony surface! The donkeys are transporting desert shrubs as fuel to nomad encampments.

At night we shared the engineer's simple meal which had for years followed the same dull pattern: pilau (the Afghan rice), tea, bread, mutton and fruit. In the course of it, he described the wretchedness of his lonely existence far from Europe, and was constantly overcome with emotion. We had broken in too suddenly upon his life, a physical reminder of his almost-forgotten homeland, opening old wounds and arousing nostalgic desires.

Budapest, the Danube, wine, the csárdás, Hungarian women – it all sprang vividly to his mind. The tears ran down his cheeks and he began to whimper like a child.

"Budapest! My beloved Budapest!"

We tried to distract him from his memories but it was no good. He seemed to be overwhelmed with sadness and yet at the same time exalted. It was not until long after midnight that we all lay down to sleep in his hut on the building site.

The following morning Helmuth had a good idea. "I know, we'll give him the salami!" In our stock of meat products (sealed for use in the tropics) which was intended to be eaten only in time of need or for celebratory purposes, we still had a fine whole salami. This we now unpacked and ceremoniously presented to our Hungarian friend, saying, "A present from your long-lost homeland!"

He was seized with violent emotion and struggled once more to repress his tears, but the salami remained in Helmuth's outstretched hand. The Afghans around us were watching expectantly but the Hungarian did not take the salami. We looked from one to the other, rather surprised. Finally he exclaimed in a choked voice, "For God's sake put that sausage away. I can't eat it! The Koran forbids it. It could cost me my entire reputation here as an engineer!"

We took the salami back to the car. I will never forget the sadness in the Hungarian's eyes as the sausage disappeared back into the provisions box.

"Farewell, and give my love to the homeland," he said quietly as we took our leave. He would gladly have come with us, but he was bound to his employment and I felt that he would never go home again. He was lost to his native land, for all his nostalgia.

He provided us with two letters of recommendation, the first of which was to the mayor of Girishk. Girishk lies on the banks of the Helmand and the Lord knows how we would have got across the river at that season (when it was swollen with melting snow from the Hindu Kush) without some help from the authorities. We found the local dignitaries in a hut made of branches to which they had transferred their seat of power during the heat. Several soldiers were constantly occupied outside, dousing the walls with water. Two others were on sentry duty in front of this rather ludicrous official building. They pointed to our shoes which we easily recognised as a command to remove them and soon our boots were lined up alongside the elaborate and richly decorated Afghan slippers and sandals. We stepped inside and were astounded how cool and fresh it was in that small space, although it was filled with people.

The most venerable of the bearded men invited us to sit down on the carpet. We were presented with hot green tea in glasses and our interview with the city fathers of Girishk began. It was very simple. We pointed to the letter of recommendation and they kept on talking, while we smiled and nodded encouragingly. This little game went on for quite a while. We had already learned that one must never get

Above: The summer residence of the mayor of Girischk. The brushwood hut was constantly doused with water, which kept it amazingly cool inside.

Above: Primitive loom, half sunk in the ground (weaver's seat in foreground).

Above: The Helmand, one of many rivers in Afghanistan with no bridges. On antediluvian ferries like this we needed all the help that oriental kismet and western luck could give.

Above: Captured bandits brought out of their dark hole by Afghan soldiers so that we could photograph them.

impatient in the East. At last, however, coffee was brought in, a sure sign that the 'conference' was at an end. A soldier was assigned to us and we assumed that he had been ordered to help us with the river-crossing, as requested in the letter.

Down the valley rolled the grey and muddy Helmand, a mix of melt water and soil. There was a heavy current, and it seemed very doubtful whether we would be able to get the car across. Furthermore, when I saw the rickety boat pitching and tossing restlessly on the waves, I confided to Helmuth, "It would be much simpler with a motorcycle!"

Could our heavy car really cross this raging torrent on a boat reminiscent of the one that carried the souls of the dead to the underworld in Greek mythology? Add to this the lack of any proper approach road or rescue apparatus. It was a desperate prospect, and no one would attempt such a thing unless he had to. If the boat were caught in an eddy and capsized, that would be the end of it. The ferry boatmen however preserved a calm oriental demeanour. They made a solemn and serious appraisal of the situation and then brought along a load of poles, beams and planks. With these, and a sort of studied carelessness, they built a ramp from the bank to the boat. I was quite certain that the whole conjuring trick would collapse as soon as the car's front wheels drove on to it, but there are miracles, apparently, in the lands of Islam, including technical ones. I could hear groaning and cracking below and felt something rocking. I accelerated and the car leapt on to the ferry, leaving behind splintered planks and cracked beams.

The current drove the boat wildly downstream. The ferry boatmen never batted an eyelid, but bent to the oars in a quiet, matter-of-fact way while two boys baled out the water that was getting in.

The crossing lasted about ten minutes, until we reached the other bank many hundreds of metres further downstream. Allah had blessed our journey!

The second letter of recommendation was addressed to the representative of Siemens-Schuckert in Kandahar. "You really must look him up," the Hungarian had insisted. "He's a real Bavarian and has a house with all home comforts!"

We asked our way to the man's house through a maze of alleyways – thank goodness the address was written in Afghan characters on the letter – but on our arrival we found not him but his Afghan servant who addressed us in very broken German.

"Engineer not here. Come back two hours."

However, he was evidently used to unexpected guests, for he immediately brought us table and chairs, bread, sour milk, fruit and his master's wind-up gramophone with a stack of records. When we asked the way to a barber's, he pointed to himself and gave us each a very decent haircut. A frequent word that we noticed in his garbled speech was Schafskopf ('Sheep's head,' also 'Numskull'). To begin with we wondered nervously whether he intended to shear us like a sheep's head, but soon realised that this was the charming name by which the good honest Bavarian usually called his servant.

An urgent desire to relieve ourselves prompted us to test this theory by calling aloud "Numskull!"

He appeared on the instant and we enquired most politely for the lavatory. He grinned. "No understand!"

As things were becoming more urgent, we tried another tack and asked, "Where latrine?"

"Me, Numskull, no understand!"

At this Helmuth ran out of patience and began to swear in Munich dialect. Half laughing, half desperate, he exclaimed, "Ja, habt ihr kein Sch ... haus hier?"

"Me understand!" beamed Numskull, and we were saved.

Above: In the villages, people had never seen a car. Although usually so courageous, the Afghans feared this strange animal, knowing only that it was capable of rapid and sudden movement. This explains why they kept a respectful distance ahead of the car!

Left: The Shikari narrows ('Hunter's gorge) in the Hindukush. Crossing bridges like these was always a gamble.

Above: Getting stuck in loose gravel on the flood plain of the Heri-Rud river between Herat and Kandahar.

Living with just the bare necessities in the Dasht-i-Margo, the so-called Desert of Death, yet this is where religious fervour is strongest.

Above: Afghan fiddler at a nomad wedding.

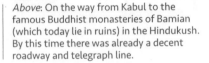

Above: On the way from Kabul to the famous Buddhist monasteries of Bamian (which today lie in ruins) in the Hindukush. By this time there was already a decent roadway and telegraph line.

Below: The mosque of Mazar-i-sharif ('grave of the Prophet'), the holiest city in Afghanistan. Early attempts at motorisation usually came to grief because of small mechanical failures or lack of spare parts. This steam-roller had been imported from the Soviet Union in the north.

Left: Clothes make the man ... Max Reisch in the costume of the Afridi. He is beginning to grow the beard which was to prove so useful in China.

Below: In the 1930s, the first bus services began in the region of Kabul, Herat, Kandahar and Ghazni. First class meant riding in front with the driver, second class inside the vehicle, but third class was accommodated on the roof in the full glare of the sun. Fixed into the primitive ladder is a lump of wood on a pole which helped with hill starts on steep gradients.

Above: Turkmen woman in northern Afghanistan. Many Turkmen tribes fled from the Soviet Union after the First World War, bringing with them their highly-developed skills in rug-making and the production of 'Persian' lamb skins.

Above: Habibullah-Khan (centre) was murdered in 1919, whereupon his son Amanullah (left) had himself proclaimed king, but his attempts to modernise the country brought about his downfall in 1926.

Below: In 1924, King Amanullah ordered the construction of the first (and only) tramway in Afghanistan. After his fall, the tramcars were converted for use as goat stalls. Amanullah had modelled himself on the Turkish dictator Atatürk, but succumbed in the face of clerical opposition. Before this, he had visited Germany and bought two Junkers aircraft, which he never paid for. In 1926, he went into exile in Rome.

Below: Proud sons of the Urlajat, the 'native soil,' or the 'navel of the world,' as the Afghans refer to their country. The predominant tribes are the Afridi, the Waziri and the Ghilzai.

Above: Border fortress, also serving as a granary for the warlike tribe of the Afridi on the Khyber Pass.

Above: Traffic regulations on the Khyber Pass. For strategic reasons, the slow and ponderous camel-caravans were not allowed to use the new motor road.

Below: British Indian Sikh troops on manoeuvres in the border area of the North West Frontier, home of the notoriously freedom-loving Afridis.

Above: There was always trouble on the Khyber Pass. To protect the North West Frontier between India and Afghanistan, the British had driven a road and a railway deep into the mountains.

Above: The border between Afghanistan and India on the Khyber Pass. Driving permits were only rarely issued, and motorcycles were completely forbidden until 1933, following the incident when Dr Stratil-Sauer, a German resident in India, caused the death of a rider who fell from his horse at the noise caused by a motorcycle.

Left: Permit No 124 allowing Max Reisch and his Steyr 100 car to travel through the North West Frontier Province, issued in Kabul 25 July 1935.

No. **124**

PERMIT FOR ENTRY OF A MOTOR-VEHICLE INTO THE NORTH-WEST FRONTIER PROVINCE.

This pass shall, after endorsement by the District Magistrate, Peshawar, be valid in the N.-W. F. P. for one year only from the date of its issue.

Certified that the undermentioned vehicle is fit for use, and the driver thereof fit to drive, on the highways of British India.

Kabul :

Date *25th July 1935*

British Legation, Kabul.

Secretary.

Note.—This Pass is the first instance merely authorises the owner or owners, on arrival at Landi Kotal to apply for authority to proceed with the vehicle covered thereby to Peshawar. On arrival at Peshawar the pass must be produced before the District Magistrate for endorsement and for separation of the reverse.

PARTICULARS REGARDING THE VEHICLE

Name	**Max Reisch**
Father's name	**Hans Reisch**
Owner of vehicle { Address	**Wien 4,Storhembergg 39**
	Austria

Description of vehicle **Motor Car 3 Seater**

Name of maker **Steyr**

Particulars of model of chassis **1935 Model A 20 20**

Serial number of model, or maker's number of chassis **G 1501**

	Number of cylinders **Four**
Motor	Horse power, or bore of cylinders **35 H.P. Brake**
	Shape **Touring Car**
Body	Colour **Grey**
	Number of seats **Three**

Weight of vehicle empty **K.G. 1000**

Number, or distinguishing marks on identity plates **Austria A 2020**

Name of driver **Max Reisch**

Father's name **Hans Reisch**

Address **Wien 4,Storhembergg 39**

Austria.

10
CLOSER TO INDIA

In Kandahar we were to see first-hand how the time for prayers affected a larger and rather more modernised city. All the traffic stopped, cars came to a halt, beasts of burden were tethered to the trees that lined the streets. People squatted by the open runnels to perform their ritual ablutions. Then they rolled out little carpets and, facing west towards Mecca, began their prayers. Even the policeman who had been directing the traffic from a raised platform in the middle of the square outside the mosque knelt down and hundreds of people with him. It felt embarrassing to go on walking upright in the midst of all these people kneeling, but our Bavarian friend led us forward, saying that this was the only correct course of action.

From Kandahar the way led along the notorious Northwest Frontier. The very name gave me a few qualms, seeing that this was the site of constant flare ups between Afghanistan and India. It was also quite clear that some sort of trouble was brewing, but we passed through escorted by tanks of the Afghan military without any mishap. The fact that one of the tanks broke down can scarcely be called a mishap, since in view of its venerable appearance we would have been amazed if it had reached its destination in one piece. What interested us more was the way they set about transporting it. They began to load all six tonnes of it on to a lorry with a load-bearing capacity of 3000kg. We took the liberty of issuing a gentle warning, but the answer was simply "Allah is great!" In this case, as it turned out, Allah seemed to lack the necessary technical foresight. With ramps and block and tackle the tank was successfully hauled on to the lorry, but after travelling only a few kilometres all the springs broke. Now we had not one, but two unusable vehicles in the column, and in the end we had to leave them both behind, but we reached Kabul safely.

We visited the brother of our friend in Vienna, Mahmudi, and we were deeply touched by the good care he took of us. Many Europeans received us with the warmest hospitality, and all insisted that we must not leave without seeing Bamiyan. We therefore set off, driving through romantic and rugged gorges (one of which stretched for a magnificent 120km) up to Bamiyan and the ruins of its Buddhist monastery, founded in the sixth century by Tibetan monks. Six hundred years later, the little centre of Buddhist culture that had grown from this foundation fell victim to a Mongol invasion led by one of Genghis Khan's sons. They crossed the mountains of the Pamir and Hindu Kush in the dead of winter at the cost of enormous effort and privation, and fell without warning upon the territories lying on the further side. Nevertheless, one can still see three colossal statues of Buddha, carved in the living rock, the largest of which is so huge that a dozen men can stand on its head. The rock is honeycombed with the cells, caves, passages, chambers and staircases of the monastery. These ruins are all that is left in Afghanistan to suggest the existence of any religion but Islam. With the exception of Tibet, it is the only country in Asia which allows no proselytising by any other faith. [These statues were blown up by the Taliban in 2001. Tr.]

A record was broken on the return journey – nothing to do with motor engineering or travel – but a gastronomic record. As we were looking ahead at all the twists and turns that led up to the 3000 metre high Haft Pass, Helmuth observed, "I think the car needs a rest, and I'm hungry!"

We unpacked the cooking box and broke some eggs into the pan. They were the only food of which we had a lavish supply. The products of the Afghan chicken are of no very great size, but it was an exceptional achievement on Helmuth's part to consume 16 of them at a sitting. He paid a sorry price for it! The next day there was a slap-up banquet at the British consul's in Kabul, which Helmuth was quite unable to enjoy, with the 16 eggs still lying heavy on his stomach.

We also had official business to attend to at the British Consulate. A special permit was necessary for crossing the Khyber Pass and entering the Promised Land of India. We had to demonstrate the car to a motor specialist and were then presented with an extensive document which would also serve as a driving licence on the roads of British India. In this were recorded not only the technical data concerning the car but also the name of my father, which only goes to show that the plodding grey horse of European bureaucracy was presently sharing a stable with the fiery steeds of the Afridis.

The area surrounding this pass is also famous, or rather notorious for the constant minor skirmishes, which here are the order of the day. The situation of the road, which in many places touches British territory on the one side and Afghan territory on the other, permits considerable refinement in the settling of scores. For example, the police once came upon a murdered man on the British side. After a short search they ran the murderer to earth and arrested him. He was most indignant, as he had only been exercising his proper rights in a blood feud, and on the Afghan side at that. His despicable victim had retained enough strength to drag himself over into British territory where the avenger could be hanged for his deed. The police checked the evidence, found traces of blood which confirmed the story of the bloodthirsty avenger and were obliged, with suitable apologies, to let him go.

It was a laborious two-day journey on bad stony tracks for the car to reach the Khyber Pass, but from here on we were suddenly in a different world. A railway appeared abruptly, as if conjured out of the earth; forts looked down from all the hilltops, telegraph wires sliced through the air, and from inside the mountains, which hid superbly camouflaged fortifications, we heard the roar of diesel engines.

We paid a visit to the commanding officer of the great fort on the crest of the pass, and received further permission to continue our journey to Peshawar. He then invited us to tour the fort and to watch a Gurkha regiment on manoeuvres. His invitation appealed to us all the more because of the aura of secrecy usually surrounding such things. Sixty men set off to run cross-country from a fort lying about 2km away as the crow flies. We saw them come charging down the mountainside, twice disappearing into hollows in the valley and finally sprinting up the steep slope towards our fort. Neither of us would have stayed even part of the course, and moreover, these native soldiers were running barefoot!

The colonel invited us for a drink in his own quarters. We were amazed to find that this block of grey stone with its embrasures, munitions stores and barracks also contained a comfortably furnished apartment. We sank into cosy club chairs. One drink became two, and then, as far as I can remember, quite a considerable number. We completely forgot that we were sitting on the Northwest Frontier where you never knew what the next day would bring. Even our host seemed totally unconcerned, no doubt because he was used to being always at the ready. The very next day he might have to mount a campaign against some robber band or other. Anyway, he seemed unaffected by the large number of whiskies, although I couldn't say the same for myself, arriving as we were from a 'dry' country where alcohol was a sin, and where Europeans were subject to a government ban on alcohol, even if they were not bound by the Koran. Each white man was allowed 50 bottles of beer per year. What a ridiculously small amount this was can only be appreciated by someone who has seen the way white people drink outside Europe and America. I don't mean that there are no teetotallers in the tropics, but they are rare and they are usually unhealthy. A certain quantity of alcohol is said to be an absolute prerequisite for the maintenance of physical well-being in the tropics. That's as may be, but when does the 'certain quantity' cease to be medicinal and become a debilitating poison, and the reason why so many Europeans in hot countries 'go to the dogs'?

Somewhat elated, we said farewell to the friendly colonel and steered merrily down the smooth winding road from the Khyber Pass into India. Night was falling and we were soon to realise that the pleasant hours we had passed in the British fort came at a price.

Arriving at Peshawar, a town with a population of 100,000, we found the gates shut and we kicked up a fuss. We could understand that one might shut the front door of one's house in the evening, but why a whole city? The sentries were unmoved by our complaints, explaining that the gates were closed at eight every evening and the key was in the garrison headquarters. We smote ourselves on the forehead. Were we still in the twentieth century or had we inadvertently stepped into some sort of "galoshes of fortune", like in Andersen's fairytale, and been transported back to the middle ages? But it was real. We remembered that in the North West Frontier Province the wicked Afridis would be keeping a watch on the town from up in the mountains.

The idyll was shattered.

Anyone arriving from Afghanistan knows that in the hotel in Peshawar he will find his first long-awaited white bed. This was now denied us, just when we would have sunk into it most gladly after our drinks at the top of the pass. But there was nothing for it. Hung over and wretched, we were obliged to go back several kilometres to the last fort, where at least we found a commanding officer sympathetic to our predicament. Soldiers erected our camp beds, and then the Englishman had us served with whatever the kitchens and cellars could offer at that late hour. At last we fell asleep contented within the security of the fortifications. The strange thing here was that we would not have risked sleeping in the open, knowing that the forts were nearby. In Afghanistan itself, where it was far more dangerous, we lay down to rest without a second thought wherever dusk overtook us.

The following morning we took a closer look at our surroundings. In an odd way, I seemed to recognise them – the landscape, certain parts of the fortifications ...

But these were no memories from a former life, as an Indian would probably have supposed. There was a much more Western explanation for the phenomenon. The commanding officer told us that a lot of scenes from the film *The Lives of a Bengal Lancer* (1935) had been shot here. So not all the magic tricks you see in the cinema are film sets! You may be sitting comfortably at the pictures back home, thinking "That's a clever bit of set building!" Yet it still sends a shiver down your spine. Out here you see everything the way it really is; you listen to the officer's stories of punitive expeditions and adventures on the Northwest Frontier, and you don't turn a hair! When you are on a trip you get used to the different and the unusual. Breakfast tasted no worse for the news just coming over the radio that a cholera epidemic had broken out in Peshawar, and that a bit further on, heavy monsoon rains had flooded whole villages. [According to some sources, much of the film shot on location in India deteriorated, so the production was eventually shot in California, with some elaborate sets. Tr.]

It was four months since our inoculations, so the first place we drove to on entering the gates of Peshawar (now wide open) was the hospital, but they did not have a single ampoule of vaccine for us. Troops were out inoculating people all over the place, and supplies of serum were eagerly awaited. Besides, in the town itself all Europeans had already been inoculated. It was not until the following morning that we were fortunate enough to lay our hands on another ampoule in the military hospital. Thus relieved, with heavily swollen arms and eighty litres of germ-free water in the cans, we set out again.

The hours leading up to our departure passed quickly, as we spent the daytime and part of the night shopping in the Peshawar bazaars, with Helmuth wanting to get a new khaki outfit. It was swarming with soldiers, English naturally, and then the Scots with their short kilts and checked bonnets, swinging little canes with silver knobs. Soon Helmuth found the cut of uniform he'd been looking for, and we learned how every Indian shopkeeper checks that the rupee you've given him is genuine. He lays the coin on his bent index finger and flicks it upward with his thumbnail. When the nail hits it, it should ring with a clear silvery tone. It flies a couple of feet up in the air, to be skilfully caught by the same hand. The silver content of a genuine rupee is so good that you can buy cheap silver jewellery of not particularly good workmanship on a weight-for-weight basis. You pay as many rupees as it takes to balance the piece.

Then there was an area full of narrow alleyways with little bays built out on the houses. The ladies who lived here leaned out of the bay windows, smiling seductively. In Peshawar, as in the other Indian cities, this was called the 'Bibi bazaar'. These beauties (and to European eyes there were some really pretty creatures among them) wore wreaths of heavily scented white flowers, little silver nose rings, sometimes a pearl in the nostril, heavy rings in their ears, and little chains or rings around the ankle. None of these flashed or gleamed as brightly as the brilliant white teeth in those narrow brown faces or the fire in their deep black eyes. Whenever we wandered into a 'Bibi bazaar' the girls were amused by Helmuth's light blond hair and made frequent attempts to grab hold of it, just in order to discover whether it was really growing on his head.

11
KASHMIR

On the Grand Trunk Road, which runs from Peshawar to Calcutta, we crossed the Indus at approximately the same spot as Alexander the Great. Before him, the Persian king Darius had already shown interest in 'where the Indus flows,' and had sent a Hellene to follow the course of the stream. Possessed by the desire to create a sensation on his return to Persia, Scylax of Caryanda allowed the Indians to tell him the wildest of tales about their country. There were people with enormous ears and the heads of dogs, rings with magic power, griffons guarding great hoards of treasure and trees whose roots attracted gold and silver by magnetism. Alexander knew all this from Persian sources, but of the terrible monsoon rains that turn half the country into a swamp from June to October he knew nothing. These were the principal reason why he came to grief in India. Not even his crushing defeat of the maharajah of Taxila in a brilliantly led night time battle could help, and Alexander was obliged to turn back. Yet even today one comes across evidence of the Greek invasion. The Indians incorporated columns in the Hellenistic style into their own architecture, even though the acanthus leaf was replaced by tropical tendrils, by rams' or even tigers' heads. Greek sculpture exerted a similar influence and in the little museum at Taxila we met with countless Buddha figures of all sizes, regarding us with faces of a pure Greek cast.

In Rawalpindi we left the broad tarmac highway and branched north. Cholera was said to be raging in the mountains of Kashmir, and so we would scrupulously avoid drinking any water other than our own supply. There was no way we were going to miss this detour into the glorious Himalaya. Indeed, there was an old saying: 'He who has not seen Kashmir does not know India.' We wanted to test the truth of this. Afterwards, we had to admit that it was so. What you experience is not the exotic India so often described by travellers. Up there, the images that present themselves are strangely familiar. You are in a client state at the northwest tip of the great Indian Empire, but it's like looking at a peepshow with a cut-out of Switzerland or the Tyrol, and then another of the English Lake District or of Venice. The cool mountain air wafted around as if we were at home. Prosperous Indians appreciate this European-type climate too. They escape from the intolerable summer monsoon to the deep green woods and mountain meadows of Kashmir, one of the loveliest countries on earth.

Kashmir has its own border with India, and while we waited in a queue of cars for customs clearance we watched the brown-skinned figures squatting motionless on the roadside. They fanned themselves with punkas – paper fans – to keep cool and made use of the popular back scratcher. A little hand with fingers curved at right-angles is mounted on the end of long wand. Depending on the purse of its owner it may be of wood, amber, ivory or jade. With this tool you can comfortably scratch all the parts of your back where the hand won't reach. When you've tired of this little game you can go hunting in the bushy hair of the man next to you. We noticed for the first time that any lice bagged in this way get eaten on the spot. Another pleasure is dipping into the betel box and chewing away, then spitting out the blood-coloured saliva to a great distance, leaving stains all over the place which Europeans find quite repulsive. On the other hand, the containers in which the betel nuts are kept are marvellous – cylindrical boxes woven out of bamboo, dipped in lacquer, polished and painted. Scenes from Indian myths and epics are frequently to be found on these tiny surfaces, beautifully depicted.

English people from the car waiting in front of ours came over and asked whether we were carrying corned beef or any tinned beef products, for which strictly Hindu Kashmir charges a particularly high duty.

"Just take the labels off the tins and say it's pork. You'll get through without any trouble."

We thanked them for their kind advice and had a quick rummage in the provisions box for the tins of corned beef, which accounted for most of those we had. It's so difficult in India with different kinds of meat. Only the day before we had been told a lovely story of how a pig had escaped from a wagon on a goods train and had gone charging around the station, squealing with delight, while the entire station staff crouched on benches and tables with their legs drawn up so as to avoid contact with the unclean creature. This station was in a Moslem area, and it took quite a while before they found someone who was not an ardent disciple of Islam, and consequently prepared to try and catch a pig.

Once we had passed the border with no difficulties and no customs charges, the land of the holy cow and the unholy pig both seemed far behind us. The houses were built of solid tree trunks. The roofs were flat and weighted with stones. There were wooden water troughs at the roadside, into which clear spring water from the mountains flowed in rough-hewn gutter pipes.

How our hearts quickened, though, one glorious morning at the sight of Srinagar and its unforgettable landscape crowned by Nanga Parbat. A heavy mist had come down the previous evening and we had gladly accepted the hospitality of a Catholic mission. Their task in this area was a long and hard one. Converting a single Moslem was all but impossible. It was easier to educate little Hindu girls to be good Christians and to take responsibility for the poor creatures. In order to rid themselves of an excess of female progeny, the usual expedient adopted by parents was to throw them into the Jhelum river. The missionaries fished them out again. Sitting around the fireside, we heard many a long tale of the difficulties facing this indefatigable brotherhood.

Next day, the cold and fog of the night time were all forgotten. The sky was cloudless and of the deepest, clearest blue. The broad valley of the Jhelum stretched out before us and an avenue of poplars led to Srinagar. Canals and lakes glittered around the houses and gardens of the town they call the Himalayan Venice, but behind the wooded slopes rose massive grey mountain walls and in the background, framing it all in a distant curve, the dazzling white chain of the Karakorum with its peaks 7000 metres high.

In between came the massif of Nanga Parbat. It is useless to attempt a description of this glorious summit, which at 7900 metres towers far above all other peaks and ranges. Suffice to say it is one of those visions that remain in the mind for a lifetime, an unforgettable gift of Providence.

The little Steyr rolled into Srinagar over a wooden bridge. The river was teeming with boats of all sizes. Traders had loaded their wares on to dug-outs with mountains of fruit and vegetables, mountains of flowers. On the steep riverbanks the houses were built so that the first floor was at street level, while at the back of the house one could step straight from the ground floor into the boat. Gables, ridges, balconies and window shutters were all richly decorated with the most beautiful wooden carvings. But the shikara, those trim little craft with canopies and plump cushions, were actually very similar in shape to the gondolas of the old city of the Doges and only the Indian gondoliers destroyed the illusion.

We were assailed by a veritable swarm of Indians, all wanting to rent us a house-boat – a speciality of Srinagar instead of hotels. Soon, for three rupees, we availed ourselves of one of these boats with two bedrooms, a dining room and a smoking room, not to mention servants to see to our wants, and finally a lotus pool just under our veranda and a panorama of the Himalayas on the horizon. Could you imagine a more beautiful spot for taking it easy, for dreaming, for spoiling yourself? If you felt too hot, you could dive straight out of bed into the cooling waters and if you got tired of the place where your floating hotel was moored, you could tell the Indian who would summon all his relations, and soon the houseboat would be rowed away to another spot. It was a thousand pities that the expedition had a time schedule and that we were endeavouring to keep to it.

This was still our ambition. For the moment, we had no inkling of how, later, the concept of time would become totally alien to us, nor how we would learn to take things as and when they happened, in true oriental style.

It was this ambition for special achievement that prompted our attempt at a first ascent by car from Srinagar to Pahalgam, then to a large tented camp at an altitude of 2800 metres used by many Indians as a summer resort, and finally to Amarnath. A proper road took us as far as the mountain village of Pahalgam, after which there were only mule tracks leading further into the mountains. We ran into difficulty on the very first slopes, but the Kashmiris immediately sprang to our aid. They are a small nation with a great capacity for enthusiasm, and in spite of being relatively untouched by civilisation they appreciate what technology can do. Lying dormant in their subconscious is something we Europeans would call a love of record-breaking. They were determined to achieve the impossible, and pushed us, eight men at a time! Little by little, we climbed seemingly impossible gradients. The way was often narrow and blocked by thick roots, which had to be attacked with spades and axes.

Slowly we moved forward. The spinning rear wheels were burning hot and the water in the radiator steamed. Then to crown it all, after taking us briskly forward over a plateau, the mule track began to twist upwards in impossibly tight hairpin

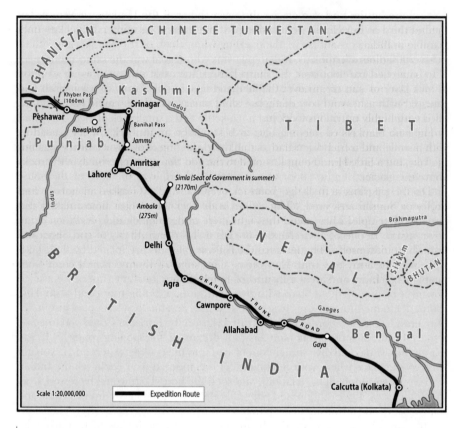

Map 4: Crossing northern India.

bends. We negotiated it by taking the slopes alternately in forward and reverse gear without turning the car round the sharp angles. This sounds easier than it was in reality. On each bend, strong Kashmiri hands heaved the car to point it in the right direction and our nerves were in a constant state of tension because of the danger of slipping on the steep terrain.

But we made it! The sound of our engine drew crowds of holidaymakers and Kashmiris from the Amarnath tent camp out to meet us. The arrival of a car was an event of the first magnitude and we were submerged in a buzz of questions. Among the many curious onlookers were groups of aristocratic Indians. As I looked more closely at them, I was struck by the thought that I had seen one of these faces before. The eyes of the tall man with the intelligent face lit up also and he hurried towards me. It was Professor Sondhi, president of the Indian Olympic Committee, whom I had already met on the occasion of my motorcycle trip to India. We shook hands heartily, delighted to see each other again, and immediately arranged to meet the following day for a proper mountain hike to the Sonasar lake. This lies at

4500 metres at the foot of a glacier of the same name. On the long scree slopes in the last third of our climb, we had one of those strange encounters which are only possible in India.

Several sadhus overtook us, Indian pilgrims whose goal was the same as our own. They marched barefoot over the sharp loose stones, not protected as we were by a thick layer of sun cream over the face and lips, but clad only in a loincloth and smeared with ashes and cow dung, like all of their kind. They carried no rucksack filled with highly nutritious food, just a tea kettle and a small sack of rice. They had brought no blankets or sleeping bag, at best maybe an umbrella. They passed us with a smile and a friendly 'Salam, sahib!' and the object of their journey was not the lake, but a little Hindu temple sacred to the god Shiva, barely visible in the rocks above the glacier.

"Do the pilgrims actually go barefoot over the ice?" we asked in horror, and Professor Sondhi answered, "The sadhus walk over the glacier almost naked and pray at the temple. They spend the night there in deep meditation and then come down again. If one of them freezes or falls to his death, then the god Shiva has taken him to himself." The feats to which these pilgrims are incited by their faith will always be a mystery to us Europeans, since some of them certainly come from the plains of India and are totally unused to mountains.

12
END OF THE FIRST STAGE

The Banihal Pass was probably the clearest experience we ever had of a meteorological divide. It separates the mountains of Kashmir from the lowland plains of the Punjab. Leaving the clear, fresh mountain air and the bright, green mountain pastures you enter a tunnel through the mountain several kilometres long. On the other side the beauty of Kashmir came to a sudden end and we were greeted by typical monsoon weather. Wreaths of mist drifted by, rain clouds came down, murky and louring, and the road was unpleasantly slippery. Here it descended abruptly for 2500 metres into the plains, where the wet was accompanied by a humid, almost unbearable heat.

We had already been driving for several days with the car closed because the tropical monsoon rains kept pelting down with a force we could scarcely believe. Then there would be a few short hours of burning sun, which made the whole landscape steam. Our luggage was moist and hot. The blankets took on a musty smell, shoes went mouldy, our laundry had green spots. We put our exposed films in tin boxes with little packets of potassium chlorate, which was meant to absorb the moisture and save the valuable material from destruction. The rainwater frequently hit the windscreen with such force that it seemed as if someone had turned a fire-hose on it. When this happened, then of course the windscreen wipers were useless, we could see absolutely nothing and had to take refuge under a tree, or preferably the nearest bungalow of the PWD (Public Works Department). Meanwhile, the whole area was soon completely covered by water, and in many places even the road, which ran on a raised causeway, was also flooded. Our brave Steyr then resembled a motorboat with a bow wave and a wake, but with its high wheelbase it managed to get through places where other cars would have been brought to a halt with a wet ignition system. Things only turned nasty when there were no trees or stones along the edge of the road by which to make a rough estimate of the water's depth. Then one of us had to get out of the car and poke around with a stick to feel where the road lay, while the other followed on slowly in the car. In the end we took to riding barefoot or sometimes even in swimming trunks.

Now yet another car had broken down ahead of us with a gentleman in rolled-up trousers standing next to it. A lady remained seated in the car with a resigned air. The Indian servant was holding an umbrella over the sahib, but this was not enough to get the car going again. We stopped.

Above: Kashmir: altitude 4500 metres, on the sacred Sonassar Lake, a Himalayan place of pilgrimage.

Right: Road-building, using people instead of steam-rollers. The heavy tampers were missing toes by a hair's breadth as they compressed the road stone.

India is not just jungle. Wandering sand dunes were a constant menace to roads in the Thar desert in the Indian state of Rajasthan.

"Can we help you?"

Soon we had an emergency operation going, in the course of which Helmuth would call out to me in German – or rather in his best Viennese – the tools he needed from our repair kit. The lady in the car leapt up as if electrified.

"But you must be Austrian!"

It now turned out that the man standing helplessly in the water with his trousers rolled up was the German consul general from Calcutta with his wife, a native of Vienna. The joy of the meeting equalled our determination to get the car rolling. I drove my Steyr behind the consul's car in first gear and at full throttle, pushing it out of the water and a few kilometres further on until the water-soaked engine fired again. The nice plate with the legend 'Corps Diplomatique' got a bit of a dent in it, but no matter. As far as we were concerned, this diplomatic encounter was to prove highly useful later on.

The immediate consequence of the encounter was a farewell party at the best hotel in Simla (India's summer resort) which involved soaking of a much cheerier kind. In fact, we then gave ourselves a second break from the monsoon floods, not for the pleasures of Simla but to visit a very dear friend whose acquaintance I'd made on my motorcycle trip to India. This was Herr Johannsen, originally from Hanover and minister for hunting to the Maharajah of Patiala. There he was again with his green hat and Gamsbart tuft, waiting outside his house 'Vaikunth' – a Sanskrit word meaning 'heaven on earth.' We had scarcely brought the car to a stop before he was turning to call over his shoulder, "Mother! Put the coffee on! We've

Above and below: The Quetta earthquake of 1935 left 10,000 dead. We would have been staying with our friend Latif Hamid in Quetta if my accident in the Tigris in Baghdad had not delayed our arrival.

Above: The state carriage of the maharajah of Indore – a Rolls-Royce, of course.

Right: Cows, although a sacred symbol of Hinduism, are nevertheless often commandeered to carry heavy loads.

Below: In 1932, the rich American Mary Foster built this Buddhist temple. The style includes traditional and modern elements.

got German visitors!" (When we had come through with the motorcycle, it had been "Fetch some beer, Lore, the gentlemen will be thirsty!") Only then did he greet me with all the emotion of a father welcoming a long-lost son. I felt very much the same when Mother Johannsen poured out the coffee and Lore appeared with a cake she had made herself. Soon after, we were allowed to relax in deck chairs with a pile of German newspapers beside us. Helmuth didn't stay with me for long, though. He found an astonishing number of things to do in precisely the places where pretty, blonde Lore happened to be busy. He, the motor car enthusiast, discovered a passion for gentle morning walks in her company. When we learned that the ferry over the Ghaggar river was out of action and that consequently we would have to stay at 'Vaikunth' longer than planned, he took the news with extraordinary equanimity.

But even this idyll came to an end. To keep us going, Mother Johannsen packed the car with a few more white bread rolls and a big pot of jam, all from her own kitchen. Lore wiped a tear or two from her eyes and down we went once more into the steamy grey wash-house atmosphere. We did not enjoy it. After Vaikunth, India seemed to have lost its magic, and when the monkeys threw nuts down from the trees on to our heads, it matched our mood exactly. They did worse. We left the car unattended for just a little while and soon a regular invasion was underway. Monkeys were swarming over the car, inside and out. They had eaten up half of Mother Johannsen's beautiful jam, and smeared the rest over the seats and windscreen. There would be no treat for us now. The cheek of it!

The struggle against the moist heat went on. It made us dull and limp. There was neither time nor opportunity to take baths during the day or change our clothing. Towelling yourself dry after the bath was the only moment when you felt anything like dry. You were always streaming with sweat, and even if you washed your clothes out and hung them up to dry overnight, they stayed wringing wet in that atmosphere. It was too hot to sleep. Wearing nothing but a body belt, you would toss and turn sweating in bed, and never get any rest until long after midnight. Some of the British had adopted a sort of sleeping gadget from the Dutch in Java. This was the so-called 'Dutch woman,' a pliable bolster about a metre and a half in length, which the sleeper would embrace and clutch between the legs. Possibly the 'Dutch wife' encouraged pleasant dreams, but this was incidental. The bolster was intended to absorb sweat and warm the belly, the latter being extremely important in the tropics in order to prevent dangerous chills on the stomach.

Cold drinks and ice could have quite devastating consequences. Experienced Europeans in the tropics drink what they call a 'warm up' as a prophylactic, and during the day, whenever we were thirsty, we bought fruit in the bazaar. If we were offered iced drinks as guests, we only drank freely if we could be sure of getting 'medicinal' brandy, gin or cocktails before, during and after. These warmers are an important component of social life in the tropics.

Once we also got invited to an Anglo-Indian club, the resort of those unfortunate beings referred to in the English saying that 'God made the white man and God made the coloured man but the Devil made the half-caste.' It might seem surprising that alliances giving rise to half-castes are so numerous, especially when you know the unbearable situation that a man of higher social class finds himself in if he marries an Indian woman, and that Hindu families, conversely, disown their daughters if

| *Above*: Benares. Corpses ready for cremation lie in the foreground, with holy cows behind.

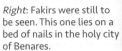

| *Right*: Fakirs were still to
be seen. This one lies on a
bed of nails in the holy city
of Benares.

they marry Englishmen. You hear stories of the appalling disillusionment facing the white woman who falls perchance for the exotic charms of some young Indian studying in Europe. However, it is not, in the main, these official alliances that the millions of Indian half-castes have to thank for their existence, but rather the position of power, the money and, in many cases, the unscrupulousness of the white man. One is inclined to put the word 'thank' in inverted commas. Furthermore, one is inclined to say, 'That was then,' since these days Asia has acquired more self-respect. Let us hope that it stays that way, and that Asians do not dwell on our past sins. How would it be if the 400 million-strong Indian nation, grown great and powerful, found that we were not buying enough of their rice and copra, and giving them a poor price into the bargain? An Indian fleet would come storming out against England, say, and anchor in the Thames. The superior weapons of the Indians would lead to victory, and London become an Indian trading post. The English would look on in amazement and 'gratitude' as Indian palaces sprang up along the banks of the Thames and they would grovel in the dust before Indian culture. English girls, albeit reluctantly, would submit to the attentions of their lords and masters, and a new age of the half-caste would dawn.

But that was only a dream, an unpleasant nightmare. We were still in the twentieth century and the half-castes I was referring to were fortunately in India, not in England.

The children, so it seemed, inherited mainly the bad characteristics of their parents' respective races. They felt drawn to the higher station, admired the British, despised the Indians, and always presented themselves as 'whites,' even in the way they dressed. Some of them look like that anyway. They are blond and blue-eyed and only one thing always gives them away: the whites of their eyes have a yellowish tinge. They try to get round this by saying to the newcomer, 'Mind you don't get malaria. It darkens your skin and turns your eyeballs yellow. Look at me, I had a bad go of malaria!' I used to be sorry for these people until I came down with the fever myself, but to this day my colour is unchanged.

All the same, I can well understand how people find Indian girls entrancing. I have only to think of the delightful little sister of Professor Roy, an Indian scholar working at the Hindu University of Lucknow. How beautiful she was, that slim girl in her colourful sari, her mouth like a red flower in her delicate, dark-skinned face, with brilliant white teeth. She spoke English wonderfully well and was so pretty and friendly, perky and talkative, just like 16-year-olds back home with us. She accompanied us to the university with her brother. Of course, as it was the summer vacation there were only a few lectures, but one was on German literature. We landed up in the middle of a discussion about the Brothers Grimm. The Indian professor who was leading it had even spent a couple of semesters in Heidelberg. He greeted us with delight and invited me to speak to his students. This was an unwelcome surprise, and left me somewhat embarrassed. These Asian students were so keen, so clever, and frequently far better-read that their European counterparts.

In India it is only the real intellectual elite who attend university. With us, many average minds are included, too. As I was never a brilliant scholar, I have to count myself among the latter.

Had I been honest and courageous, I would have said that I probably knew less

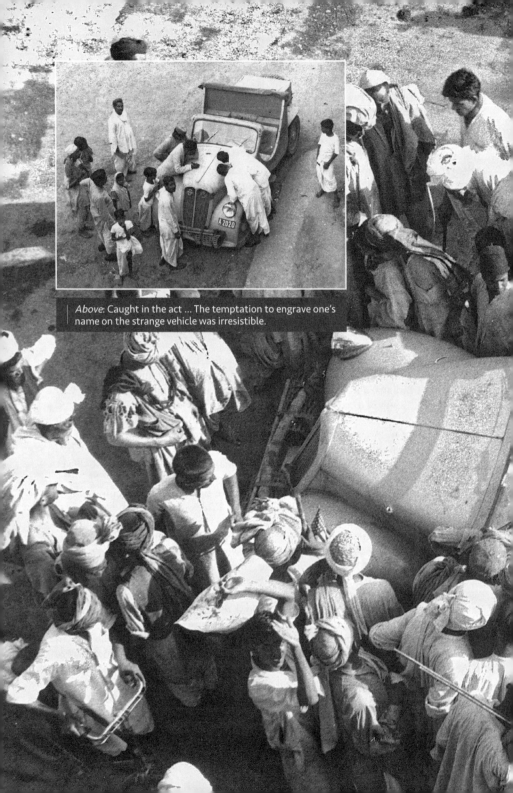

Above: Caught in the act ... The temptation to engrave one's name on the strange vehicle was irresistible.

Main image: The oddly-shaped Steyr was always besieged by curious sightseers.

than they did, but I was neither, and imagined that in this case I had to keep up the prestige of the white race.

My first thought was to present a paper on Klopstock which I remembered from my middle years at high school. The memory was particularly strong since the examination question on Klopstock had earned me a resounding 'unsatisfactory,' thus obliging me to make rather a close study of this gentleman during the school holidays.

This thought no sooner crossed my mind than I rejected it outright. I lacked the deeper knowledge of English and the proper expressions in that language for making a really good presentation. I would never be able to stand up to the Indian students, who actually spoke very formal English.

They were all looking at me expectantly, and it was high time to get started, so I talked about our trip and how necessary it was for young people to get out and see the world. I ended up assuring them how delighted we would be to welcome our colleagues from the University of Lucknow to Vienna.

With this simple but heartfelt address I came out of the affair quite well, receiving generous applause from the Indian students of both sexes. I'm pretty sure it was genuine, but anyway, I still had to answer a lot of questions, which included some rather clever ones, and I was glad when the session was finally over.

As we continued on our journey we also visited the imposing buildings of the University of Allahabad. After that, the only city of any size remaining between us and Calcutta was Benares (Varanasi). A few days previously, I had been most insistent on prolonging our stay in Agra so that Helmuth could see the Taj Mahal, the loveliest building in India, both by day and by night, and come away with the same unforgettable impression of that "monument to a great love," as I had had on my first trip to India. As for Benares, I was just as insistent on leaving it as soon as possible. For every Hindu, this is the holy city to be visited at least once in a lifetime, and where, if at all possible, he will want to be cremated after death. For a European, it means witnessing some of the most gruesome and disgusting scenes that human imagination could ever conceive. Only fanatics or holy cows could take any pleasure in them.

It was quite otherwise in the former capital of British India, Calcutta (Kolkata). With its three and a half million inhabitants, it is proud to call itself the second largest city of the British Empire, and is English in every respect, but for the climate, which is dreadful. A year in Calcutta is equivalent to two normal years out of your life.

When we drew up in front of the Calcutta Consulate in Fancy Lane on September 2nd, the odometer registered 13,372km since the beginning of the journey, putting the first half of the trip safely behind us. Countless names had been scratched all over the car's bonnet and wings, making it probably the oddest autograph collection ever to be carried round the world. Some American teenagers in Haifa had started this craze as a way of achieving immortality, and the Asians had enthusiastically followed their example. They included the secretary of the Grand Mufti of Jerusalem, Arab sheikhs, Persian khans, Afghan robber princes in disguise, and now the Indians. Indian newspapers had written all sorts of nonsense about us and the car, for instance that it could float, it could run without petrol, and more in the same vein. No wonder, therefore, that we were constantly besieged by inquisitive people. Even upper class Indians were not averse to engraving their names with a knife in the paintwork of the bonnet. Later on, these engravings began to rust so that the different handwritings and characters made quite impressive reading. The autograph collection continued to grow and, together with the car, was destined for the Technical Museum in Vienna. Nobody could have foreseen then how differently it would all turn out.

Our fame also drew a visit from the son of the mayor of Calcutta. He praised our car, and after a short conversation he announced with modest pride:

"I'm a pilot. I don't suppose you'd care to have a look at Calcutta from the air?"

Now, I'm no pilot, but the crate to which I imprudently allowed myself to be dragged off by Mr Roy looked a bit on the ancient side, with a lot of tin plate and a lot of rattling wires.

I got in, we took off and pretty soon my hair was standing on end and my stomach turning over. Roy wheeled about over Calcutta and the Bay of Bengal, and soon I had no idea which way was up and which way was down. We landed again after half an hour. I was completely exhausted and unutterably grateful, not so much to the pilot but rather for the fact that, even though my knees were trembling, I was back on firm ground once more.

Laughter echoed round the club that evening. "So he found another one, did he? Don't you know that nobody here in Calcutta will fly with him? But Roy only enjoys flying if he's got someone with him to perform to! He may be an excellent pilot, but ..."

Somebody called for another round. "Let's drink to the second birth of Mr Reisch! Anyone who's flown with Roy feels weak as a new-born baby!"

So I was born again and setting out on the second stage of the journey. It was quite possible that I was going to need that renewal of energy. Driving from Europe to India was nothing significant. For a craftsman, it would represent a simple demonstration of skill. The log book recorded the broken differential in Palestine, the remodelling of the bodywork in Baghdad, several broken springs in Persia, damage to the radiator in Afghanistan. Add to that the broken spare wheel holder, changing the steering knuckle pins because of excessive play and finally, because of the humidity in India, innumerable faults due to leaking electric current. Helmuth's careful servicing and maintenance of the whole car gave us the feeling in Calcutta that A2020 was in good condition, and would continue to take the strain.

This was vital. What lay before us, namely Southeast Asia and China, was the test that would raise us to master craftsmen, but I had my doubts: it might be too hard a task. I'd had these doubts right from the beginning, but had never told anyone about them, otherwise the managing directors at home might not have come up with the cheque. Helmuth once told me I had been bluffing about the car's reliability, and it is possible that as a coolly calculating engineer this was the way he saw it. But the trip threw up innumerable problems that could not be solved with the accuracy of a slide rule. If you're not ready to call on your imagination for help, then better stay at home!

Above: Honouring the shoes of the leader of one of India's numerous sects.

Above: What greater pleasure than being deloused as you wait for a bus on the roadside!

Above: Not much credit to the hunter for this catch. When vultures have eaten their fill they are so heavy that they can scarcely get off the ground, which is how this splendid bird got run over.

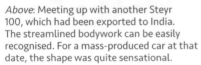

Above: Meeting up with another Steyr 100, which had been exported to India. The streamlined bodywork can be easily recognised. For a mass-produced car at that date, the shape was quite sensational.

Above: Sedan chair carrying a woman in India. This is really a Chinese invention, where the passenger sits in a sort of chair with her legs hanging down. The Indian sedan chair, used mainly by women, necessitates a crouching position.

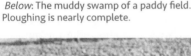

Below: The muddy swamp of a paddy field. Ploughing is nearly complete.

Below: The strictest rules apply to natives and foreigners alike at the Golden Temple of Amritsar.

13

THE LAND OF THE
SMILING BUDDHA

"To drive from Assam to Burma by car is virtually impossible without taking the car to pieces. In the monsoon season it is doubtful whether one could even get through with pack animals, besides which the Naga border tribe is in revolt. This presents a great danger to security." This was typical of the information we received. I compared these reports with the ones I had previously secured back home from the Royal Geographical Society in London with the help of Professor Dietrich, and from the British Automobile Association via the Austrian Touring Club (ÖAMTC). Nevertheless, I paid a visit to the University Geographical Institute in Calcutta.

"The knowledge you already have about the situation is essentially true," was the opinion of lecturer Willard Bayley and his Indian colleague. "In theory you can probably get from Assam to Burma if you make the effort, but the unrest on the border means that you will most likely be turned back by the Anglo-Indian military.

"There might be an alternative. You could travel all the way along the coast from one fishing village to the next. You'd probably find some paths through the jungle between the villages, with the advantage of being on flat ground. However, a lot of rivers go into the sea there, and there's no guarantee that you'll find ferries to get across, just little boats. At a guess, you'd have to get about twenty ferries built out of dugout canoes, or take the car to pieces.

"But the main thing to consider is this – it would add nothing to the future of transport geography. It would be a total waste of effort on your part, because that is certainly not going to be the site of the future Trans-Asia highway. The only sensible course for the short distance from Calcutta to Rangoon is to take the mail boat."

We eventually realised that the main thing holding us back was the revolt of the Naga. On the other hand, the prospect of building twenty ferries or of taking the car apart was grotesque. At least, this was our opinion in Calcutta. We did not know that later on this would be the only means of achieving the goal we had set ourselves, namely the crossing of Southeast Asia and China. Nobody has ever really managed it by car, and our success was only what you might call nominal. If you have to take a car apart and ship it piece by piece on jungle rafts or have it carried by coolies, then you can't really claim to have 'driven' anywhere.

"We've heard that your car floats on water," said some rich Burmese merchants in

Rangoon. This was after inviting us to dinner one evening with plenty of rice wine, which they hoped would loosen our tongues. "I would very much like to become your sole agent ..."

The desire for an amphibious vehicle in Lower Burma, with its numerous rivers, swamps and lakes, is understandable. The whole area seems to consist of nothing but floodwater for months at a time. Unfortunately we had to disappoint all such inquiries and moderate the reports appearing in the press. Getting your name in the papers is a tricky thing in Asia (as it probably is all over the world). How proud I had been when the first big article about us appeared in Tehran. It was written in Persian and printed in Arabic characters. The bit I cut out of the newspaper and carried smugly around with me for a long time might well have been a song in praise of the Trans-Asia Expedition, but it might also have been a report of the latest camel market.

In the Anglo-Indian papers it was at least possible to read up the next day what you had said and what was imputed to you. This is by no means such an interesting or amusing exercise as one is at first inclined to think. We began to find journalists tiresome, and we avoided them where at all possible, in Rangoon as previously in the Indian cities. We paid the price for this of course, as the articles about us and our jalopy grew more and more fantastic. We were usually referred to as 'round-the-world travellers' and you would scarcely believe how far our supposed affiliation to this clan could discredit us in European eyes. 'Round-the-world travellers' are the bane of all white people in Asia. They bum around for years, sometimes all their lives, usually on foot. In cities, their first port of call is the newspaper so that they can soften up their victims with a slushy 'world travel' article. Then they home in on their countrymen, the consulates and finally the remaining Europeans. Whenever I came across one of these round-the-world travellers, I realised to my embarrassment that they were usually better dressed than we were. However, the right turn-out is important for them, since they make visits, armed with their 'golden log-book.' Anyone rash enough to allow himself to be immortalised therein is constrained to pay for the privilege. Others offer better value for the demands they make. They sell postcards bearing a picture of themselves with pith helmet and borrowed hunting rifle. The really serious ones even offer a small booklet with tales of their own adventures.

Thus, to be known as a 'round-the-world traveller' does you no honour at all. You get a frigid reception from your compatriots, and you can tell from our look of resignation that we are waiting for you to pop the question. Mostly there was no other way round this than for them to say straight out, "But, my dear countryman, we do not want your money!" Only then did we become people who spoke the same language, delighted to be meeting up in distant Asia.

I wouldn't like to be thought arrogant by many of my young friends who are now planning trips of their own. I wouldn't want them to think "It's easy for Reisch to talk. Travel's no big deal when you have money like he did." It wasn't like that. Reisch had no money at all. It came from the university, from the Austrian Sports Authority ('Sport- und Turnfront' as it was then), and from industry. All things considered, it was not a lot of money at the time of the Depression in the 1930s, but it was enough to make a decent showing abroad on behalf of one's country.

Above: These delicate-looking bridges built of thin (but strong) teak wood and tough bamboo can carry amazing loads. In the background are typical Burmese farmhouses with banana groves.

Below: Small rivers were crossed by ford. Jungle dwellers were always ready to help us up steep river banks, and were often delighted with the little presents we offered them.

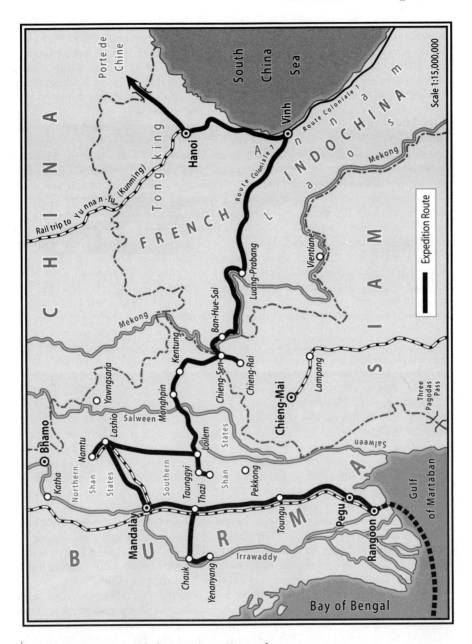

Map 5: Southeast Asia with the excursion to Yunnan-fu.

Curious rumours concerning our vehicle were rife in Rangoon, including the myth that it ran without petrol. However, it was not the purchase of fuel that was giving us a headache at this point, but the loss of the entire tool kit. It had simply been stolen. Although we were able to reconstitute some of it from garages and workshops, many of the special gadgets were irreplaceable. Helmuth was dreading the time ahead of us which was bound to bear out that well-known law of motoring: if you have a tool, you won't need it, but if you lose it, you will.

On 15th September 1935 we left Rangoon, a city of over a million inhabitants with an incredible mixture of races where Indians, Chinese, Burmese, Shan tribes, Japanese, Siamese, Tonkinese, British, Anglo-Indians and half-castes of dubious origin all lived side by side. Ahead of us lay the country where we would make our first real acquaintance with the true Burmese people. Can it be religion that has such an effect on the peoples of Asia and moulds them so decisively? We had met with so much fanaticism and hostility in the lands of Islam – veiled women, shouts, curses, filth – while those glorious mosques with their wonderful domes and minarets towered overhead. Here we found pagodas, pointed turrets, sinuous ornamentation, but above all the smiling golden Buddhas. The purest and most basic form of Buddhism prevails here. There is no conjuring of spirits, no particular cult, and no fear. All the people smile along with their Buddhas, and rejoice in the beauty of existence. Their unconscious motto is 'live and let live.' There is tolerance, not fanaticism. Everyone is peaceful, polite, delicate and clean. Everyone seems to smile with happiness and contentment. Nowhere did we feel so much at ease as in South-East Asia. The people are like children, trusting and curious, open to any joke or prank. Whenever we got into difficulties they would help, smiling, delighted when everything turned out well and never thinking of a reward. If we offered them a few cigarettes, they would smile their thanks.

Actually, in Burma what they really smoke is cigars, which can be up to a quarter of a metre in length and so thick that sometimes a pretty little girl's mouth will scarcely go round them. And yes, it's quite true that in Burma everyone smokes, old and young, boys and girls. Schoolboys can be seen cheerfully puffing away at their thick cheroots, and the charming, slim-hipped Burmese girls also go around smoking these dreadful rolls of tobacco. Otherwise they appear quite delightful as they go tripping across the roads in their closely fitting skirts, with a long plait wound round their heads in a cylinder-shape, always adorned with a fresh flower.

These entrancing creatures bathe in the muddy waters of the Burmese rivers, but swimsuits are unknown to them. Nevertheless, they manage their narrow sarong in such a sophisticated manner that all you see when they go in is their brown arms casting it off, and when they come out, all you see is their brown arms slipping it on again. That is all – and we made a very close study of the procedure!

It was 800km from Rangoon to Mandalay. For the first 30km the road was tarmac but after that it became a track which slowed us down considerably. The first sizeable place we came to was Pegu (Bago). In 1930 it had been almost totally destroyed by an earthquake. Only the great reclining Buddha remained intact. It is no wonder that since then it had enjoyed the reputation of an exceptionally holy site, while at the same time being the largest reclining Buddha in the world. Not only did its incredible size cause the Burmese to approach it with deep reverence, but

Above: Buddha statues in Burma are often of colossal dimensions. The Buddha of Pegu is sixty metres high.

Above: Buddhist nuns on their way to the cremation of a dead monk. The dead man is consigned to the bliss of nirvana not with sorrow, but with celebration and a lavish firework display.

even American tourists were stunned by it. From a distance you could see the lofty steel scaffolding surmounted by a corrugated iron roof soaring over the bamboo jungle. You would have thought it was covering a half-built factory rather than a shrine. This canopy was erected by rich Burmese, who were probably labouring under a guilty conscience, and so here lies the Buddha of Pegu. The amazingly well-proportioned statue is 40 metres long and built of bricks with a coating of plaster painted in bright colours and decorated with gold. The finger-nails are each the size of a small table top. The gigantic body rests on lotus petals. It is possible to walk all round it, but because of the steel scaffolding on every side, you can't get a complete view of the Buddha from any direction.

Strange bells and gongs hang down from the corrugated iron roof, plates of brass in the shape of an anchor. They are set spinning by blows from a wooden hammer, and a clear singing note emerges, which gradually dies away into the depths of the jungle. A monk who was evidently on duty set two of these bells going and then brought a flower vase, telling us to press our hands against it.

"It will make you strong, master," he promised solemnly.

At sunset we came to Taungoo on the Sittang river having made 290km that day. The road had not been as bad as I had at first thought. Like so much in life, it's a question of what you are used to. After the tarmac ribbon of the Grand Trunk Road in India I had become critical, and had cursed the road in Burma, which, compared with conditions in Afghanistan, ought really to have seemed like a driver's paradise.

Taungoo lies on marshy ground in the middle of the jungle, between papaya stems and paddy fields. Houses are built on stilts, with walls of bamboo matting and roofs thatched with rice-straw. These miserable conditions were scarcely relieved by the presence of a proud Anglo-Indian gendarme and a modest shopkeeper who actually stocked petrol. The high spot was undoubtedly the Italian mission station, opposite, at which, as a counterbalance, someone had set up a cinema showing trashy films.

The mission had been going for 72 years, and was a boon not only to the local inhabitants, but to all those travelling through.

"We've had high-ranking British government officials staying here before now," recounted friendly Father Rasinelli, who had left his hometown of Padua just forty years previously. His kindly features were framed by a beard which could only be described as patriarchal.

"Don't you ever want to go back to Italy?" I asked him.

"Yes, there's nothing stopping me. After 25 years of missionary work I'm due for a holiday. But what would I do there? Burma has become my home. I've spent my life here among these children of nature and this is where I want to die. As for Italy, it would be a fine thing to see Sant'Antonio di Padova once again, but the rest would be rather too much for me."

I couldn't help wondering what my feelings would be if I were suddenly projected forward into a European city of the year 2000.

Father Rasinelli seemed to have guessed my thoughts when he added, "Yes, life is more peaceful here, believe me. Of course, the first few years were hard."

We accompanied him on a short evening walk through the village and noticed how respectfully the priest was greeted by all the Burmese, even the Buddhist girls. This was yet another instance of how tolerant this religion is.

Sugar cane market in a Burmese village.

A little later we were sitting in what they called the cinema. The projector was rattling away like a machine gun as Tom Mix charged across the flickering screen before us. Excitement gripped the whole of Taungoo, and pretty Burmese women calmed their frightened and crying children by offering them the breast, or a cigar. Although the whole cinema was only a bamboo hut, there were no fire regulations to disturb the comfort of the audience. About a hundred spectators of every age and sex were crammed into the auditorium, puffing on their cigars.

The following day we planned to reach the oilfields of the Burmah Shell Oil Company at Chauk on the Irawaddy river. The road as far as Meiktila was tolerably good and the needle of the speedometer touched 70kph on occasion, at which Helmuth would shoot me warning glances meaning 'too fast.' He was always concerned for what might happen to the car.

Just as in India, flocks of vultures were camped out along the roads, ready to descend on animals that got run over. People all over Asia hold this 'waste disposal service' in high regard. The Indians have even declared these creatures holy. Without the scavenging vulture, southern Asia would most certainly be afflicted by far more frequent epidemics. Vultures are insatiably greedy, and they feed until their bellies are near bursting, making them so heavy that they can no longer get into the air.

As we rounded a bend we saw one of the waste disposal team sitting lethargically in the sweltering sun in the middle of the road. The vulture rose up, or rather tried to, but without success. His repast, the remains of which were lying on the edge of

107

Left: Buddhist pagodas in Burma are slender, well-proportioned structures, with spires on which little bells ring. The pagodas are solid, and thus have no doorways.

Below: Nothing like changing a tyre to get you going first thing in the morning! 'Semperit' had established depots of tyres for us in Tehran and Calcutta, so we were always well-equipped.

Bottom: Elephants can be hired in the villages of Southeast Asia in the same way as taxis in Europe. They were often useful helpers, but their smooth feet could not get a hold on jungle paths that were frequently steep and boggy. In these cases, the only answer was a block and tackle and manpower.

the jungle, had been too lavish. Now he was running towards us, and, having no idea of the hidden force of the car, launched an attack on the vehicle. The brakes went on, but it was too late. With a strength born of despair the gigantic bird had managed to take off and flapped straight into the radiator. Somehow he got hurt and blood spurted over the bonnet. Then the injured creature hit the ground and the wheels went over him. The vulture was killed and the car got such a jolt that it nearly left the road.

This vulture was a whopper, with a good two metre wingspan. I confess that, apart from the spiny lizard in Mesopotamia, this was the only game that we bagged on the whole of our journey through Asia. It was not particularly glorious, I admit, but still interesting enough to record on film.

Beyond Meiktila, our road was overtaken by the fate of all Asian roads. It mutated into a pathway, became first sandy and then boggy, crossing streams and rivers with no bridges or proper approaches. The track went steeply down over the bank at the river's edge, and our wheels disappeared in the ooze. The way grew more and more wretched, and our hopes of reaching Chauk before nightfall sank in proportion. There were countless obstacles, mostly with the same effect. Once again the car zoomed into a mud hole where treacherous stones lay hidden. There was a frightful crash and we stuck fast. I started the engine again and watched the oil pressure gauge with my heart in my mouth. The needle climbed to four atmospheres and stayed there. Thank God! The crankcase was undamaged and no oil had escaped. If that had happened, it would have meant a delay of several weeks.

It was still with mixed feelings that we climbed out of the car and sank up to our calves in mud. Since we were only wearing khaki shirts, shorts and sandals, this was unimportant. We began the work of digging under the chassis. Stone after stone was extracted from the mud like some priceless treasure, until the undercarriage was free again. Then we held a conference. Should the car now be moved forwards or backwards? Forward was the direction we were going, but reverse gear had a shorter transmission, and thus more power. It might be simpler to get the car out backwards and then drive round the awkward spot. Our opinions were divided on these two possibilities. In the end it came to an argument, with Helmuth's technical experience pitted against my driving technique.

"Just dig down at the back there," said one of us, "and you'll see that we can only get out forwards!"

"No, you've got it wrong," retorted the other tetchily.

Consequently, each of us set about constructing his own track, one in front and one behind. The argument went back and forth and we got really angry with each other. Meanwhile night had fallen. The headlamps shone at the front, the searchlight was turned towards the rear and the stark light shed a ghostly glow on the figures of two Europeans scrabbling around in the mire, raging bitterly at each other and at anything to do with automobiles or Asia.

The problem was finally solved when we tried driving alternately forwards and backwards to get out of the hole. Suddenly, we were free and sitting peacefully side by side once more, the angry words forgotten. On we went through the Burmese night. The mud on our arms and legs soon set to a hard coating and we amused ourselves by flexing our muscles and watching the crust come off in flakes.

A peculiar atmosphere seemed to hang over the countryside in the tropical night. A violent monsoon storm was breaking just ahead of us. Lightning flashed and gave momentary glimpses of a cone-shaped mountain. This could only be Mount Popa, the only significant outcrop for miles around. Some activity had sprung up to left and right of us in the forest; strange cries and other sounds pierced the silence of the jungle and were added to the noise of the engine. Things kept flashing in the thick vegetation. This was the light of the headlamps glancing off the numerous little bells and hanging brasses which decorated every pagoda. Single huts stood here and there along the way, where the Burmese sat round big fires to protect themselves from predators, a ghostly spectacle slipping by.

Suddenly, wild cries penetrated the darkness. We stopped the car and turned off the headlights. Silently we advanced in the direction from which the shouts were coming. A statue of Buddha, garlanded with flowers, was fitfully illuminated in the uncertain light of a flickering lamp. Around it crouched people with hands clasped before their foreheads, bowing to the ground repeatedly from the waist. We were gazing upon the distraught faces of young girls, almost howling in an ecstasy of prayer to their god, as if to drown out the thunder of the tropical storm.

Deep in thought, we groped our way back to the car and our lights blazed again, cleaving the tropical darkness, which is so much more stifling than night in a German forest. The journey seemed endless, and the kilometres ticked by reluctantly on the odometer. Then suddenly, as if by magic, the jungle cleared and we looked down from rising ground on a sea of lights reflected in sluggish waters. It was the Irawaddy, the 'river with stinking water,' as the Burmese call it. The lights came from the derricks that, day and night, pump oil, oil and more oil from the bowels of the earth. The world's biggest business!

Here were more people, and they were Europeans. Soon we found ourselves in the comfortable guesthouse of the Burmah Oil Company in Chauk. Alternate hot and cold showers pepped us up in no time, and sandwiches and ginger ale did the rest. Only a quarter of an hour before, we had been battling with the jungle, and now we were secure in the lap of civilisation. Contrasts such as these, the strangest imaginable, make travelling in Asia an exciting experience.

14
THE AGENCY COMES TO CALL

Who would have thought that we should find a workshop equipped with all the latest gadgets in the middle of the jungle? However, what the Burmah Oil Company could offer us in Chauk was so impressive, with an English engineer and Burmese technicians, that we rubbed our hands with glee and immediately drew up an extensive list of all the work the Steyr needed to have done. Apart from anything else, it had already covered 14,721km over Asian roads, and a thorough service could only be beneficial. In view of the high qualifications of these 'car doctors,' Helmuth for once decided to take a holiday from his responsibilities. Using a car belonging to the oil company we made various excursions, starting with the extensive oilfields.

In amongst the forest of derricks there still existed the wells of the Twindsars, a Burmese tribe who had been extracting liquid gold from the earth for about three hundred years. Clad in inadequate diving suits, with masks as a protection against gas, they let themselves down on ropes, re-emerging every day from the depths with around ten to fifteen full oil cans. These were bought by the Oil Company at a specially high price with the object of protecting as far as possible the local tribe's ancient rights. Any petrol company in Burma could certainly afford to be generous.

Next on the list for our reconnaissance trip, after the oilfields, came the surrounding villages. We even decided to make a two-day journey on board a rickety old paddle steamer. The middle deck was full of Burmese, all shackled together with heavy chains, who were being taken to forced labour in the tin mines. One of them kept calling out, "I am not a murderer. I am not a thief. I am a political prisoner and proud of it!" So even in Burma, land of smiles, there was seething discontent which manifested itself from time to time, as in India, by periods of friction and rebellion.

When we arrived back in Chauk, the car had been cleaned up, bright as a new pin, and every part had been checked over. We were somewhat surprised to find large letters applied to the bodywork in oil-paint announcing, "Decarbonised and revisioned, Chauk, Burma." [sic] Of course, the bodywork was already decorated with inscriptions from many lands and in many languages, scratched into the paintwork with sharp objects, but this bit of painting, nearly a metre long, was really over the top. We put a good face on it so as not to spoil the mechanics' pleasure. Why shouldn't these big Burmese children, with their ready laughter, have some fun with us too?

When we left the oilfields, the decarbonised and revisioned car had a new and cheerful sound to it, which I might almost qualify as Burmese.

The roads were still in very decent condition and we reached Mandalay, capital of Upper Burma, and the home of Mr Price whom I had got to know in India a couple of years back. He had then been taking his holidays in the Himalaya and we had spent a lot of time together. He had always insisted, "If ever you come to Burma, I'll be delighted to see you!" Whether he had ever considered this as a real possibility I didn't know. The resort of Simla in the Himalaya is as far from Mandalay as Vienna is from Gibraltar. At the time I had absolutely no idea that a new trip would really take me all the way to Mandalay. I was naturally on tenterhooks to know whether Mr Price was still here, and what his reaction would be when suddenly confronted with the visitor to whom he had so casually issued an invitation.

On asking after the companion of my Himalayan days, I found that he was indeed still living in Mandalay. "As if I could forget!" he said warmly. "You and your friend are most welcome." Mr Price exercised the rather gratifying profession of brewer, and I found his beer an excellent remedy for malaria. During the day, when our host was at the brewery, we two lay around on the terrace of his bungalow, leafing through old magazines and relaxing.

One fine afternoon, one of the houseboys came tiptoeing softly in bearing a card with the words: "Minh Hla Mei Agency"

I was not surprised to find a Burmese woman running an agency. We had already realised that Burmese women were very industrious and played a significant role in commercial life. Women enjoyed absolute social equality and took on economic responsibilities quite early, whereas men of a young age retired for some time to a monastery.

Madame Minh Hla Mei was in the prime of life, and cut an elegant figure in a long Burmese skirt of shimmering bluish-pink fabric and a jacket of petal-white silk. Her black hair was pinned up in a sort of turret, with a coquettish white blossom for decoration. Our visitor sat herself down ingenuously in Helmuth's rocking-chair and began a sort of interview with us in English. We were used to this sort of thing and let it go on quite happily. She told us a number of useful things about the country.

Secretly I was thinking, "What does she really want? When will we come to the agency's business?" But we were already half way to being Asians, and accordingly had both time and patience.

"And did you know that in Burma all marriages are very happy? Once upon a time, in the dim and distant past, they say it was not so. In those days there was a long war, much too long, for the men got so used to their own company that there was a noticeable fall in the number of marriages and in the birth rate. This was a great worry to the king of the Burmese, and so he invented a form of dress for women which is still the one most worn today. Our tamein is not a sewn skirt, just a long cloth tied round the body and open at the side. In walking, the bare left leg peeps out of the side-opening and disappears again, a sort of provocative hide-and-seek! Since this invention, Burma is again a land of many children."

This was certainly a nice little story and I made a couple of notes about it. Our strange guest went on: "Girls are completely free to choose their own husbands and they are so wise that they are never jealous. Monogamy is the usual way in Burma, but if the marriage is childless, then the wife has no objection to welcoming another woman she likes into the home."

"Very interesting," murmured Helmuth.

"The beauty, grace and cheerful disposition of Burmese women are unique in the world!"

Unflustered, and as if quoting a schedule, she continued.

"Even Europeans are not immune to the charms of Burmese women, as you cannot have failed to notice."

"Of course, the girls are enchanting!"

"That makes me very pleased for my country. So now you are travelling through our beautiful land of Burma quite alone? Isn't that rather sad?"

"Indeed it is, but unfortunately it must be so," interjected Helmuth. I suppressed a sigh.

"Burma is the land of cheerfulness and joyful surprises. Do you not know that we have such a thing as temporary marriage? It is contracted for the duration of a journey or for a stay of any length in the country, just as you wish. Life is beautiful with us, is it not?"

Gradually we began to see the light. Now the cat was out of the bag and a series of photographs made their appearance. The agency swung into action and individual photos were described and extolled.

"How is this temporary marriage contracted?" I enquired out of interest.

"Exactly like any other in Burma. There are no official formalities. The two partners share the famous pickled tea with their families at a small celebration with special ceremonies, and the marriage is made."

"How very practical."

"Now take this photo, for example ..."

"Well, now, the photos would be very nice to have, but as for the originals, we have no room in the car. All that in the papers about the miraculous car is, I am sorry to say, quite wrong. We scarcely know how to fit ourselves and our piles of luggage into it."

"But see photo number seven! Such a delicate little creature. Why, she weighs 90 pounds at most!"

"Now that's 45 kilograms," Helmuth pointed out in a matter-of-fact way. I added the last straw. "Madame, I must respectfully remind you that there are two of us, and that twice 90 pounds is far too much weight for our car. Sorry, very, very sorry!"

"That is a pity," said our visitor, "and just how great a pity you will probably only realise when you are old and unable to count amongst your memories one of the most beautiful experiences in Burma."

Amid many formulaic expressions of politeness and good wishes for our long and lonely journey, the Agency made a dignified exit down the steps and through the garden, the left leg slipping gracefully out of the folds of the tamein at every stride.

When Mr Price returned home that evening and we told him of our experience, he smiled knowingly and pronounced his opinion.

"You are my dear guests and I wish you would stay a long time. But if you don't go soon, you will fall under the spell of Burma, agency or no agency. You know what they say about us British: wherever we go we are meant to be haughty, unapproachable and racially arrogant. However, Burma is the exception. Look behind the scenes in those white bungalows and you'll often find them keeping one servant girl more than is really necessary. And that's not all. There are British men here who are legally married to Burmese women. If you ask them how this came about, they will say, 'I couldn't help it. But I'm very happy!' In addition to their natural charm, Burmese women are credited with secret powers by which they can bind the will of the strongest man."

I just failed to stifle a private smile.

"You may laugh, just as I laughed when I came to Burma. In the meantime I've seen, heard and experienced so many extraordinary things to do with the whole question that nothing surprises me any more. And if you, too, were to find yourself tied down in some jungle village, the European community in Burma would find it totally understandable and the only comment would be: There goes another one!"

15
DEEP IN THE JUNGLE

In the Mandalay club I attempted to elicit from businessmen and army officers some information concerning the next part of our journey through the Shan States to China. They would smile and say, "You've just got over an attack of malaria, haven't you?" In other words, they were treating my questions as the aftermath of delirium. When they realised that I was in deadly earnest, they stopped smiling.

"You're mad," we were told, "and I suppose you've each still got your appendix."

To this we assented somewhat guiltily. "And you're travelling through jungle in that condition? You do know you might not run into a doctor for months and months?"

Condemnations of our criminal negligence were pronounced in every tone of voice. We got no information at all.

Nevertheless, the day came when we simply packed up our stuff and left. With petrol, oil, food and a whole crate of Mandalay Beer on board, we turned east towards the Shan States. In spite of belonging to Burma, according to the political map, this group of small principalities enjoys considerable independence. There are the Southern Shan States and the Northern Shan States. All the principalities together formed a kind of buffer between Burma on the one hand, and China, Indochina and Siam on the other. They made a pretty good living from teak and from growing and smuggling opium. The area is also known as the Golden Triangle. For reasons which had to do with the controlling position of Singapore in South East Asia, there was as yet no connecting route through the Shan States to the neighbouring countries. This was the gaping hole in our Asian itinerary and we knew that hard times lay ahead of us.

For quite a way beyond Mandalay the roads were quite decent and we had as yet no idea of the skills we would later hone to perfection. These were of two sorts. One concerned the use of stakes and ropes, by which we managed the arduous business of heaving the car out of mud-holes and out of the deep ruts full of stinking water made by passing ox-carts. The other was a virtuoso use of sign-language, and dictionaries which we compiled ourselves for the various Shan languages.

To the right and left of our road the slender towers of pagodas appeared regularly in the jungle, some of them already falling into ruins, poking up over the tops of the trees. In Hsi-Par too, a small town along our route, we came upon several fine pagodas with both rounded and straight-sided towers, and between them moved the yellow-clad monks with sunshades of the same colour. Even schoolboys wore this yellow robe resembling a toga, even though they were only in the monastery for a short while. In Burma and the Shan States (at this time) the entire responsibility for educating young people lay with the monks. Everywhere, in the tiniest villages, one came upon monasteries, even far into the jungle where they were mostly sited idyllically on hilltops, so that their towers provided a welcome sight from across country. Around each monastery clustered several pagodas – large, cone-shaped towers, solidly built with no entrances. They were covered with whitewash and gold leaf. The monks themselves lived in the nearby pundijaung, the monastery building proper. They led the most simple and spartan form of existence, remained celibate their whole lives, and, following a vow of poverty, were forbidden to own money. They were supported by the village inhabitants. Young monks and pupils went from house to house every morning to collect food.

Every practising Buddhist must spend at least one day of the year in monastic seclusion. Young boys are usually put into a monastery for several years, where they become acquainted with the teachings of Buddha, and with reading, writing and arithmetic. A Burmese may also return to the monastery at any time. Should he fall upon hard times, he can be sure of finding help either there or from his extended family. Thus suicide is practically unknown in this country, where life is seen as a gift to be enjoyed with laughter and never to be voluntarily abandoned.

Not only Burmese, but anyone, irrespective of religion or outlook, may find food and shelter in a monastery for as long as he wishes. Unlimited hospitality is one of the prime commandments of Buddhism. Food and clothing are provided without obligation. In remote areas even the British frequently used the monasteries for an overnight stop. One of them told me the following typical episode. On one of his trips through the Shan States he spent the night in a bamboo hut belonging to a Buddhist. In one corner sat a man who was evidently a Hindu. The Englishman asked who he was. "I don't know," replied the Buddhist. "The man only enters my house to sleep and to eat."

"How long has he been here?"

"A year and a half," was the answer.

The Buddhist habit of hospitality also rubbed off on Europeans. In Lashio we asked an Englishman the way and he never thought to answer our question, but sprang straight on to the running board, explaining that we should follow his directions to his – the police district commissioner's – house, where he asked for our papers. It was impossible to tell from his expressionless face whether the two well-worn passports filled with stamps meant anything to him. He handed them back, remarking dryly:

"A few days' rest wouldn't do you any harm. You'd better stay with me."

We stared at each other in amazement. But the prospect of having to put up our tent that evening in some more or less desirable spot did not attract us, and if the police commissioner meant what he said ... While we were still considering, Mr Millan had already got his various household genies running hither and thither. Beds were made, a meal prepared, and in the evening over a good glass of whisky our travel problems were discussed. Mr Millan, an expert on the Shan States, smiled and said, "I know you are here in Lashio near the Chinese border, and I know you want to go to China, but this route is impossible. What are you thinking of, taking a car into the Yunnan mountains? There's only one other possibility. You can try going southwards through the Northern Shan States until you hit the postal road at Taungyyi. It runs via Kentung to Siam. Of course, these are not roads. They are not even tracks, just the trails made by buffalo carts."

It was a glimmer of hope, all the same. Off we set, following Mr Millan's instructions, deep into the jungle. The noise of our engine unsettled small parrots and monkeys. Brightly coloured parakeets flew up, cursing and squawking loudly and the monkeys fled screeching. The air trembled in the heat and swarms of mosquitoes shimmered in the sun. It was a real paradise for these malaria mosquitoes, with ponds, stretches of standing water and puddles everywhere. Even the water of the little rivers that crept between the bamboos was dark and sluggish, whilst overhead the gigantic stems came together almost like a vaulted ceiling. The way was quite deserted. Now and then we met Shan men, carrying their great bush knives on their backs. These bush knives, which we also acquired for ourselves later on, and which did us good service, were three quarters of a metre long and were usually manufactured from old motor springs.

The people wore wide sun-hats made of dry bamboo leaves. The bamboo is truly a jack-of-all-trades. Young shoots of bamboo are a delicious vegetable. A young stem forms the shaft of an umbrella, and split stems make the umbrella ribs. Full-grown bamboo provides the solid framework for houses and open buildings. Bound together to make rafts, it permits the most turbulent rivers to be crossed in safety, since its air-tight chambers give great buoyancy. Cut into strips, it becomes the fabric for mats that are used for wall and floor coverings. When it is really thick and fully developed, then segments of the shaft are used as water containers and as quivers for arrows. European housewives will be envious to know that the inhabitants of Southeast Asia cook their rice in these segment containers, and know that it is ready when the outside of the pot is just beginning to get charred. Nothing is easier than to cut a new pot from the nearest thick bamboo in time for the next meal. Bamboo fibres are used to weave the ropes that carry suspension bridges at dizzying heights. The ropes sway, shudder and stretch, but do not tear apart. Fibres and shavings of bamboo of varying strengths are used to weave baskets, plates, bowls, boxes and bottles, and many such articles are coated with lacquer and painted so that the wickerwork becomes quite invisible.

For building, one is spared the bother of nails by lacing scaffolding together with bamboo cords. Water is conducted through bamboo pipes. The child sucks food through a bamboo tube, as the smoker his tobacco or his opium. The flute-player conjures provocative rhythms from it. The treacherous foe blows his poisoned darts through it. The hunter in the forest bends a bamboo bow to loose a bamboo arrow with enough force to kill a tiger. Bamboo makes the child's cradle, the rich man's litter, the poor man's bed, and the mat in which the dead are wrapped to be consigned to the flames. The funeral pyre is ignited by firing bamboo rockets, the same rockets that go blazing skywards at festival time. There are hundreds of species of bamboo, each with a thousand possible uses for humankind. With the aid of bamboo, dark thoughts of murder can be realised in a manner both cruel and untraceable : its fibres are as sharp as knives, but if mixed into food, the victim will notice nothing. However, the gut will be pierced by thousands of needle points and over a period of weeks the victim will die a slow and agonising death with symptoms resembling dysentery. A real jack-of-all-trades, bamboo is the friend and enemy of man, from the cradle to the grave.

Our night stops on the jungle trip varied considerably. On several occasions our tent would be standing quite alone in a clearing, surrounded by massive forest trees. On others, friendly monks would offer us a room in their monastery. In larger villages we used the Dak bungalows. These were a very agreeable institution, first established by the British on the Indian subcontinent and eventually introduced into South-East Asia. The name 'Dak' is Indian, and means 'post.' They are the only better sort of accommodation, and are used for overnight stays by political officers, government officials and other travellers. You set up your camp bed and pay a penny or two to the Indian or Burmese khansamah, or attendant on duty there.

However, one of our stays in a Dak bungalow was less than enjoyable. It was in an advanced stage of dilapidation. Rats scurried away as we stepped on to the veranda, the balustrade was covered in a thick layer of dust, and the corners were full of old newspapers and empty tins. We sounded the horn, we shouted, but there was no sign of the khansamah. Although we could enter the hallway from the veranda, the doors to the bedrooms, the dining room and the kitchen were locked. In the end we had no choice but to clear the hallway of the worst of the rubbish and put our camp beds up there.

The next morning, up popped the khansamah, stretching out an obsequious hand and demanding, "Two rupees for each master!"

We made it clear to him that he had done us no service at all, and furthermore had shown criminal neglect of the Dak bungalow entrusted to him by the government.

He shouted curses after us, but we stepped on the gas and had soon forgotten the whole incident. However, the old grey horse of bureaucracy had a better memory, as became clear later on.

16

FOLK FESTIVAL AT INLE LAKE

In the state of Jaunghwe, preparations were under way for a big festival. It was the end of the 40-day fasting period and the celebration of ear-piercing for young girls. The Sawbwa (hereditary ruler) Sao Khun Leng had his hands full with the organisation of the ceremony and little time for us, so he sent along Georgy to be our guide. Georgy was what in high school back home would be called a bright lad.

We arrived just as a procession was gathering to bring presents to the monks from the local population. The gifts lay on bamboo racks, and were a colourful profusion of pots, dishes, knives, kitchen implements, pocket torches, yellow fabric and other useful things, each one bearing a label showing the name of the donor and the price of the gift.

A colourful mix of peoples jostled around the market stalls in Jaunghwe. There were the Kareni, the Taunta, the Lato, the Intha, the Palaung, and the Manu. They were all different and all brightly dressed. Every tribe was speaking its own language, and our ears could detect no similarities between them, although they all derived from Mongolian. It was the isolation of mountains and valleys and the lack of traffic routes through the thickly wooded areas that had fostered the development of different dialects, costumes, customs, and habits. Watching a festival like this when the tribes are streaming in, you can't help rubbing your eyes and thinking it's all a dream. The figures and individual types strike you as so fantastic that it's as if people from every corner of the earth were squeezed in to one small space. All the same, the strangest and the shyest of the Shan peoples put in no appearance at the festival, namely the Padaung. If they would not come to us, we would have to go to them. We had already heard about them so often, and every time we could only shake our heads and say, "Strange! Very, very strange!" I wouldn't believe it until I had seen for myself.

We sent Georgy off to hire a boat – the usual local dug-out – which would take us on a three-day journey to where this mythical tribe lived. We shopped for food, partly on land and partly on the water from the boat. On Inle Lake they grow vegetables – sometimes flowers, too – on floating gardens that rock gently on the rippling surface, just a bit of soil on woven bamboo matting, but enough nourishment to grow plants both useful and pretty, and which never need watering.

Everything was stowed neatly in the boat – sugar, tea, rice, bananas, bread, eggs, and pineapples. Far too many pineapples! We adored this fruit – who doesn't? We ate dozens of them every day, but unfortunately we had to pay for it. How restrained people were back home – one, or maybe two slices with a nice blob of whipped cream on top! Now we learned that such restraint was no bad thing. This delectable fruit has fibres – not as nasty as bamboo – but irritating enough. First the lips and mouth get rough, then sore, and finally become hideously inflamed.

As well as food, we packed camp beds, cooking gear and the necessary luggage. At last we contrived to get ourselves in as well, by sliding under the curved bamboo roof. That done, we were ready to go.

I watched in fascination the movements of the two Intha men who had, like all the rest of their tribe on Inle Lake, a unique method of rowing. They stood with one foot on the outside edge of the boat with the other tucked around the oar. The oar dipped into the water like a human leg elongated by a metre and a half, pulling through the water with a powerful yet harmonious swinging of the hips.

Of course, we were obsessed by the whole thing and wanted to learn leg rowing too. The evening of the first day out was given over to it. News of our intentions spread with astonishing rapidity and we were soon surrounded by a swarm of boats. Little girls giggled, dignified Intha men waited patiently, boy leg rowers manoeuvred their boats nimbly here and there as if to say, 'Look how easy it is!'

For a novice it was not so easy, though, and after I had lost my balance and fallen in the water a second time, I gave up. Satisfied, the Intha boats followed us back to the village. Nobody thought of scorning my failure. On the contrary, the friendly lake-dwellers were delighted that I had wanted to have a go at their special skill.

Everyone on Inle Lake knows the famous story of how a couple of boats with Intha rowers were invited to the great regatta in Rangoon. At the end of the proceedings (probably just to lend a little local colour) the Inthas were set to race against the winning eight from the English Boat Club, and would you believe it, the eight leg-rowers beat the trained English crew by several lengths!

The following day we left the lake behind, the boatmen no longer using their legs but their powerful arms to pole the dug-out forward through the narrow jungle channels. Near to a small village, we startled a group of Red Kareni women. When we made as if to moor the boat, they dropped everything and ran toward the huts, if their comical waddling could be described as running. Below the knee, these good women had hundreds of metres of black-lacquered wire wound around their legs, forming a thick and shapeless tangle. This meant that their gait was about as graceful as that of telegraph workers walking with their angled crampons still on their feet.

The explanation for this custom is given in one of countless Burmese legends. One morning a young prince, dressed as a hunter, struck up a conversation with a beautiful girl. He told her he was on his way to kill a tiger. The girl laughed and said, "If you bring home the tiger, I will make you my husband." That evening the hunter returned with the tiger skin slung over his shoulder. He called to the girl, "Come with me and I will marry you at once!" Then she burst into tears and confessed that in the morning she had only been joking. She had already been long married and was even the mother of a son. Then the prince became incensed and ordered that from then on all married women should wear rings wrapped around their legs so that they could be recognised from afar for what they were, and be discouraged from teasing other men.

But the knee-wear of the Red Kareni was as nothing compared with the ornaments of the Padaung women, the first of whom we saw in Pekkong. A spiral of heavy brass wire, fifteen or even twenty centimetres high, encircles the neck. Girls have their necks stretched from a young age in order to aspire as near as possible to the Padaung ideal of beauty. We were told that it is not the women who set so much store by this extraordinary custom, which condemns them for life to hold their heads in an extremely uncomfortable position, but the men. These gentlemen would never dream of marrying a girl with an 'ugly short neck.' Only 'longnecks' are really desirable, and where is the woman who would not do anything to be desirable? Only occasionally were Catholic missionaries able to persuade women to remove their adornment, which had to be filed apart at the soldering points. It was then discovered that the neck was unnaturally thin and its muscles completely atrophied.

The neck rings were by no means all that a Padaung woman was bedecked with. Whole collections of silver coins were being worn, from Burma, China and Siam, not to mention Maria Theresa thalers and rupees, strung in little chains, along with semi-precious stones and silver balls, broad silver bands round the wrists, and another armour-plating of spiral wire around the ankles. A high-born Padaung woman carries a good 15kg of decoration about with her! She is a living bank deposit box for her husband, who relieves her of part of her burden of silver when business is bad. This is the origin of a law in the Shan States, which specifies that even pierced coins carry full value.

Helmuth just missed a good bargain. He was struck by a pretty little Padaung girl whose rings sparkled as if they'd been polished with Brasso. He photographed her and then inquired, with Georgy's help, the age of this young beauty. "About 12 to 15 years," answered the mother. Just for fun, Helmuth then asked whether she was eligible for marriage. "Right away!" the mother informed him. "You can take her now if you give me 30 rupees!" A bargain as wives go, especially as she was bringing several kilos of brass with her into the marriage, not to mention the possibility of being shown in a circus in times of economic depression.

We travelled back along the same forest channels as we had come. I lounged on my back in the boat, trying to catch sight of a piece of open sky through the crowns of the trees and the tops of the bamboo stems. Grass as high as a man brushed along the sides of the boat. Sometimes overhanging branches slapped the naked torsos of the boatmen. Again I experienced that contentment of being close to nature in all its tropical extravagance. Free from care, I gave myself up to the enchantment of the jungle journey. I was being allowed a glimpse into this dark Asian world, which to us appears only dark, but which is in reality large and free to its inhabitants. In such a mood I could well understand how any European who had settled here would never again want to stand on a crowded station platform or struggle to cross the street as cars roared by. The thought of entering a Buddhist monastery, as many an Englishman had done in Burma, seemed perfectly comprehensible. A life like that, although apparently monotonous when seen from outside, could be so rich in inner experience, that all our so-called achievements would call forth only a pitying smile. I have met people who have reached that stage: once, for example I met a Buddhist monk in Calcutta who spoke wonderful German, which was not really to be wondered at, since his father's house was situated somewhere in the Lüneburg

Heath. I spoke a number of times with Buddhist monks who were originally from England. It always turned out that they were neither adventurers nor down-and-outs. One of them had come to Asia as an accountant in a British company in Mandalay, another had given up the comforts of his farm in Siam to find greater spiritual rewards wearing the yellow robe. My own 'great' plans and aspirations seemed embarrassingly ridiculous after talking to these disciples of Buddha, who had opted for a life of apparent renunciation, and my own life then struck me as a small and sorry one.

This contemplative journey through the jungle waterways gave me some inkling of those values planted by the Creator in the minds of many people in Asia. These were the happiest days of the entire trip, and it pains me that outside circumstances allowed me only these feeble glimpses into the miraculous world of Asia, so hard to comprehend. These outside circumstances can be summed up in the single word 'car.' Time and again I perceived it as an alien body, which hindered me from turning the deep insight that I once or twice achieved into a long-term view. But most of the time I was still a slave to my own locomotion. I scarcely regarded the beauty of the jungle, only the difficulties of getting through it. My thoughts revolved around petrol supplies and breakdowns, and conquering Asia by car.

I would have been far happier crossing Southeast Asia with a rucksack and walking pole or on the back of a water buffalo. However, this would have brought little satisfaction to my taskmasters in Europe, so the object was still to tackle the 'southern route' for the first time by car, to put the car through a massive test of its performance, and incidentally to investigate the possibility of the next generation driving on metalled roads all the way from the Atlantic to the Pacific. For the sake of these endeavours, no doubt perfectly laudable for us white men, I had allowed myself to be, as it were, chained to a car that I must drive through Asia. However, you can take it from me that it wasn't all good. Sporting ambition certainly helped us to see the project through. But of course, when everything we saw in Asia – the landscape, the people, the attitudes to life – seemed to tell us that ambition was reprehensible, then we could not avoid some inner doubts. We tried to shake off the chains that shackled us to the car, but alas for us if we succeeded! In the next big town we would be sure to find several letters, which always began something like this:

"We are very surprised that you have only just reached X, when we thought you would already have got at least as far as Y, and according to your schedule you should surely have been in Z anyway ..." We would be brought down to earth with a bump once more, and thoroughly annoyed by the officious tone of the letter.

17
ſPECIAL DELIVERY

Inle Lake and the Padaung had been a romantic diversion, and now life had to be taken seriously once more. We must succeed in getting through from Taunggyi to Keng-Tung, capital of the Shan state of the same name, lying right on the border with Siam.

The determination with which we set about our preparations caused our friends in Taunggyi to abandon their initial distrust. One after another they came and studied the car, eyeing the bundle of mail in their hand, searching our faces and finally deciding to entrust us with their letters and newspapers. The mail was destined for the Italian missionaries, the American Baptist mission, the Sawbwa and the political officer in Keng-Tung. The authorities in Taungyyi laid special stress on the bundle of letters for Mr Kingsley, saying it was very important, with the result that I tucked it into my breast pocket. If we were lucky, we should be able to deliver it in Kentung within the week, beating the record for pack animals, which stood at nine days' travel. If not, we engaged to hand the mail over to the postal caravan when it overtook us.

Provisions, luggage and mail were ready, and all that remained was to take our leave of a friend we had made in Taunggyi, an English eccentric who, when we approached him for the first time, greeted us as follows:

"I hate the British, I hate all whites, and I hate you, too, but you're my guests, so come in!"

He showed us his paintings, consisting of a whole series of portraits taken from different Shan tribes, flowers, animals, buddhas and landscapes. He seemed to be an excellent hunter, as his walls were decorated with the heads of tigers and leopards, the horns of every species of antelope and gazelle, the skins of big cats, stuffed birds and elephants' tusks. His wife was a pretty and intelligent Burmese woman and his two children had inherited soft round cheeks from their mother and from their father blue eyes and fair hair. He was evidently so happy and contented, sitting there in his nice little house, surrounded by his hobbies, that you had to ask yourself whether he was really an eccentric misanthrope or simply a fortunate man who had succeeded in devoting himself exclusively to the things he enjoyed most. Was it any wonder that he wanted no one to disturb him, deep in the Burmese jungle?

Our friend was a genius at languages, and it was him we had to thank for compiling our private dictionary of the Shan languages. We asked him questions

123

in English, and he dictated them back in the requisite dialect. We wrote everything down phonetically, and a page of the finished dictionary looked like this:

Is this the way to ... ? *Lam be masi le?*
Are there any rivers to cross? *Lam poma tschaum?*
How deep ...? *Sidela?*
How far to the next village? *Be ne nai se da le?*
Does anybody here speak English? *Ingalesage bit ta delu si de la?*
Get four buffalo to pull us! *Tschoe legaun jamai dala!*
How much does it cost? *Tagaun belauw le?*
Are there poisonous snakes here? *Une si de la?*

It was touching, the hours he spent helping us to lay in these valuable stocks of words for our journey.

We began our drive towards Siam at 9am on 21st October 1935.

In the Pun Lung mountains, a spur of the Himalaya, there was a pass to be crossed. It had no name, but if it had been in Europe, any motorist would boast of having crossed it. Here in the mountainous country of the Southern Shan these things were taken for granted and not even worth a name. However, the road was in disproportionately good condition, that is to say, the swing axles of the car made the bumps and holes less noticeable.

At one o'clock we reached Loilem, so we had taken only four hours to cover 400km, mostly in second and third gear. In Loilem the road came to an end and what followed did not bode well, as it actually became an ox-cart trail, with two deeply worn ruts and high grass on either side. The landscape had changed character and we had left the mountains for rolling steppe with only a few groups of trees dotted about, teak, Scots pine and the odd forest giant. The immensity of the tropical sky arched above us, sending down now showers of rain, now sunshine, and from time to time a huge rainbow bridge would span the heavens from east to west.

We made slow progress. In between the wheel ruts ran a strip of high grass in which lumps of rock and tree stumps lay treacherously concealed. The axle of a buffalo cart has a ground clearance of about 60cm, while our car could only manage 28. This is a lot for a European car but frequently insufficient in Asia.

Dusk had already fallen. It would have been more sensible to make camp, but we were obsessed with getting the mail to Keng-Tung as quickly as possible, and this drove us on. However, our speed was about half of what we did by day and on top of that we were constantly tormented by the niggling fear of being on the wrong track.

After two long hours the beams of our headlights shone suddenly into a void. The undergrowth through which we had been groping our way had disappeared and black night yawned ahead of us. The car came to a stop on the edge of a chasm from which the sound of rushing water echoed. Helmuth pointed the searchlight downwards. Fifty metres below us, the light reflected off the waves of a broad river, which could only be the Salween. It had to be crossed on the way to Keng-Tung, but here, in this place? That seemed out of the question. Not even a buffalo cart could have negotiated the almost vertical fall of the river bank. We must have taken a wrong track, driving through the night. Having just passed a little hut, we thought we could ask its occupants the way, but only one Shan man lay sleeping under the primitive thatched roof. With great difficulty I shook him awake. His eyes stared vacantly and he relapsed immediately. By his side glowed a dying fire with a pipe and a tin can lying beside it. Opium! It was the same old story. Whole villages were enslaved by it. No matter which house you entered, the men would lie restlessly dreaming and the women would run away. Then you had to wait until the gentlemen had come round from their smoke. It is not in the ante-rooms of busy company directors in Europe that you learn what waiting means. It is in the East where you learn the true meaning of the word, where the concept of time has virtually no currency and waiting exerts the same charm that work does with us.

Hadn't we seen a light just before the chasm appeared? We turned round and drove back along the track. The faint beam was coming from a lonely Buddhist monastery. We stopped the car and stepped barefoot into a room that was half in shadow. An old monk was sitting with his pupils around a petrol lamp and reading aloud to them. From the depths of the room came the ghostly golden shimmer of many buddhas. Nobody took any notice of us. When the reading was over I ventured to ask .

"Keng-Tung lam be masi le?" Which is the way to Keng-Tung?

Luckily the monk understood. With the babel of languages in South East Asia one can never be sure of choosing the right one. He came out with us into the dark night and pointed in the direction from which we had just come.

There was nothing else to be done but wait until morning and find out where and how we could cross the Salween. Once more we turned the car about and set up our camp near the hut of the opium sleeper.

I do not know which number to assign to this camp in relation to the start of our whole journey as I have no notes on the subject. If I could refer to it as 'Camp 87, Salween River' this might enhance the expedition's reputation in Europe, but such details seem to me irrelevant. Nor did our camp conform to the usual definition of 'expedition camp' as recognised in other great journeys. This time we dispensed with erecting the tent, since the reed thatch offered enough protection, and we could forget about mosquitoes because of the cold, so we simply folded out the camp beds. They measured a hundred and eighty by sixty centimetres. Their only resilience came from the sailcloth stretched over the frame. Once you have got used to it, you can sleep like a god on such a couch and any town bed becomes sheer agony because of its softness.

Once the beds were set up and made, hunger made itself felt. Should we really start all the business of cooking? Tiredness finally triumphed over all other physical demands. I switched off the car's headlamps. Only the light of the rekindled fire betrayed a human presence. The Salween roared far below us.

It was a bad night. I dreamed that the car had plunged into the river as we tried to drive down the bank. I watched as the car was seized by the current and dragged down into the depths. Funnily enough, I wanted to plunge in after it, and then I woke up.

It was six in the morning and Helmuth was still asleep. The nearest path led to the chasm. I now had a clear view of what the searchlight could only hint at the night before. Looking down into the chasm I saw the wide river flowing sluggishly along the bottom. It was impossible to drive the car down the steep bank. Even a tank would have tipped over trying it.

Helmuth was already making cocoa when I got back to camp, and as we held our steaming mugs we discussed what we should do. The whole landscape had a godforsaken look about it. The only detail worth noting was an object which, after due regard to all technical considerations, might possibly be called a ferry. It lay in a little cove of the river. We decided to take another look at the place after breakfast. Meanwhile things were getting busier down on the river. Two boats with men in them were afloat on the waters, steering towards our bank. It was the postal service from Keng-Tung to Taunggyi which crossed the river at this point. An English-speaking Shan was with them.

"Is this really the only crossing?" we asked him.

"Yes, the only one. Now, at the beginning of the rainy season, the river is low and the banks are steep. In a few weeks the water will be ten metres higher. Why on earth are you travelling by car? You can hire an ox-cart for two rupees a day, and an elephant for four rupees! Then you can be sure of getting where you're going!"

"Yes, but slowly," I replied.

"Why are you in such a hurry?"

There was no answer to this that an Asian would understand, so I simply said, "We have mail for Mr Kingsley and want to get it to him as quickly as possible."

He gave us a rather pitying smile. "And do you really think you will be faster than the postal caravan?" The postal agent, as he proudly called himself, could not possibly imagine it. He feared no competition from the motor car. He was even willing to help us in getting the car across the river. The first thing to do was to fetch some coolies from the village of Takau. They were tough little lads and never work-shy – unless they happened to be under the influence of opium.

Ropes were hitched to the car's frame by which the people could let it slowly down the steep incline, with me sitting at the wheel, steering and braking. That was how we envisaged the manoeuvre, and Helmuth was even hoping to film it. I slipped gently over the edge of the bank, and to begin with all went well. However, in one place where it was not so steep the car stuck fast in the mud. We had not expected this. Instead of holding back, the people now began to push, which seemed to them the better course of action. Helmuth could do nothing to prevent the car beginning to slide again, faster and faster. He could hear me shouting, heard the coolies shouting, saw them falling over and piling up in a heap, and thought:

"That's torn it! Brave Steyr meets its end in the waters of the Salween!"

In spite of everything, it was the coolies who saved us. Although they had fallen over, they never let go the ropes, and used their body weight as a brake. The car came to rest just at the water's edge. Somehow it even got over to the other bank aboard the primitive wobbly ferry, but the moment had not yet come to breathe freely again. There was another steep slope to overcome, and this time upward, which scarcely made things easier. While the coolies were heaving the car up backwards, there was a cloudburst. The coolies pulled in front and pushed behind. After every metre they managed to raise the car, Helmuth pushed billets of wood under the back wheels.

The engine was not much use because the wheels spun on the slippery slope. I believe that even the most powerful caterpillar vehicle would have failed here, and human strength would have been of little help because the intrinsic weight would have been too great. I was often delighted to observe that our relatively small car, because of its lower weight, was at a distinct advantage compared to a heavier one, not only on steep slopes but also on rickety ferries.

It was late in the afternoon by the time we had scaled the bank, wet through with the rain and dripping with sweat. We had no thought of food. Hunger was assuaged with cigarettes. Onward, ever onward was the only urgent command in our European minds, alas, restless as they were. We still had to conquer two mountain chains, which ran north to south. The land around the Salween lay at a height of 250 metres, but the passes to be crossed were at 1250 and 1700 metres, meaning that there was a considerable difference in altitude to be overcome.

It was to be less of a problem than we feared.

On this leg of the journey, it was not mountains but water that conspired against us. Only the next day we came to a halt after 12km, this time on the banks of a brook. It was small, but it was a torrent. It went by the name of Nat-Tengh, if I remember right. Helmuth waded across, leaning on a stick. The water only came up to his knees. He prodded the bottom carefully and pointed out the way to me. The bed of the stream was full of round stones, not too big, which promised to make a ford, albeit a bumpy one. Even before reaching the middle of the stream, I could feel that the sideways pressure of the water was becoming dangerously strong. Then it happened: the car was forced downstream, front first.

The engine had cut out. Nevertheless, the car was still moving slowly forwards down the bed of the stream, driven on by the water.

"Brake!" yelled Helmuth.

"I am braking!" I yelled back. The water was gushing in through the pedal holes. I stood on the brakes with all my might but the car continued to slither forward, bumping over the smooth stones. The water was getting deeper! All at once the front of the car sank in right over the headlamps. The only sound I could utter in my dismay was a strangled croak, while Helmuth behind me was roaring something at the top of his voice.

I waited for the catastrophe and got ready to bid farewell to the car, but the catastrophe never came. On the contrary, we were saved! The car had gone into a deep hole with its front wheels, tipping up the chassis. It had got itself wedged in the rushing brook and had stopped moving. Helmuth rushed forwards, slipped and fell flat in the water. He picked himself up again and we nearly hugged each other for joy.

The water was up to the seats, so we clambered on to the luggage space. There was jungle to our left, with a torrential stream running by. In the middle of this stood the car, half in and half out of the water, with the 'expedition' sitting on the roof, drying its clothes. All around us the only sound was the rushing water, with now and then the cry of a parrot.

But were things as peaceful and idyllic as they seemed? All we needed was one of those downpours reminiscent of Noah's flood, and the brook would be massively swollen in no time. We needed help, and quickly. The task of fetching it fell to

Helmuth. Meanwhile I stayed sitting on the car. My eyes went back and forth to the threatening clouds and I called on all Christian and Buddhist saints for aid. No tropical rainstorm, please, not now! Then again I would look down from my lofty seat into the gurgling water. The empty thermos flask floated in circles around the gear stick in a contemplative, almost philosophical manner. It was a sad picture! I tried to count how many times the flask went round the stick and then gave up. I was distracted by the louring clouds and anyway, I had no heart for such a pointless game.

It was a relief when at last I seemed to hear human voices, and indeed it was Helmuth coming back! With him were about a dozen Shan men, followed by women, children and dogs, the whole group lost in a buzz of shouting, laughing and yapping. Salvation was nigh!

With the equipment they had brought, the salvage operation was soon put into effect and the car was hauled out of the brook in triumph. It was a field day for the forest dwellers and must have given them plenty to talk about for years to come. All the stuff white people owned and carried around with them was little short of miraculous! Most of it was really quite incomprehensible to the natives, and went far beyond the bounds of their imagination. Our gloves were the greatest sensation. (When clearing a route through the bush we frequently wore gloves because of the thorns, and especially the razor-sharp splinters of bamboo.) What a great invention these gloves were! We had to put them on and take them off again and again, to endless amazement and laughter. Fancy white people having another pair of hands to go over their own! It was as comical as it was marvellous.

The spectacle of our luggage which we had spread out to dry on the river bank, and especially the performance with the gloves, constituted a veritable funfair for our helpers. They seemed to feel that an entrance fee would not have been out of place, and when we gave them ten rupees for their help, they took it only reluctantly and seemed almost offended.

Meanwhile, Helmuth had dried out the plugs and the distributor, and the engine began to turn over hesitantly once more. The carburettor spluttered and coughed, and the water that had found its way into the exhaust spurted out. Everything else was in order. It had been just one small episode among many. You get inured to these things and take for granted what in Europe would be seen as a massive operation.

We had covered 80km that day when at ten o'clock at night we reached a little mission station. The Italian priest looked rather startled to be disturbed at such a late hour by two tired and dirty people. He led a hermit-like existence among his flock and had not seen another European face for many a long day. After the first surprise, he insisted on celebrating the occasion in the proper manner, and produced a small bottle of communion wine.

The 20 litres of petrol he gave us next morning delighted us even more. We had used far more of this commodity than we had calculated in the Shan States where it was very expensive, and were very grateful that the good father let us have the supply he kept for his petrol lamp. He was almost sorry that we wanted to drive on so soon, but soon consoled himself, saying,

"You'll be back soon, in any case. The rains have been unusually heavy in the last few days. I needn't tell you what that means for the state of the roads."

His gloomy prophecies could not shake our confidence. The sun shone. It was a fine night. It was only a 140km to Keng-Tung and we would do it in no time.

A little way beyond the mission station the road began to rise steeply. The muddy ground was overshadowed by giant forest trees which allowed barely a glint of sunlight to reach the earth. It was so slippery that we had to put on snow-chains. Where it was particularly steep, the wheels would frequently be turning forwards while the car slid inexorably backwards. The higher we went, the deeper and softer the mud became. The ox-carts had carved out deep tracks. When the car's undercarriage rested on the mud with the wheels sunk in these furrows, all driving skills proved useless. There was nothing for it. All you could do then was to take a shovel and dig away the soil between the furrows. That sounds like a recipe in a cookbook, but it was a laborious business. The mud was as tough as glue and mixed with leaves and half-rotted lianas. The stench of this sticky mass as we dug it out was indescribable. We watered it copiously with our sweat and even this made it no more malleable.

Slowly, very slowly, even this day drew to a close. We found rest in a village and immediately our car became the hub of all social activity. Men, women and children sat around the wonder in a circle, discussing it in one of the country's hundred and sixty languages.

We refused an invitation from the owner of one of the huts, preferring to keep our sleeping bags at a respectful distance from certain little creatures, which are as common in the jungle as in third-class hotels in Europe. Bedbugs as such are rare in Southeast Asia, but their place is taken by ticks, which are even more of a nuisance. A bamboo roof which apparently served as some kind of shelter would be sufficient for that night. In the hours that followed we suffered the consequences of these modest demands. It began to rain heavily during the night, and under the leaky roof our beds got wetter and wetter.

We were shivering with cold as we shook out our sodden blankets in the morning. We had felt nothing like it since going over the high passes in Persia and Afghanistan. Skeins of mist were rising from the valley, heavy clouds hung amongst the mountains, cutting off any view. We took our time getting under way and spent a lot of loving care on the preparation of a lavish breakfast. For eight annas we acquired the finest chicken in the village, and six eggs along with it. You have to turn your hand to everything when travelling, such as plucking a chicken like a professional and preparing a menu, which went as follows:

Pea soup with sausage and eggs
Rice with tinned beef hash à la viennoise (since the tin came from Vienna)
Chicken soup with bamboo shoots
The chicken in person (with a lot of downy feathers)
Fat Burmese cigar

This was not so much breakfast as a lavish luncheon, and had to last us the whole day. Eating to lay in reserves is an ability well worth cultivating, which both Helmuth and I had brought to a fine art. In Asia it is remarkably useful, and in the course of the journey one's stomach adjusts completely to this way of taking in food.

After our lavish breakfast we stowed the luggage in the car and started off. I must say right now that this day was one of the hardest. After thirteen hours we had driven all of 11km. 'Driving' is not the correct term to use. Dragging, pushing, pulling, shovelling, cursing, overtaxing the engine, overheating the clutch, scuffing the tyres − it all came under the heading of 'driving.'

At the same time, Helmuth had a bad attack of fever. He sat in the car, huddled in blankets, eyes glittering, and whispering over and over, "Don't be angry with me. I can't help you."

The illness of my good friend and companion in misfortune weighed heavily on my spirits, although I was forced to admit that one man's strength, more or less, meant little when the efforts of twenty coolies were all in vain. Shall I write more about how I shovelled in competition with the coolies? How the coolies hung on to the ropes? How they pushed? How I trembled lest the differential fall apart? Shall I write about how dirt clung in thick crusts to skin and clothing? About the appalling stench of the rotting swamp into which one could sink up to the knees and never find a foothold? It's pointless, because there would be no end to it.

Around nine o'clock in the evening we came to the hut where I had found the coolies. They worked as lumberjacks in the teak forest.

Helmuth was put to bed near the fire and went straight to sleep. My hands were bleeding and my feet were covered in cuts from the razor sharp bamboos. I stared into the flames and thought: "Why am I doing this? Why, when in Europe I could be walking around with a neatly tied tie and clean finger nails, maybe going out to Grinzing for a drink with a nice girlfriend from the university ..."

Shoes dried slowly by the fire. Rice steamed in the pot. There was only a little water in the hut, as the lumberjacks had to carry it in from a distance. That was normal − and washing was out of the question, not to mention contrary to the custom of the country. The mountain tribes of Southeast Asia are not known for their grasp of personal hygiene. That said, they are only filthy up to a point, a sort of patina, and the rest falls off naturally.

Helmuth felt better in the morning, but I would not be able to count on his help. If we were to believe the map, there were still 55km between us and Keng-Tung − a day and a half's march. Would we do it by evening? As a precaution, I took four coolies with me. Over treacherous ground they were able to help with the pushing and digging, and when the track was drivable they would run behind the car. They could easily work up a speed of 8kph, and the car would travel no faster than that. I often had to call on the coolies for help, but the situation had improved, in that it was now downhill all the way to Keng-Tung from a height of 1700 metres. At four in the afternoon we reached the bottom of the valley. Now it was easy. We dismissed the coolies, and covered the last 10km to Keng-Tung on our own.

At five o'clock the brave little Steyr drove through the city gates. We had taken five days and beaten by four days the record for the pack animals. We were so pleased with ourselves that we felt like driving into town with a fanfare on the horn.

Even without the fanfare our arrival was a sensation. Everyone was excited about us, for us, about the car, about the mail we had brought. We handed round the latest edition of the *Rangoon Gazette* and everyone immediately began an animated discussion of the headlines. Soon we were even sitting in front of Mr Kingsley, for whom we had brought that very important 'special delivery' of letters.

He excused himself briefly and opened it, still in our presence, cast an eye over it and said:

"Gentlemen, this letter from the political officer in Taunggyi will certainly interest you. Here, read it!"

Rather flattered that we were found worthy of perusing the correspondence of two political advisers in the Shan States, I took the letter from him and began to read:

"Dear Mr Kingsley,

A kansomah has informed me that two young Europeans in a car with grey paintwork ..."

Here I faltered and then read on in subdued tones,

" ... used the Dak bungalow and refused to pay the overnight fee. If these two have actually got as far as your area, namely Keng-Tung, I advise you to keep an eye on them ..."

Without delay I began explaining in some detail to nice Mr Kingsley how this apparent failure to pay our bill came about, but he wouldn't pay attention to my story. He was too highly amused at the idea of our having carried our own 'wanted' poster all the way from Taunggyi to Keng-Tung, and made a special effort to do it quickly. "Very sporting! Very sporting!" he kept saying, clapping us on the shoulder in appreciation. In the end we were the ones laughing most of all at the joke, and admiring the rapid and effective way news was transmitted in Southeast Asia, to which we ourselves had contributed in no small measure.

10

DEAD PRINCE AND LIVING PRINCE

If our first official visit had been to the political officer, Mr Kingsley, then our second approach in Keng-Tung must be to its prince Sawbwa Sao Kaung Tai. His name forms part of the autograph collection on our car, standing next to that of his servant, Hla Pei. This did not bother the rajah. Most princes in Southeast Asia preserve their dignity in a relaxed fashion. Even their letters are surprisingly informal, for example, "Shall I come to you or will you visit me in my palace?" This would never have happened in India! There one must first make two petitions to His Highness's private secretary and if His Highness has not too many "demands on his time" then one is graciously and magnificently received. However, one must be the rajah's friend of many years standing before he will deign to play garam – the national game of India – with a European.

It was different in Keng-Tung. From the very first weeks of our stay we would sit with Sao Kaung Tai and his minister in the haw, the prince's palace, in a gloomy hall decorated with pictures. Helmuth asked him once,

"How many ministers do you have, Your Highness?"

"Six or seven, I believe," was his reply.

The Sawbwa indicated a heavy golden sarcophagus standing two metres from us. "My father died five months ago," he told us. "You Europeans call it 'dying.' We, on the other hand, treat the dead as living persons until the moment of their cremation. See his throne standing in front of the sarcophagus. I give pleasure to my father every day by letting him watch us play garam."

The hall was filling up with visitors as we continued to flick the ivory figures, (which resemble the pieces of nine men's morris) across the board with our fingers. There was a constant coming and going. The people of Keng-Tung were bowing down before the throne. This had been the way while the old prince still lived and so it was now. Every day at eleven o'clock he received his subjects. A small orchestra with bamboo instruments appeared for the amusement of the dead prince. I played on absent-mindedly. My thoughts kept returning to the coffin and the empty chair, and I often missed my shot.

Around midday Sao Kaung Tai's three charming sisters entered the hall. Each of them carried a dish of food and flowers, which they placed before the throne. Then they, too, knelt down and remained there in silence. Simultaneously, eight Buddhist priests were lining up on a raised platform. The music ceased and then the monotonous chanting of the priests echoed through the hall. Strange to say, the young prince, unmoved by the atmosphere of reverence, went on playing his game of garam. He even gave orders to his servant to bring two bottles of beer. It was labelled 'Made in Pilsen,' although the Japanese characters betrayed its true place of origin.

Sao Taung Tai spoke perfect English. He had studied for four years in Cambridge and in the haw at Keng-Tung hung photographs showing him in tailcoat and dinner jacket. In his own country, however, he dressed entirely in silk, the only reminder of Europe being his sock suspenders. "They never stay up," he declared disapprovingly, pulling up his trouser leg. I observed that the young prince's legs were tattooed with images and Buddhist maxims.

The monks were still praying, and Sao Kaung Tai's sisters were still kneeling before the empty throne. They seemed to be waiting until their dead father had consumed the food.

There was a curious contrast between this ceremonial and our playing and drinking. "I'm going to buy a car soon," said Sao Kaung Tai conversationally. "My old one I had brought over in pieces six years ago from Siam. It's a bit rickety now. I've already had several proposals for a new one. Do you want to see?" The young prince spread out some English motor car catalogues. He seemed to be finding difficulty in making a choice. The car had to be small and manoeuvrable, suitable for the tropics and sturdy enough for roads in Southeast Asia.

"Buy a Steyr, then!" I interjected, to which he replied:

"You car would suit me very well. Its power and resilience have already been proved. It's just the sort of car I'd like ..."

"But?"

He hesitated a moment. "My father ... I don't know. He only understands English cars."

We all gazed at the empty throne.

"No, no," went on the prince hastily, "my father knows nothing about your car. I do not know whether he would allow it."

I wrenched my gaze away from the sarcophagus and the empty chair of state and tried to concentrate all my attention on the garam, but it was no use. The monotonous prayers of the monks echoed round the hall. To my ears it sounded like, "My father will not allow ... my father will not allow ... my father ..."

We had many more games of garam with the prince and our conversations covered all sorts of topics. However, no more mention was made of buying cars, or of the old prince who continued to lie beside us in the great hall, a dead man among the living. I longed to ask when the cremation would actually take place. One day, Sao Kaung Tai broached the subject himself. "I'm having trouble with the government just now," he declared frankly. "You will have heard that 500kg of opium has been smuggled from Keng-Tung to Siam. Now the Anglo-Burmese government is holding me responsible. As a punishment they are proposing to postpone my appointment as Sawbwa of Keng-Tung for three years. It would be a matter of indifference to me personally, but the people are grumbling, because, according to ancient custom, the deceased ruler may not leave the palace until his successor has assumed his rights. My people are already looking forward to the festival of cremation and they will be unwilling to wait years for it. I have now refused to sell my tung oil seed to the English Tung Oil Company. They are desperate for this seed!"

The prince kept coming back to this tung oil of his, so I asked him what it was.

"My friend, have you never heard of tung oil? It is extracted from the seeds of the tung tree, a member of the spurge family which in Southeast Asia grows to a height of several metres. It is called Aleurites fordii, which is the name bestowed on it by western science. I thought you would have known this."

There was an embarrassed silence, until Helmuth had a bright idea which saved the situation.

"We are still students, Highness, and have not yet got as far as tung oil!"

At this the prince laughed. "But of course! The letter T comes quite near the end of your alphabet. However, tung oil is very, very important. It is used in the painting of aircraft and to impregnate fabrics and much else. In the Keng-Tung jungle grows a very special variety, the montana. It is far better than the one introduced from America. The whole world is after my montana seeds!" said he, with a smile of satisfaction.

We drove the car three miles out of Keng-Tung. The prince himself took the wheel and proved excellent at steering. He drove with confidence and changed gear skilfully. While we were out, he had himself photographed among his beloved tung trees.

During our very first audience with Sao Kaung Tai he had remarked quite casually, "And when will you start your return journey?"

We were taken aback. "Return? But we are going on to Siam and Indochina!"

A fleeting smile of disbelief crossed the prince's features.

"Well, of course you will find good roads in Indochina, but as for what lies between Keng-Tung and Indochina – I fear you will not get through."

"But there is an ox-cart trail through the jungle from here to the Siamese border, isn't there?"

"Yes, there is, but in difficult places the goods are unloaded and the carts are taken apart and carried by coolies, even the wheels."

Some time had elapsed since this conversation, valuable time which we had been forced to spend there until the worst of the rains were over. But it was also time in which we had gradually won the prince over to our project until at last he was willing to help us in any way we wanted.

Even the new ideas I proposed did not seem too extravagant to him. What would happen if human assistance was no longer sufficient to get the car moving? On the way to Keng-Tung this had nearly happened on several occasions. The only solution was an elephant! That would be strong enough to get us out of any hole we were in.

"Not a bad idea," agreed Sao Kaung Tai. "I have elephants in all the villages along your route, and I can give orders that they are to be placed at your disposal. But you must first make sure that an elephant will not be frightened by a car. There's a perfectly ordinary swamp just beyond the bazaar. Drive the car into it and I will order an elephant to come down so you can get an idea of its capabilities."

One could tell that the Sawbwa had studied in England and absorbed some of the sporting spirit of that country.

Naturally he took care not to miss the fun as we drove the car headlong into the swamp and got it stuck in the mire right over the axles. Two elephants were standing by with ropes and chains and their handlers waited for orders. I knotted one of the ropes to the front suspension at the point where it was secured to the frame with strong clamps, which seemed the best place. The larger of the two elephants was harnessed to it and began to pull – but the rope broke. We used a double rope. The animal braced its legs and leaned its body forward, supporting itself on the ground with its trunk – it gave a heave and the double rope broke too. Next we tried the chain. Once it was fixed to the hook on the elephant's saddle, he settled into it carefully like a good draught horse and jerked at it a couple of times. The car jerked too but stayed put. The elephant then took a step back with the obvious intention of creating momentum. "Stop!" I yelled at the top of my lungs and Helmuth ran like a madman straight into the elephant's path. The movement was stopped just in time, for the giant creature would certainly have ripped the front axle right out of the car, together with the wheels. The fright that Helmuth had had over his beloved car inspired him to have it pulled out backwards. There was a strong tube running through the frame at the back which would resist any heaving and tugging.

We set about it directly. The elephant was harnessed the other way round, heaved, stood on his hind legs and leaned his whole weight against the chains, which was an amazing sight, finally bringing the car on to dry ground.

We tried it once again and the elephant seemed to enjoy himself as much as we did.

The people of Keng-Tung howled with enthusiasm, their prince was delighted and the very same day saw an addition to our letter of recommendation, requiring elephants to be placed at our disposal whenever we wished.

10
HONOUR THE
YELLOW ROBE

We had arrived in Keng-Tung at the end of October. Christmas was coming, but travelling on was still out of the question. We were pinned down by the sudden and violent rainstorms, added to which Helmuth and I suffered bouts of fever by turns. We were fortunate in having at least some sort of home to call our own. It was a small bungalow made available to us by the Italian mission. They presented it to us complete with a servant, Mang-Te, a Shan boy aged about 14. Together with him we explored the little Shan city of Keng-Tung.

Keng-Tung could be described as a focal point in Southeast Asia for the trading and smuggling of opium. Chinese are the main dealers in the Golden Triangle's poison, and although they enjoy only guest status in Southeast Asia, they nevertheless use their knowledge and influence to have plenty of fingers in the pie when it comes to this line of business. Although the smoking of opium is universally permitted in the Shan States, it is nevertheless subject to a high rate of taxation. Concessions for smoking parlours are issued by the state.

Chen Wu provided the official purchase coupons and the gadgetry necessary for smoking a proper pipe of opium. The house name and also the sign over the door were international and in many languages, as a strange mix of peoples came together here. I found Chinese characters, cunning and intricate Burmese daubings, Shan curlicues, and just to make sure that we Europeans knew what was going on, the magic word 'opium' one more time in clear Latin script for all the world to see. Chen arrived with Yew An tripping along behind him, bearing the utensils. Many are needed, and they are difficult to manipulate. There were two small dishes of liquid opium, two separate pipes, a coconut-oil lamp and long sharp needles whose purpose I was at first unable to guess. There were also pieces of split bamboo used for shaping. We found ourselves a space. The room was dark and I had to be careful not to tread on anyone or disturb them. On one side of me lay two old Chinese and on the other a Shan. Although still smoking intermittently, they were already staring into the void and making the convulsive movements which marked their uneasy passage from consciousness to unconsciousness. Their pupils were contracted and they lay listlessly, their skin stretched like paper over their wasted bodies. Even the establishment's owner was crouching in one corner, and Yew An pushed him calmly aside, for there were only a few hours in the day when old Hwang Ho was in his right mind. To keep his business going he employed two non-smoking servants. They bustled about, bringing fresh opium, shaking the sleepers awake to refill their pipes, and tending to the lights and lamps. Thus old Hwang Ho was free to indulge his habit while his business ran itself. The dish of liquid brought by Chen had cost two annas. A quick calculation suggested that this was a cheap form of entertainment. Next to me, Chen was busying himself with forming the sticky, syrupy mass into a ball to be inserted into the pipe. With his finely jointed hands that bore witness to addiction and long habit he made me a bed on one of the benches running down either side of the room. The smoke was thick, and I considered drawing a sword from the sheath of one of the generals immortalised in the wall paintings, convinced that fine figures could be etched on that solidified smoky mass. Coloured prints showing gruesome events in China's civil wars were also attached to the walls, and there had been no stinting the red paint for the quantity of blood spilt. My contemplation of these images was interrupted by a shock to the senses as an old Chinese struck me smartly on the back of the neck. Grasping wildly in the air at some vision, he lit on me, a hapless innocent, and releasing myself from his embrace was a slow and delicate business. Overcome at last by deep lassitude, he rolled over and collapsed. He had come through the euphoric stage and now, totally reconciled to his surroundings, he sailed on into dreamland. Yew An, the servant, had refreshed the lamps and placed a cylinder of coloured glass over them. In other corners of the room, oil lights were still flickering, and the sweetness of the white smoke was overpowering.

The preparations are such a tedious business that many opium enthusiasts light up a cigarette in between stages. I watched Chen in fascination as, with a knowing smile, he explained the tricks to me. First he dipped a long metal needle into the opium, which had the consistency of honey, so that a blob remained sticking to it. Then he held it over the flame for a few minutes, turning it until it was the size of a fingertip, continuing to shape it, heat it and show off his skill. He turned and compressed the bubbling mass with extraordinary elegance and dexterity. Sometimes the stuff was half solid, sometimes it was a boiling hot liquid, but finally a mathematically perfect sphere emerged, which was further smoothed off with the bamboo spatula.

When a travel writer asserts that he has 'filled' his pipe with opium, then you can be sure that he has never taken a look inside an opium den. Chen handed me the pipe into which he had carefully inserted the plug of opium and I heated it for a moment longer above the lamp. When it bubbled up I drew the opium smoke into my lungs through the long tube. The pipe was empty after only a few draughts and Chen was already offering me the second one, but I refused it. I had the same, strange sensation as after my first cigar. Chen tried to persuade me to go on smoking. He was sure I would tolerate six pipes. He himself would take twenty or twenty-five. But already the room was turning and receding from my sight, although I could still make out the Chinese general with his sword poised ready to strike and the troops on horseback surging forward to some new battle. I decided that now was the time to leave.

England had prohibited the cultivation of opium in India and Burma, while Siam and more recently China had done the same for their territories. Only the tiny Shan State of Keng-Tung still allowed the poppy to be grown. Of course that did not prevent thousands of secret opium fields from flourishing in the sunny Yunnan Mountains. Many tonnes of the dangerous narcotic were still being produced every year, and it was big business. The figures spoke for themselves: in Keng-Tung, 1 viss (1.6kg) of opium cost 28 rupees, but in neighbouring Siam the price rose to 900 rupees. Imagine how much it cost in Singapore, Aden, Casablanca, Amsterdam, New York or San Francisco!

Our little bungalow became more like home every day. Buddha statues decorated the walls, along with weapons and other strange objects we brought back from our forays into the country. But it cannot be denied that even in this snug little house, lashed by the monsoon rains that kept us from pursuing our journey, we had to rely on our own company – me on Helmuth and Helmuth on me. We had been together since April, seen each other through good and bad times, had become faithful companions – and now we were getting on each other's nerves in no uncertain terms! A polar explorer will recognise this phenomenon, as will the leader of any expedition, but you only have to listen to married couples carrying on about how to put up with the same person, day after day. Helmuth made the shrewd decision and moved out. He wanted to be alone for a while, to put some distance between us and stop the ridiculous petty arguments that had suddenly become the order of the day. It was probably our relative inactivity and the consequent boredom that caused the tension.

On one of his excursions into the neighbourhood Helmuth had discovered, about an hour's journey away, a wonderful pagoda and a monastery inhabited by only three elderly monks. Hoping that he, too, might find refuge there, he set off one evening in that direction. He kept a detailed diary of his experiences, so here is the story in his own words:

"Off I went with a small suitcase and my blankets tucked under my arm. Night was falling, but I knew the way even in the dark.

"I greeted the priests according to the custom of the country, kneeling with folded hands, and asked for shelter. They pointed me towards a hut that was standing empty, and brought me a bowl of rice and a jug of water. At this time, the opportunity of living far from civilisation meant a great deal to me. Seclusion of this sort is rarely granted to people in Europe. You can never get your thoughts so well in order as when you are obliged to live quite alone and in silence.

"All the same, I was quite pleased when, after a few days, a young lad interrupted my solitude, making himself understood in broken English. A pampered European finds it hard to live on nothing but rice and pumpkins, and so I took the opportunity of sending the boy off for eggs and fat.

"These he brought me the next day, and invited me to go with him to the nearby pagoda where there was to be a pwhoa, a great festival. I simply left my luggage – no Buddhist would think of interfering with someone else's possessions – and off we set.

"People could be seen coming from all directions, climbing the mountain in small groups, calling to each other, laughing and joking. Around the pagoda stood many little booths and tables. People were eating, drinking and playing games. They had spread out their mats and blankets on the meadows, intending to spend the night up there after the festival and not to go home until the following day. The temple doors stood wide open. The buddhas were clothed with fresh yellow robes and lit by many small oil lamps and candles. On one side knelt the men, headed by the congregation of priests in their yellow togas, and on the other side were the women and the shaven-headed Buddhist nuns similarly dressed in yellow. The monks sang out in a monotone and the people answered them. Meanwhile darkness had fallen and the golden buddhas, the towers and the intricate decorations on the temples were illuminated solely by the light of many torches. It was a scene of deep peace and intense piety.

"The murmuring of prayers gradually died away and when it finally ceased came the muffled sound of monotonous music and the rhythmical beat of drums and gongs. Beside the buddhas, two temple dancers appeared with golden helmets and face masks, fluttering wings and jerky movements – evil spirits attempting to bewitch the worshippers. The helmeted figures danced scornfully and contemptuously around the buddhas, striding with slow, circling movements, then they gave a sudden start of terror, whirled about madly and then collapsed, the whole body shuddering through to the tips of their fingers.

"A movement passed through the crowd of onlookers. Some stood up and followed the movements of the two dancers with a rapt expression. Women stared in terror with bated breath. Children whimpered. The monks looked on calmly.

"Then the dancers awoke, came to life again and expressed in a most compelling manner their acknowledgment of the divine. They bowed down before the buddhas, knelt to pray with folded hands, leaned so far backwards that their helmets touched the ground, then rose again and danced around the holy figures with the greatest reverence. For one last time they reared up to their full height. Finally, they sank to the ground, covering their bodies with their trembling wings and ceasing all movement, as if redeemed in death.

"A sort of redemption also seemed to traverse the crowd, who had perfectly comprehended the symbolic meaning of the dance. The music played on in the same monotonous rhythm and the people began to dance, but only the men. All were enraptured by the drumming and the sound of the gongs. How it happened I don't know, but suddenly I found myself amongst the dancers, making the same jerky, dislocating movements. Nobody took any notice of me. Rice brandy and rhythm had brought us all to the same state of intoxication.

"Meanwhile, in the deep blue sky sprinkled with stars, a delicate sickle moon had risen. Pinewood torches were set up around the square, salvos were fired from bamboo cannons and little rockets shot upwards.

"A gigantic hot-air balloon was being filled over a fire. It was made of paper glued together, and had a diameter of at least six metres. Long before Montgolfier hit upon this idea in Paris, people in Burma had been sending up balloons raised by hot air. Our magnificent specimen rose quickly too, to be closely followed by nine others which hung in the sky like enormous stars. Suddenly there was a loud crack as the rockets attached to the balloons went off and a glorious firework display burned and died away high above our heads. The balloons were still visible many hours later, while the lights on the ground were extinguished one by one.

"I made my way back to my monastery, but I could still see the glow of torches as folk returned home.

"Tauma Tillee, the senior priest at my monastery, often allowed me to be present when he was instructing his pupils how to pray. His prayer was a hasty droning, but

I got someone to explain the words to me in Keng-Tung and translate them. It went like this:

Prayer to Buddha, who knows all:
O divine image, I honour you!
O law, I honour you!
O yellow robe, I honour you!
O nirvana of contentment
O never-ending nirvana,
O eternal nirvana,
Could I but attain you!

"Tauma Tillee also showed me manuscripts, paintings and buddhas of great beauty. A monk in the monastery carved them from teak wood, but I also got to see figures made of stone, bronze, lacquer and even glass. The glass one carried a small but quite clear mark 'Made in Czechoslovakia.'

"Every day for ten days I would hear before sunrise the seven strokes on the monastery bell, a decorated triangular plate of bronze. Every day for ten days the evening breeze would waft the melodious chime of little wind bells to my ear and far into November I could lie in the open air and look up to the stars overhead. Then I returned to our bungalow next door to the Italian mission, resolved to avoid all discord between us in future. Max confessed to me later that he had been very much afraid that I would fall completely under the spell of Buddhism, 'get stuck' in Burma and marry a local woman. Wasn't this the danger Mr Price in Mandalay had warned us against? Certainly, my parents would have taken a dim view of my 'round-the-world trip' ending in this way!"

I too was to become acquainted with Tauma Tillee, for he came to visit us one day in our bungalow. He entered with some hesitation, and sat down modestly on the edge of a chair, saying nothing. His eyes opened wide with wonder as he examined the things we had brought with us from Europe, especially the typewriter. As I tapped away at it, a smile of comprehension lit his features. I had been rather afraid that he'd thought it was some kind of musical instrument. All the same, he seemed to take particular pleasure in the way the little warning bell sounded as the end of a line came near. Eventually I took the paper out of the machine and handed it to the monk. I saw immediately that he understood the process.

Soon afterwards he left as silently as he had come and I was afraid I had offended him. This was not the case. On the contrary, he reappeared the next day at the same hour bringing a present. It was a gilded statue of Buddha. A few days previously in the market at Keng-Tung I had bought a yellow cap which I now presented to him in return. He then expressed a wish to try the typewriter, so I showed him how to move the keys with his fingers. He soon got the hang of the machine and was studying the printed sheet with interest. He then explained to us in sign-language that we should go with him. We walked for two hours on deserted jungle paths until we came to a beautiful old monastery. We entered the inner courtyard through a gatehouse, and it must have been one of the largest monasteries I ever saw in Southeast Asia.

The disciples were just returning in droves from their daily round of begging in the surrounding villages. Tauma Tillee led us to a side building. There we made the discovery which at last explained the monk's great interest in the typewriter. We were in a printing shop! An old monk sat on the floor making the type, carving the characters into little blocks of teak wood. In another 'department' of the print shop these were being set up. They had even made a block showing Buddha in a halo of light! The printing press stood in a dark corner of the room. It consisted of a stamp plate that could be pressed down on the paper surface with a foot pedal mechanism. I was unable to discover what the printing ink was made of. It smeared easily, and seemed to present the only problem in this amazing workshop. The paper was likewise manufactured in the monastery. I rather supposed that this press deep in the jungle had been set up without reference to any other model. Maybe the inspiration had been no more than a sheet of newspaper that had somehow ended up in the monastery. This impression was strengthened by one of the American missionaries, to whom I showed one of the printed pages. Mr Bucker examined the page closely and then exclaimed, "But this is Khun!"

This aroused my interest too. "What is Khun?"

"It's the language spoken in the mountains around Keng-Tung. The written characters differ in several respects from the other Shan languages. Until now, no printer anywhere in the world has had type for Khun. I must get them to print copies of my psalm and prayer books!"

So, while a simple Buddhist monastery was turning out nicely printed books of the Four Noble Truths of Buddha, schoolchildren in the American Baptist mission in Keng-Tung were writing their fingers to the bone copying out biblical texts. The American was quite embarrassed when he became aware of this disparity. I could not resist asking why he had not set up a similar printing press himself. He excused himself by explaining, "I've been intending for some time to have type like that cast in America, but so far the cost has been prohibitive ..."

Whether the Baptist preacher actually paid a visit to the Buddhist monastery to see how printing can be done with very simple equipment, I do not know. We certainly visited the monastery on several more occasions, on one of which we were present at the cremation of a priest, an unforgettable event.

The coffin stood on a platform richly adorned with coloured paper, paper snakes, and carved heads of mythical beasts. For nine days it was an object of pilgrimage for the people of Keng-Tung. They came and knelt, made sacrifices and placed all kinds of food in shallow bowls before the platform. On the tenth day was the funeral. The coffin was placed on a wooden sled, also richly decorated and mounted with dragons' heads. Long ropes were attached to it before and behind. The women seized hold of the rope at the front, and the sled began to move slowly towards the cremation site. Meanwhile, the men had taken hold of the rope at the rear and were holding the sled back, with much howling. An enthusiastic tug-of-war arose between the women and the men. The older folk lined the roadway and shouted to the two groups to spur them on. First the women would prove stronger, the men would relax, and the sled would move a little way forward. Then they would strain on the rope again and haul it back a metre or two. Slowly, and in spite of all opposition, the vehicle drew closer to the pyre. Everyone was laughing and

The Khun typeface.

howling, shouting and egging each other on – it was really nothing like a funeral procession!

Only the priests moved in a slow and dignified manner, striding along behind the coffin, accompanied by all the monks and novices of Keng-Tung, stopping whenever it slipped backwards and continuing as it inched its way forward.

I could only conjecture at the symbolic meaning of the actions. Ultimately it must have represented the triumph of death over all the strivings of the living to keep the monk among them. In the end, the call of nirvana proved stronger and the sled came to rest at the cremation site.

The coffin was raised high on a pyre of logs, surmounted by the tower of a model pagoda constructed of wood and paper. The coffin was broken open with an axe and from it fell ashes in which the corpse had been packed. It now lay completely in the open, wrapped in yellow cloths. The monks stood around it in a tight formation and prayed.

Suddenly, from all around there was a hissing sound and fuses, mounted on strong wires in the same way as cable cars and driven by rockets, plunged into the petrol-soaked pyre of wood and ignited it like an explosion. When the body began to burn, the air was suddenly filled with a strong smell of opium. The dead man's lungs had been stuffed with it, and now it was released.

The people shouted and laughed, and finally they all departed for home in joyful mood. What a wonderful funeral, in which death itself became a festival of gladness! And only possible in the Buddhist country where laughter reigns.

20
LAUGHING WITH SIMBA

O n December 28th we quit Keng-Tung at last. We had spent two months there, waiting for the return of the dry season, two months until we could tackle the last 180km to Siam. Two months was also the approximate time it took to send a letter from Keng-Tung to Ban-Hue-Sai in Indochina, although it is only 160km as the crow flies. It would be sent by pack animal, taking nine days to Takau – which was back the way we had come – from Takau to Taunggyi, by rail to Rangoon, from Rangoon by sea taking 14 days round the Malacca peninsula to Hanoi, from Hanoi by motor to Vientiane, and from there up the Mekong by motor boat to Ban-Hue-Sai – that is, if it had not got lost in the meantime.

The fact that we managed to reach Siam without any significant wear and tear was thanks to the support of Sao Kaung Tai, who eased our passage in every possible way. He sent coolies on ahead to clear the road through the jungle; he provided us with labourers who laid boards every time we came to a bottomless swamp, and helped us to cross the hundreds of little rivers. On this journey I came to appreciate the buffalo. When our car was bogged down, they were often our only means of rescue, and they were more reliable than elephants. On January 10th we reached the river that forms the border between the Shan States and Siam, the Mesai. Here stood a bridge that the Siamese had built precisely as far as their border; that is to say, to an island in the middle of the river. At this point it terminated in a vertical face, with only a long ladder to reach the top of it. In view of this beautiful modern bridge, it was doubly annoying for us to have to be hauled through the river by a team of oxen. Helmuth took a picture of it. It showed us struggling through the river with the elegant arched shadow of the bridge falling on the waters.

Siam (Thailand) provided some delightful surprises. What was actually known about the country? Not very much, except that it was the home of the white elephant, and that in the previous century it had witnessed the birth of conjoined twins who had eventually become a circus sensation in both Europe and America. However, Siam had been quietly developing into a modern state, skilled at playing off the interests of the great European powers amongst themselves. The king of Siam had allowed many European powers a part in opening up the country to commerce, in building roads and railways, without giving preference to any one over the others. He had apparently pursued a very clever course in exploiting the riches of his country without betraying its ancient name 'Muang-Thai' – land of the free.

The wide all-weather road running from the half-built bridge to Chieng-Rai was a new experience after all the swamps in Burma and the Shan States. The road was bordered by numerous villages. Teahouses had become bus stations where the departure times of the buses were announced by gongs. In fact, these gongs were the brake drums of old cars, a bit of an eyesore and the consequence of motorisation, but sights like this were only disturbing for Europeans, the Siamese owners being proud of their modern acquisitions.

Chieng-Rai was a town of about 10,000 inhabitants, with asphalt roads, concrete buildings, charming little Siamese villas, and pretty gardens. The main traffic consisted of hundreds of rickshaws which were totally different from the Chinese and Japanese sort. It is wrong to think that the rickshaw was an Oriental invention. In fact it was an Anglican clergyman, the Reverend MB Bailey who, in the early 1890s in Tokyo had the brilliant idea of mounting a chair on a handcart and having it pulled by a man. In Japan this form of transport was dying out, and little motor taxis were in use everywhere. It was well-known that tuberculosis limited the life of a rickshaw boy to only a few years, which was why this type of rickshaw had been banned in Siam in favour of a bicycle with a light sidecar.

In Chieng-Rai we found accommodation at Mr Thorwaldsen's hotel, which bore the very un-Siamese name 'Asgard' on its very Siamese façade. The proprietor was a massively built old Dane, a former officer of the gendarmerie, who rejoiced in a Siamese wife, with children representing every stage of development from three to 25 years old.

He was not the only Dane among the couple of dozen Europeans in Chieng-Rai. There were also some French people who gave us a warm welcome. Madame de Camp, the wife of the French consul and director of the Compagnie Asiatique et Africaine, was a charming hostess. As we sat in her garden, our conversation began with Paris and Vienna, and led on to the wonders of Indian temples and the white elephants of Siam.

"Have you seen the elephants in the teak forest yet?"

"No, unfortunately."

"Oh, but you must!" And turning briskly to her husband, "Couldn't the company arrange it?"

"Our herd of elephants is engaged in felling giant trees 80km from Chieng-Rai," explained M de Camp. "You should be able to get there in your car. You must have come through some difficult country already. Do you want to try?"

To this we eagerly assented, and de Camp sent a messenger to M Martincourt at the forester's lodge in Honai Ta Ho to announce our arrival.

After about 52km we came to a tributary of the Mekong. There was not a bridge in sight, and because of the unusually high water level, even the ferry had been swept away. We had experienced the same thing many times before during the expedition and had always found a solution, but in this case it was pointless to expend much effort. We turned around and drove back to the last village. Here we looked for the post office and we did indeed find a sign on the wall of a hut proudly inscribed 'Post Office' with a letter box beside it, but that was all. Contact either with Chieng-Rai or with the forest lodge was impossible. We had more luck with the mayor. His son spoke some English and was delighted to show off his knowledge. He

Above: The first crossing of Southeast Asia by motor car. The worst bits were the steep slopes where neither elephants nor buffalo carts could help. In these situations we had to rely on heavy stakes and block and tackle.

Left: The leg-rowers of Inle Lake are unique. They pull the oar through the water by powerful and rhythmic swinging of the hips.

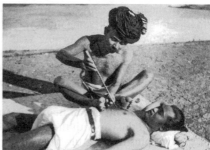

Above: Tattooing. This customer's legs have already received the 'beauty treatment.' Now for the torso ... Snakes and ornamental motifs are the most usual designs. Even Sao-Kaung-Tai, prince of Kengtung, showed us his tattooed legs with slightly self-conscious pride.

Leg-rowers on Inle Lake hold a boat-race. The enormous dug-outs each have a crew of twenty men. They were once invited to Rangoon to appear against a British rowing eight. At parties in the British clubs we heard widely differing accounts of the results of this race!

introduced himself as Sanong Punyedyana and solemnly presented us with his own hand-written card.

"How do we get to the Honai Ta Ho forest lodge?"

"You can't, at least, not with the car." He advised us to arrange with Martincourt to pick us up with another car on the other side of the river. I hastily scribbled a few lines which Sanong Punyedyana sent off immediately by messenger on his own horse to the lumber camp. Meanwhile he had organised accommodation for us, but the rider returned the same night with the answer. "All right!"

At eight o'clock in the morning a car would be waiting for us on the opposite bank and at eleven o'clock a car really did turn up, although M Martincourt, who had come himself, apologised for its being more of a work vehicle.

"Of course," he added, "we had several breakdowns. You know what these native vehicles are like."

We did not know, not at that time, and not from our own experience. Helmuth walked round the car with the suspicious eye of the expert. He discovered that one of the two pins holding the front springs on to the frame was broken. Simba (that was the driver's name) laughed and repaired the damage with a building clamp and several lengths of wire

We set off at midday. Martincourt had tied a handkerchief over his nose as protection against dust and mosquitoes. On each of the mudguards sat a coolie, and he kindly enlightened us on this point.

"The people like riding on the wings, and anyway, they have to hold on to the radiator cap."

"Why can't it be fixed? It's only a little job."

"But we've got the coolies!" explained Simba the driver somewhat haughtily.

There was no answer to this. The vehicle moved off, creaking and groaning. We soon noticed that Simba was a good driver, an excellent one even! No European would have been able to drive that car. The play on the steering was 270 degrees, and the gearbox was in a parlous state. Simba steered essentially one-handed, just as the Arabs did. The other hand was always busy with something else. He might be tugging on a cable, doing some other 'little mending job' or blowing his nose conscientiously and thoroughly. Besides, the gear stick required his constant attention. The gears had a tendency to slip out and disengage. To prevent this, Simba had a comprehensive system of hooks fixed to the seat and the dashboard, by which he could keep the gear stick fixed in any position he wanted.

Simba drove at full throttle into hundreds of holes, over ditches and ruts. He had no foot brake, at least, his foot never touched the pedal once throughout the entire journey. The handbrake was a rusty piece of decoration that wobbled uselessly this way and that with every jolt.

"The truth is," sighed Martincourt, "that a trip in this car is more dangerous than a run in with a tiger."

We had only gone a few kilometres when, in spite of the coolies, we lost the radiator cap. The gears were changed down in a crescendo of ear-splitting bangs, while the whole crew howled with pleasure at this feast of musical delights. At last we stopped, and one of the coolies ran back. Simba laughed, and we laughed too because it wasn't our car, was it? We should have got going again at this point, but the engine refused to start. Simba laughed and cranked, and cranked and laughed. The coolies got down off the mudguards, and then the rest of the crowd, who had been sitting on the carrier at the back, also got down to watch Simba cranking the engine, and, while they were about it, to perform all kinds of bodily functions with a complete lack of inhibition.

Finally, Simba opened the bonnet. For us, if for no one else, it was a sad sight. Simba, however, whistling some jolly little Siamese tune, plucked away at the leads and eventually laid bare the distributor. Lacking the right tools, he borrowed the bush knife belonging to one of the coolies, a kind of sabre of terrifying dimensions. With this, he poked around between the contacts and, lo and behold, a new attempt at cranking was crowned with success! Well satisfied, the driver settled himself once more behind the wheel. We three Europeans squeezed in beside him on the wooden bench. Two coolies took up the seats of honour on the wings, the rest crowded on to the platform, and away we went.

About 15 years back, Simba's car must have been a large and elegant limousine. Now, all that remained was the rickety chassis surmounted by an open 'body' of roughly joined planks of wood. Every time the clutch was used there came a strange noise, which kept on getting louder.

"Oh, that will soon stop," Simba assured us.

Sometimes the road improved for a distance, and we would rattle forward at high speed. Then the unbelievable happened: Simba fixed the accelerator open with one of his special hooks, and suddenly, there he was with both feet in the air. I'm not kidding! He gradually drew his feet up past his belly until they were resting on

Above: Hot-air balloons made of thin homemade paper are a favourite toy of children in the Shan States.

Right: The Shan States comprise several dozen small independent princely states. Lack of communications has led to the development of a variety of different tribes of Mongol origin. The ideal of beauty among the Padaung is the longest possible neck. These heavy coils of brass can never be removed.

Above: After an arduous two-day journey by jungle waterways we reached the village of the Padaung. The people were very trusting and mothers were only too willing to sell their daughters for thirty rupees. No charge was made for photography!

Above: Among the Red Kareni the ideal of beauty is to carry as many metres of wire as possible wrapped around the legs.

Below: A team of oxen was often a good means of traction on swampy jungle paths.

the steering wheel. He wedged his toes cleverly round the spokes of the wheel and so steered the car. Then he fished out a tobacco tin, and began thoughtfully and appreciatively to roll a cigarette. Would we like one too?

"No, thank you very much!"

Simba grinned, and I got the impression he was going to take plenty of time rolling that cigarette. At last he took his feet down off the wheel and we all breathed a sigh of relief.

The two coolies riding on the wings could no longer hold on to the radiator cap, which was getting hotter and hotter. It was as much as they could do to stop themselves falling off the car. Suddenly there was an explosion, the radiator cap shot into the air, followed by a jet of steam and water which poured out over the two boys. "Bang, bang, BANG!" went the gears as Simba changed down, until we finally stopped once more. I thought the two poor lads must have been badly scalded, but miraculously they leapt off the car and there they were, laughing. So was the driver! One of them fetched the errant radiator cap, and on we went again. The squealing and screeching was getting worse all the time, and eventually Simba remarked innocently, "There doesn't seem to be any oil left in the gear-box." All the same, he drove on as if he hadn't a care in the world.

After repeated stops for all the usual reasons, we reached the forest lodge of Honai Ta Ho after a journey of four hours. Martincourt showed us the specially trained elephants at work. They were pulling and rolling the heavy tree-trunks towards the river with incredible strength, and showed an astonishing understanding of the laws of leverage and objective. The logs then floated 2000km down the river to Saigon, where they were sawn up into ships' planking, to spend the rest of their existence sailing the seven seas. On returning to the forest lodge we looked around for the car. Simba's face lit up as soon as he saw us coming. He was holding out a couple of melted bearings and blue gearwheels.

"I was right! There was no oil in the gearbox!" he announced happily, deeply satisfied that his suspicions had proved correct.

Martincourt simply shrugged his shoulders. "The first thing you have to learn in Asia is not to get annoyed too often. If you do, your nerves go all to pieces, and you are under enough stress from the climate as it is."

This was too true, and before long we would have cause to remember it, as we stood holding a couple of ruined parts from our own car. It happened on the return journey to Chieng-Rai. We heard a noise as if a branch had got caught in a back wheel and was hitting something at every revolution. Helmuth got out to look but could find nothing. However, the knocking continued and varied with our speed. We exchanged increasingly ghastly looks until we exclaimed in unison, "The differential!"

Helmuth unscrewed the cover and went all over the housing like a doctor investigating an injured ribcage. Two teeth, one half and one whole, fell out of the crown wheel into his hand. A leading authority in Vienna had assured us that the differential was infallible. Consequently we had loaded ourselves with over a hundred kilos of spare parts for the journey, but nothing that bore the remotest resemblance to a differential or any of its component parts. The first time it had played up was in Palestine and now it had happened again in the Siamese jungle. I

Shan people are consummate performers of this balancing act for separating chaff from wheat.

Above: Two dug-outs of teak and a bamboo mat were all it took to make a ferry capable of transporting our car, once it had been unloaded.

Above: The churned-up morass. Half-rotted lianas and teak tree leaves spread an evil smell. Malaria is endemic here.

Right: Around 1930 two Padaung women with their Burmese guardian were brought to Britain. While there, they made this advertisement. Name the Edinburgh brewery!

A LONG DRINK FOR A LONG NECK.—Burmese women in Edinburgh enjoying a long drink in a local brewery.—PHOTO, C.S.A.

looked at Helmuth. "Has it gone?" He nodded. "Oh yes. If the other teeth get stuck, then the whole housing can break up. Better to tow it in straight away ..."

'Towing it in' meant hoisting it on to an ox-cart for the journey back to Chieng-Rai and then waiting for the necessary spare parts to arrive from Vienna. We ordered them by telegraphing to Luang-Prabang in Indochina, reasoning quite rightly that the French colony would be served by Air France which would be the speediest method of delivering them to us. Of course we might also get one of those nagging letters from over there, demanding to know why we weren't already in China.

All the same, it had been a bit of luck that the accident happened where it did in northern Siam. According to the best-informed sources (and for once they were all in complete agreement) we could never have driven the car to Luang-Prabang. It had to be taken apart and shipped down the Mekong, and the only suitable water transport was at present lying in Luang-Prabang. Until it arrived back in Chieng-Rai we would simply have to wait. Perhaps this would correspond with the time it took for the air mail parcel on its long journey out to the Far East. We estimated that this would take about three weeks, and this turned into a sort of compulsory holiday from the car.

Every time we crossed a river we took everything out of the car, so that if the worst happened, at least we would save our food and equipment.

Above: Crossing an unnamed jungle river somewhere between Keng-Tung and the Siamese border.

Above: The prince of Keng-Tung and his wife had, as Buddhists, a very modest lifestyle. Even their palace boasted no particular splendour. They were happy to be photographed alongside Max Reisch and his car.

Below: Our bungalow in Keng-Tung. We sat out the rainy season with all home comforts, waited on by a native servant.

155

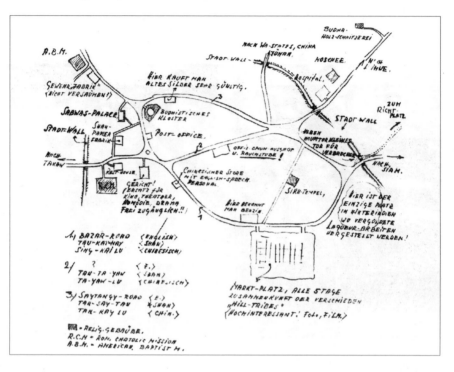

Above: Keng-Tung: Our enforced stay during the rainy season meant that I had time at my disposal to make an exact map of the city of Keng-Tung. The little jungle town of 7000 inhabitants was originally totally surrounded by walls, of which only a few traces remained, in particular the fortified gates and associated stonework. On the far right next to the gate to Siam can be seen a small gate through which criminals were led to execution ("zum Richtplatz"). Strong Chinese influence makes it probable that there were more executions in times past. On the other hand, the presence of two Christian missions, a Sikh temple, a mosque and several Buddhist monasteries is proof of great religious tolerance. In the centre is the public house for opium, with its smoking parlour ("Rauchstube!").

Left: Our homemade dictionary for use in the Shan States.

Above: Dormitory in an orphanage in Keng-Tung, scarcely the last word in luxury, but practical for all that. Note the means for conveying away "waste products" by means of a bamboo gutter.

Above: Sign in four languages, openly advertising the premises where opium may be officially smoked.

Left: Signed photograph of Sao Kaung Tai, prince of Keng-Tung. The dedication is dated 27/12/1935. His riches derived from his teak forests, and from the cultivation of opium and tung oil.

Above: On the banks of the Salween river. Even four-wheel-drive would not have helped very much. At the time, it was only available on certain specialised heavy military vehicles.

Above: Behind the bars, pipes and little dishes of gleaming black opium lie ready for the customers.

Above: A confirmed opium smoker needs twenty pipes. At the second pipe I beat a retreat.

Above: When we were over the axles in mud, it was often hard to attach the tow-rope to the car.

Below: The Messai river formed the border between the almost medieval Shan States and relatively modern Siam. There was now a semblance of western civilisation.

Above: Smoking opium is a complicated business. The viscous opium is formed into a ball by turning it on a needle over the flame of an oil lamp. This ball is introduced into the small bowl of the pipe and the opium smoke is drawn swiftly into the lungs with a few short pulls.

Above: The print shop run by monks in the jungle, where the first type for the Khun language was made. This was quite a surprise for sophisticated Christian missionaries.

21
TWO MOTORCYCLE FIENDS

In the course of our social round in Chieng-Rai, for which we now had plenty of time, we visited Monsieur Guenagar. A servant took our cards and ushered us into the spacious entrance hall of his bungalow, adorned with hunting trophies, Buddha statues and silk pictures. Guenagar soon came in with our cards in his hand and invited us to sit down. Over several Pernods the conversation began to flow, and Guenagar seemed particularly interested in the technical side of our expedition.

"This is certainly quite an achievement, but wait a moment. Not long ago I was reading in an English magazine about two Austrians who rode all the way to India on a motorcycle. That might have been even harder!"

I was about to speak but Guenagar was already on his feet. He returned with a whole stack of *Motorcycle* magazine from which he extracted a copy to show us.

"Do you know these two? Their names are Reisch and Tichy. If you're Austrian, you must know them!"

We exchanged a smile.

Helmuth picked up my card from the two lying on the table and held it out to Guenagar. "If you would just read this again ..."

"Parbleu!" exclaimed Guenagar in a flash of Gallic emotion. "This is my lucky day! Is it really you, the very same, in person?" He nearly embraced me on the spot, repeating over and over, "Welcome to my home! Consider me at your service!"

Dispatching his servant to the cellar, Guenagar called for a bottle of Veuve Clicquot, though it was only the middle of the morning.

There was a simple explanation for our friend's enthusiasm: he was a fanatical motorcyclist, a real motorcycle fiend.

"A la santé of all motorcyclists!" pronounced Guenagar solemnly as we clinked glasses.

Then he told us about all the bikes he had owned when in France, a new model every year. It was obvious that he was over the moon at finding someone with whom he could talk shop after so many years.

"You know, the other Frenchmen here think I am a bit crazy. I have a company car, of course, but – ," and here he dropped his voice, "– I've got my own motorcycle here too. I can't live without one!"

At the time I couldn't help thinking him a bit crazy, but today I have more sympathy. As a car driver, I like nothing better than to go roaring off on my Puch

250 TF Gelber Blitz to indulge in some elegant banking and weaving. It blows away all your worries and all your headaches. (Personally, I don't suffer from either, which doubles the pleasure!)

Today, I can totally understand what Guenagar meant when he said, "If I didn't have my bike, I would feel old, and if the time ever comes when I don't enjoy riding it, then I'll know that I am old."

After the second bottle of Veuve Clicquot, Guenagar made a sort of declaration of love, in the motorcycle sense. "You, Monsieur Reisch, are the only man I will allow to ride my BSA. Furthermore, I beg you to do so. It will do honour to my machine."

I was overcome with emotion. We were all overcome with emotion. We had lunch with Guenagar, which allowed us to recover a little, and then we were overcome once again, and then again. Finally after supper Helmuth and I staggered back to Thorwaldsen's hotel.

Down in the courtyard stood the crippled Steyr, and I was suddenly overwhelmed with rage. I began to give Helmuth a detailed account of all the highlights of our trip to India, and it was only when he started to snore that I gave it up. After all, he was only a four-wheel man.

In the days that followed, I proudly whizzed around Chieng-Rai on Guenagar's BSA. It was the only motorcycle in northern Siam. Like all the cars, it had come by train the 1500km from Bangkok to Chieng-Rai, the terminus of the Siamese railway. There were no roads where the railway ran. It was only where the track ended that a modest network of small roads began to radiate in all directions, although sooner or later they all ended up in the jungle. Lorries could therefore only circulate within a very limited area, and the only way out of this northern Siamese motor enclave was again by rail to the south. We were an exception with the Steyr, since we had arrived from the north through the inhospitable Shan country and were going to travel on to Indochina in the east. This was something absolutely new, and in spite of there being plenty of cars on the road within the enclave, the natives regarded us with admiration, while the Europeans considered us slightly insane. This impression was no doubt reinforced by my frequent appearances on Guenagar's BSA.

Of course we spent a lot of time visiting our friend. One day he declared that he really must get a new machine. In France, he'd had a new one every year, and he had already had the BSA much longer than that. It was high time for a change. He had already decided on a Belgian machine, and now he brought out a folder with prospectuses for all the latest models and extensive correspondence with the various manufacturers. I was burning with enthusiasm to look through all the literature with Guenagar and assess the pros and cons of each model. Just by way of comment and purely theoretically, of course.

"How about a Puch, then?" I asked.

"When I read about your trip to India in *The Motorcycle* from London, I was very excited and I thought: That's the machine for me! I wrote off to the factory via the consulate in Bangkok. In French, naturally. The consulate passed the letter on and I did receive an answer, but the letter was in German! I couldn't read it and I threw it out. I can't believe that no one in Austria speaks French! I would have loved to buy a Puch, but the 'Saroléa' is already on its way."

Helmuth, who was not so engrossed in all this motorcycle chit-chat, had meanwhile discovered other sporting entertainment in Chieng-Rai. One of the numerous festivals celebrated with alacrity by Shan and Burmese alike included boxing matches. Men, women, children and babies sat around the arena. The front row was reserved for the yellow-clad punjis, who always showed a great interest in sport. The spectators all clapped as the boxers appeared. They were thin, wiry brown lads wearing shorts and boxing gloves. The contestants took up their places in opposite corners of the ring and opened the first round with a prayer. They knelt down on the ground, raised folded hands – folded as far as boxing gloves would allow – and went through the various exercises associated with the usual prayer ritual.

Then they sprang up all at once and began to fight an unseen enemy. They boxed in the air, taking swings at the invisible foe, slipped under his guard and finally defeated him. The referee then blew his whistle to signal the start of the fight proper. The Siamese game allowed boxing with knees and feet and they accordingly made good use of these. Whenever I thought a contestant was done for, he would leap up and skilfully kick his opponent in the face with his bare soles, so that the other flew out of the ring and landed among the audience. Of course this occasioned a lot of laughter and applause. Revenge was not long coming, for the other was also a 'knee' specialist, which meant pushing his knee into his opponent's stomach while at the same time administering an uppercut to the chin and knocking him out.

It was fascinating to watch them throwing these hooks to the chin, now with the hands, now with the feet, and when an opponent was nearly KO but slowly struggling to his feet, he would receive such a kick in the stomach or face that he would give up the attempt and lie still. They wasted no time awarding the victory on points. Only knock-outs counted. To round things off, the victor performed another solo fight with the spirits and then a prayer of thanks, while music blared out and the spectators cheered wildly.

We ended the day with a visit to the cinema, one of the great Siamese national pastimes. They showed American films with subtitles. Chinese films specialised in a terrible lot of shouting, grandiose costumes and frightful music, while modern Siamese ones had all the actors in European dress, the women frequently in magnificent evening gowns. This was accompanied by modern dance music and European hits, with the women singing in squeaky voices. We found it all absolutely ghastly and got much more pleasure from the opening number, which was usually a film of traditional shadow-plays, old dances and Siamese costumes.

Meanwhile, the great day came when it was announced that the Shing-li-wang, the boat we had been waiting for, would soon arrive in Chieng-Sen. Off we set, with Thorwaldsen towing the crippled Steyr, to this village on the Mekong 40km away. It had once been the greatest city in Siam, but Burmese and Shan princes had wrangled over it for so long that it had gradually decayed and sunk into oblivion. Now only ruins testified to the greatness of its former palace. Of particular interest was a pagoda, very much damaged, about 30 metres in height. Long stalks and grass grew in the shattered walls. The tip of the pagoda was broken and hung down sadly at a sloping angle like the broken wing of a bird. My attempts at climbing up to solve the mystery of this contravention of all the laws of structural engineering were, alas, unsuccessful. Presumably the original builder of the pagoda had incorporated iron rods or wires into the stonework to give the tip more stability, and this was what was now holding it fast. This building method seemed to me a sort of forerunner of our reinforced concrete, which caused a small sensation in Europe when it was invented around 1870. Of course, the pagoda at Chieng-Sen is much older.

Only the name of this insignificant village on the banks of the Mekong recalled the former royal city, but when Siam's ruler had undertaken a progress through his country five years previously, a hunting lodge had been built for him in Chieng-Sen. The king had rested there for several days, and we too found welcome accommodation here.

Each of us was given a large room in the completely empty building. There was a veranda and a bathroom, not to mention the mayor who lived next door and provided our meals. The heavily spiced dishes were very satisfying, but we never had any idea what we were eating. The only indisputable ingredient was rice at every meal, and more rice, and just as we were feeling we couldn't face any more of it, Guenagar turned up on his BSA, bringing bread! Just what a pleasure this can be is only appreciated when travelling in Asia, and our kind friend rose high in our estimation when he proceeded to send a loaf of white bread down to Chieng-Sen every other day.

When the Shing-li-wang finally came in, we had to spend a long time with the Chinese captain discussing the best way to stow the car on the boat. It was certainly a most ingenious construction, with its two colossal dugouts and connecting timbers and a diesel engine mounted in the centre, but no European seaman could have been persuaded to sign on with such an extraordinary vessel. We were extremely glad of it, however. Our expedition was loaded on to it in three sections; first, the chassis, from which everything that could be easily dismantled, had been removed in order to reduce the weight; second, the bodywork, and third, an enormous pile of luggage, spare parts and other equipment. The chassis was placed up front, at right angles to the dugouts and the bodywork in the same position at the rear. The rest of the gear disappeared into the hold of the dinghy. The cargo also included a large number of bales of Japanese silk which had come on a long detour via Siam to enter Indochina. We were told that this was a way of paying less customs duty, but it may have been contraband. It didn't bother us.

On 3rd March the curious ship abandoned itself to the mercy of the Mekong currents. It was only a three-hour journey to Ban-Hue-Sai where we would cross the border between Siam and the French province of Laos, but what a three hours that was! At first the banks were flat, with jungle right down to the edge of the river. Wild peacocks played about in the water and crowds of monkeys screeched down at us from the high teak trees. Then the river bed narrowed, the banks became steep and the current carried us forward at greater speed. Water sprayed up and drenched the whole boat. With incredible skill, the steersman manoeuvred us through swirling rapids often only a metre or two away from the rocky bank or a reef suddenly appearing in midstream. The Chinese stood motionless at the wheel, with typical Asian serenity, only the wheel itself spinning back and forth between his hands. With the most dangerous stretch of the river behind us and Ban-Hue-Sai coming into sight, we were ready to heave a sigh of relief when we remembered that we still had to negotiate the rapids of the French customs. It was reported that the local

French customs official was particularly strict and conscientious. Just for now it was impossible to speak to him because it was Sunday. A native soldier took away our passports. He was bemused and annoyed because he did not recognise the name of the country from which these travellers were supposed to come. "Aus-tria? Where on earth is that? Australia!" He corrected us reprovingly and we nodded meekly because we were quite used to this confusion.

We then asked for the bungalow of the Resident of Ban-Hue-Sai, Monsieur Beauregard. Not for the first time on our journey we were playing postmen, and had a lot of mail to deliver. We sweated and toiled up the hill to his house. A gentleman coming towards us called us by name.

"I thought it might be you," he said and introduced himself as Beauregard. "I've been waiting eleven months for you!" We were speechless. "I had a message from Paris in April last year saying you were travelling out to Indochina by car. So here you are at last!"

The French embassy in Vienna had provided us with a letter of recommendation and simultaneously alerted the authorities in Indochina. The bureaucratic machine had functioned so perfectly that even a little customs post in Ban-Hue-Sai had the information, although it was by no means certain that we would pass through here.

Beauregard offered us hospitality in his own home, apologising nevertheless. "It is only a small place in an out-of-the way post like this, not exactly up to the standard of a reigning power." The house turned out to be an elegant villa, tastefully furnished. We put our most urgent question to the Resident straight away.

"Can you introduce us to the customs officer?"

"No, I can't," was his laconic reply.

The Resident felt very lonely in his outpost. He seemed to be on bad terms with the only other white man in the place, namely the customs officer. The two men would only meet on official business, and in private had no more to do with each other in the middle of the jungle than they would probably have done in Paris.

Everything in our host's home was redolent of western culture, and he talked endlessly of his own region of France and how he longed to return there. In the evening we sat on the terrace looking down on the huts of Ban-Hue-Sai and the Mekong, with melancholy Breton songs echoing from the gramophone beside us.

The next morning we went down into the village to seek out the customs officer, who seemed to be leading a humdrum existence in company with his wife, an elderly native woman. We hoped he wasn't going to make a drama out of examining our luggage. At the little house we sent in our cards with due formality. Soon we were being greeted by a chatty little fellow who immediately announced, "I got the message about your arrival!"

We presented the documentation for the car. Everything was minutely checked and declared valid. Then we enquired apprehensively about dutiable goods, since we were actually carrying two cine cameras, five other cameras, two new tyres, spare parts and a lot else besides. The very strict customs officer dismissed us saying, "That's all in order. You can go through!" I believe he was even more delighted at his own generosity than we were. Rumour had done a deep injustice to Ban-Hue-Sai, or were we just particularly lucky?

22
SUCCESS AT LAST

If our reception by the French authorities at the border post had been friendly, in Luang-Prabang it was somewhat unusual. It was the first time a car had come this way, as Monsieur Lacoste the commissaire de police confirmed to us in writing. In addition, he provided us with a dozen convicts to build a roadway up the steep river bank from the Shing-Li-Wang's anchorage. Amid much groaning and rattling of the chains with which their feet were fettered, the prisoners pulled the car up. One Indochinese soldier of the Garde Indigène was allocated to every two convicts, which was not a bad idea, for otherwise we would not have felt safe among this sinister rabble. Our helpers were essentially a gang of vicious thieves and murderers.

As the boat was being unloaded, another small incident occurred. They were building a ramp so that the chassis could be rolled ashore.

"That's not going to work," said Helmuth. "The ramp is too weak."

"Too weak? Don't make me laugh! I'm responsible for transporting your car and that includes landing it," insisted our Chinese boatman.

"Of course, but who will foot the bill if the car falls through and gets damaged?"

The Chinese smote his chest. "I will pay for it!" he cried. "You need pay nothing for the whole boat trip if that ramp breaks!"

All right, then ...

At that very moment the car fell into the water with a splash. It was not especially deep and nothing worse happened, but we had won the bet. The Chinese praised us as honourable men when we nevertheless paid him half the agreed fare. Since he was charging us three times the fair amount in any case, he didn't do so badly out of it.

The convicts lugged all the dismembered parts of the Trans Asia Expedition to the workshops of the Travaux Publics, a sort of builders' yard for public works. The workshops were good and Monsieur Mathieu kindly gave us free access.

"I wish you well," he said, "and I hope you manage to get a whole car out of this load of bits and pieces!"

Thanks to Helmuth's skill, that was a sure thing. But had the spare parts for the differential arrived yet? This was the great question that had been filling us with apprehension over the past few weeks.

At the post office there were a few letters for each of us.

"Any parcel? Parcel from Autriche? Not arrived yet?"

The Indochinese clerk disappeared into the back of the post office. It took a long time. Helmuth slipped through a little door into the sorting room and helped with the search. Soon a cry of joy went up and Helmuth came running back with a small wooden crate marked "Absender: Steyr-Daimler-Puch AG." The post office was submerged in a flurry of wood-wool as we dug out the eagerly awaited treasures: a pinion, crown wheel and differential cage, bearing, slide blocks and several little boxes with nuts, rings, cotter pins and other odds and ends. A swing axle differential is a complicated construction in which even the smallest part can be crucial. I felt uneasy at the sight of this mysteriously abundant delivery, but Helmuth immediately began to count the teeth on the crown wheel and pinion. His face grew longer and longer. I saw him count it all once again, and then he heaved a deep sigh: it was the wrong ratio! This was a bitter blow. One moment we had been dancing with joy around the crate in full view of the whole post office, and now the mood had gone sour. We had started by laughing and joking, and now Helmuth was asking frostily:

"Didn't you ask for the lowest possible gear ratio when you telegraphed?"

"No, I didn't," I admitted shamefacedly.

"Well, I'm telling you, it will work somehow because it's got to work, but you'd better forget about fourth gear straightaway. Consider third as an occasional gift from the gods. You'll have to live in second and you'll swear at first gear because you'll find it far too high."

We left the post office in silence, feeling that tension between us on which many an expedition has come to grief. We had experienced this before, and we feared it. Later on, of course, you realise that the causes were all petty and you can smile about it. When I sit down with Helmuth today and we sift through our memories, we are always agreed on one thing: we actually got on each other's nerves quite often, sometimes dangerously so.

We began to rebuild the car in silence and working together brought us close again. We talked the whole business through once more and my sin of omission seemed less as a result. It was the manufacturer, after all, who had provided the chassis with the small differential, and wouldn't you take it for granted that the factory would keep notes of all the mechanical alterations? They had gone to a lot of trouble and expense to equip the expedition and get it on the road, and if we now telegraphed an order for spare parts from Siam, then surely it would have made sense to ask which parts had been used in the first place?

Helmuth helped to resolve the last of the tension between us.

"You didn't actually tell them we needed a differential for a Steyr-100. Let's be glad they didn't send us spares for an old Steyr-12!"

We had good laugh at this and happily carried on working. If some detail didn't go right, then we might lose our tempers, and this could be put down to the madness of the tropics, but we were sensible enough not to let it influence our relationship with our sponsors.

Monsieur Mathieu's three little sons 'helped' us to rebuild the car, when they could, but they got terribly in the way. When one of them was stung by a scorpion as he was dragging up a plank, the excitement in the workshop provoked by the first-ever car reached a climax. Fortunately the event had no serious consequences, but to our relief Madame Mathieu forbade her offspring to give any more 'help.'

This was not the only encounter with wildlife that we had during the rebuilding. A mouse jumped out of the crate in which the engine had been packed. It had nibbled all the oil paper and sacking, and also given birth to two pretty little baby mice. It must have crept into the crate in Siam and travelled to Indochina as a stowaway, braving the wrath of the customs officer at Ban-Hue-Sai.

When we dismantled the brake drums for cleaning we found, in the left-hand rear drum, a large spider's web containing the mummy of a desiccated spider. It must have been subjected to at least a million revolutions on the way from Vienna to Indochina!

Back in Vienna the French consul had solemnly presented me with a brochure published by the Office du gouvernement de l'Indochine containing a reference to the Route Coloniale No. 7, a road from Luang-Prabang to Vinh. Vinh lies on the Gulf of Tongking. How many times we had talked about Vinh on the long six-month crossing of Southeast Asia! In all our journey through Asia it was one of the stopping-places we longed to see most.

How we had looked forward to that beautiful new road from Luang-Prabang to Vinh! Now we saw that it was clearly an editor's dream. Like many a European travel agent, the brochure promised more than the reality of the situation would bear. Even so, simply to invent 600km of metalled road through the middle of the jungle was pulling a bit of a fast one! Not for the first time we found that the best information, even presented in black and white, is useless when it doesn't fit the facts. Let them take note, all those clever people back home who thought we would get to Shanghai in nine months. It took us fourteen months and we were lucky to get there at all.

For those who are interested, it should be mentioned that this optimistic, nay, utopian brochure was six years old when we received it, and the Route Coloniale No 7 was only now being built. We expressed our concern to M Mathieu, the manager of the workshops and director of road-building for the province of Laos.

"Gentlemen, you are in luck, nevertheless! It will be years before the road is completed, but the route has been marked out and you will probably take no more than a week to drive over it. You were the first to come from Siam to Luang-Prabang and you will also be the first motorists to use the Route Coloniale No. 7 from Luang-Prabang to Vinh. Does that not please you?"

"Oh certainly, but how can that be managed in such a short time?"

"There are only about twenty places where the basic track is not yet wide enough for a car. At these sites I will muster all the workers I can and let you know when you can start. Meanwhile you can relax and go on rebuilding your car."

At the same time as working on our car we were enjoying the interesting social life of Luang-Prabang, capital of Laos province. For the first time in a long while we were able to speak German again with Madame Lacoste, wife of the police chief, who had lived for many years in Vienna.

Madame Lacoste showed us the sacred object which is the city's emblem and to which it owes its name – a statue of Buddha, sixty centimetres high, made of pure gold and bolted to the rock by the great pagoda of Luang-Prabang. There was a particular reason for this. During a war between Siam and Laos the precious statue was carried off to Bangkok, where robbers attempted to steal it. They did not get

République Française

Ville de Luang-Prabang

Indochine Française

Attestation

Je soussigné L acoste Stéphane, Commissaire de Police de la ville de Luang-Prabang, déclare que Messieurs Max Reisch et Helmuth Hahmann sont les premiers touristes qui passent en Indochine Française, venant du Siam et des Etats Shan en empruntant la route Houei..., Luang-Prabang, Xieng-Khouang, Vinh, Hanoï avec une automobile.

Marque de la voiture Steyr N° A2020)

Luang-Prabang (Laos) 12 Mars 1936

Confirmation of the first crossing of Southeast Asia by motor car, given by the French colonial authorities in Luang Prabang, Laos Province.

very far, as the Buddha grew heavier and heavier in their arms so that eventually they were unable to carry it. It was found in the streets of Bangkok and brought back to the monastery. As the robbery had failed, the Siamese also began to feel that this piece of plunder would bring them bad luck. They had returned the treasure of their own free will, and now it stood again in its old place in the capital city of Laos, to which it gave its name of 'sacred golden image.'

On March 12th 1936, Mathieu announced that we could make our attempt, and, as we were not superstitious, we left on the thirteenth. Mathieu also gave us nearly all his petrol reserves from the workshop, which was not much, since there were no motor vehicles in Luang-Prabang as yet. For the first 50km the going was bumpy, but we made good progress. Then we entered the mountains of Laos where the track consisted only of the rough base layer of big stones, gravel and clay. The whole route

Above: Rickshaws, lung-destroying invention of the Reverend Bailey, were banned in Siam. All the same, the bicycle with sidecar was almost as unhealthy for its driver.

Above: A letter of recommendation from the Siamese Embassy in London. The expedition had official recognition at the highest level. All countries we drove through had been informed, and they issued on-the-spot directives in support of this first-ever motor journey from the Mediterranean to the Yellow Sea.

Above: Driving over this innocent ditch we heard an ominous clicking, which told us that the differential had broken yet again.

Above: Small people – big wheels, big people – small wheels! Comparing developments in Europe and Asia over the centuries.

Above: This shows all the parts of the extremely complicated swing-axle differential on the Steyr-100. Now we would be stuck in the jungle in Siam for several weeks.

Left: Siam. Did they have reinforced concrete five centuries ago? In the former royal city of Chieng-sen, now choked by jungle, we came across this pagoda with a spire supported by iron rods in the masonry.

through the Laos mountains and the Annamite Range was a 680km switchback. Of the first 300km, scarcely one was anything like level, or without a couple of bends.

The difficult terrain in this peculiar landscape, all chopped up by ravines, had transformed the building of a road into a colossal engineering feat.

Soon we stopped at the first roadworks. It was clear from the freshly moved earth on the steep slope that there had been nothing here a few days previously, except maybe a narrow pathway. The coolies had dug into the angle of the hill to make a rough and ready carriageway. They had been alerted by the sound of the engine and were now approaching the car. Evidently they had been expecting us and were excited to be face to face at last with the vehicle which had cost them such hard labour. The way they had carved out for us was narrow and the soil at the edges suspiciously loose. The outside wheels could have sunk in and the car was in considerable danger of sliding down the slope. The only safe course was to use ropes. Strong cables were hooked to the front and rear of the car, and the coolies pulled and held on until the car was out of the danger zone. Similar dramas were repeated over the course of the next two days. By then the hardest part of Route Coloniale No 7 had been covered, and we reached the roadworks bungalow Sala-Pu-Khum at an altitude of 1600 metres.

There was no petrol here. We had used up a lot more than our estimate, so we set off on the next leg of our journey as economically as possible. The route began to climb steeply through the jungle. We were oppressed by the knowledge that we had only a few more litres in the tank. Then the engine coughed and cut out. Helmuth quickly switched over to the reserve tank, but we knew we could only go another 20km.

We crept slowly forward. Then a light flared up and we made out a bamboo roof, four natives and a small fire. This was a good place to stop. The jungles of Annam were notorious for tigers and panthers. We cooked our evening meal under the bamboo shelter while the natives looked on in a friendly and curious way. We treated ourselves to pea soup with sausage and then hashed meat, finishing up with a bottle of wine from Luang-Prabang. We set up our camp beds and dosed ourselves with the inevitable quinine.

When the sun woke us, the road had come to life with Buddhist monks, brightly-dressed Annamites, and occasionally a few riders on horseback. We stopped an intelligent-looking lad who attempted to explain in French, "Another three miles to the nearest village. There's a big festival there!" We checked the contents of the tank and thought we might make it.

We reached the little mountain village at 1300 metres with almost the last drop of petrol. Could we believe our eyes? There stood a car, a small Peugeot. A gentleman in uniform introduced himself as chief of the Garde Indigène at Mong-Sen. He had driven 30km to get here on official duty.

It was only thanks to the festival that we chanced upon the commandant from Mong-Sen. He was happy to give us a bidon full of petrol and our progress was thus assured. At midday we reached the first place of any size in Annam.

"When you get to Cua-Rao I would advise you to go to the postmaster," Mathieu had said in Luang-Prabang with no further explanation. So we found the postmaster of Cua-Rao and presented greetings from Monsieur Mathieu.

Above: Overnight camp in the mountains of Laos. The two camp beds are standing next to the car. Helmuth is tending the camp fire. The local people, who had scarcely seen a white man, guessed what we wanted from our facial expressions and treated us almost as demigods.

Below: In Siam we had to take the car apart for loading on to the boat that took it down the Mekong to Luang Prabang.

"It is very good to see you, although I was expecting you yesterday and the dinner's gone cold by now," he said. Our jaws dropped.

"Oh yes, Mathieu telegraphed and ordered a nice dinner for you in celebration of getting through on Route Numéro 7."

This was the height of French hospitality.

We were happy to wait while the meal was heated up. We sat at table with the postmaster and drank his health. We drank the health of Mathieu and we drank to the completion of Route Numéro 7.

Then we hastened onward once more and nobody will appreciate just how delighted we were to join the Route Coloniale No. 1 in Vinh, a real metalled road at last. After so many months we could not resist the pleasure of rushing along it at high speed and driving through the night.

On the morning of March 17th 1936, we reached Hanoi. We had crossed Southeast Asia, the first crossing ever by motor car.

We were at the Chinese border.

With helpers hanging on to the ropes for safety, Max Reisch steers the chassis down the steep bank of the Mekong.

Above: Low water on the Mekong. The teak tree trunk on the cliffs, 15 metres above the river, had been deposited at high water.

Above: Helmuth Hahmann sitting on the chassis of the Steyr 100 which he maintained with exemplary care throughout its 40,000km journey around the world.

Above: Guarded by Indochinese soldiers, convicts drag the chassis up the steep river bank of the Mekong.

Above: Road building in Southeast Asia: the local substitute for shovel and wheelbarrow.

Below: The French colonial authorities mustered great numbers of coolies to improve difficult stretches of mountain track in Laos so that our expedition could pass. They provided enthusiastic help, even though a French car was not involved.

Left: The Steyr appears tiny next to these giants of the rain forest.

Below: Four coolies at a time work this treadmill to raise water to the paddy fields on the next level.

Opposite above: Driving through Tonking. Local people wear their beautiful traditional costume. This was their first sight of a motor car.

Opposite below: Steep rocky inlets on the coast near Haiphong provided a hideaway for numerous pirates.

Above: The French colonial authorities had good diplomatic relations with the governor of the neighbouring province of Yunnan-fu. This led to the building of a dramatic railway to replace the old caravan path of the 'Thousand Steps.' Normal passenger trains took three days, but the rail car pictured here, with pneumatic tyres on its iron wheels, could cover the distance in a single day. Gliding soundlessly through the grandiose mountain landscape up to an altitude of 2000 metres was a wonderful experience. The luxury rail car was known as the Micheline because of the innovative use of tyres. Our high-level contacts with the French allowed us to make a business trip to Yunnan-fu with the appropriate visa. This was the first step in trying to alter our original visa, which only authorised entry to China by sea. It was quite a struggle, necessitating eight separate visas for all the provinces between Hanoi and Shanghai.

HELD UP IN HANOI

Now we were at the gates of China, without a visa. You will be wondering how an expedition to China could possibly lack a visa. I'll tell you.

We did have one, of course. We'd had it ever since leaving Vienna, and exhibited it proudly in our passports, but the Chinese consul in Calcutta had been kind enough to point out that this was a visa for entry by sea only, through the ports of Shanghai or Canton. It had to be, since there was simply no other point of entry.

This might be applicable in the case of 'normal' travellers, but there was nothing normal about the Trans Asia Expedition. People had told us this so often along the way that I was almost inclined to believe it myself.

Lüneburg, the German consul in Hanoi, suggested helpfully "There's a railway from here to the Chinese province of Yunnan. Try going there to get a visa. It might be the best place to start."

"But we don't want to go to Yunnan-fu! It's a dead end in the mountains on the Tibetan border. What's the point? There's a railway going there, true, but the only way out is by mule-track."

"How do you know that?"

"Our information from the Royal Geographic Society in London."

"They could be right. Nobody knows much about the Chinese interior. But I will vouch for the fact that you can only get to Yunnan-fu by rail. There is no double-track road."

"Are you saying we should transport the car to Yunnan-fu by train and find out when we get there whether it can go on under its own power?"

"It's a possibility, but I had envisaged something else. People travelling on business normally have no difficulty in getting a visa. This way, you would have permission to enter China by land and after that you might also be allowed into Kuang-Si province. There are roads there, or so I have heard. At least you will be in the country, and then God be with you! You will get from one province to another, I'm sure."

"Off to the Chinese consul, then!"

"Yes, but don't mention the car. The Chinese are taking a dim view of motor expeditions. Only recently the French Citroën expedition stirred up a lot of trouble. These people made a really excellent film which nevertheless contained a few disparaging remarks about China. Of course, it got people's backs up. Do you have film cameras?"

"Certainly we do."

"On top of everything else ... Well, just act harmless and stupid, and good luck to you!"

We debated whether Helmuth or I should be first into the lion's den. In the end we went together, in one fell swoop, as it were. We acquired the visa under the slogan "Steyr Top Class Ball Bearings for China!" and since we could find out nothing at all in Hanoi about travelling conditions in the Middle Kingdom, we decided that we would first make the journey to Yunnan-fu (modern Kunming) by rail without the car.

Alongside railways in Abyssinia and the Andes, this was one of the most beautiful as regards landscape, but also one of the most expensive in the world. Armed with our glowing letter of recommendation from the French Legation in Vienna, we approached the management of the Yunnan Railway. Monsieur Petit, the Secretary-general, made us explain our project and show him photographs of the trip. Then he went off to report to the Chairman and was back after only ten minutes.

"Well, gentlemen, you will travel by wagon-lit to Lao-Kay, and on the Chinese side you will take our Michelin-Railcar. It will be a very interesting trip, as you will see. Our only request is that you will allow us to use any pictures you take for our new brochure. Here are your tickets and your reservations for tonight in the sleeping car. I wish you a most pleasant stay in Yunnan-fu!"

To what did we owe this generosity? Was it to the letter of recommendation from the Legation in Vienna, or the photographs we had produced, or just the personal kindness of Mr Klein from Alsace? Anyway, our expedition was once more a going concern.

We took a hasty farewell of Consul Lüneburg. He gave us a letter to take to a German engineer, the representative of Siemens-Schuckert in Yunnan-fu, who, with his wife, had been living there for the last thirty-five years. He would certainly be able to tell us all sorts of things and provide valuable information. In our hotel we threw a few basic items into a suitcase, saw the car put away in the garage and then stretched out luxuriously in the sleeping car and let ourselves be rocked gently to the Chinese border.

There, next morning, we changed over to the Michelin-Railcar which crept slowly upwards all the way, almost soundless on its quiet pneumatic tyres. Because of regular landslips and rock-falls this section could only be travelled by day. The driver of the rail-bus had to be constantly changing gear, as the steep gradient and many bends made it impossible to gain momentum.

The track turned up a little side valley, bored through a mountain and emerged in a different valley. Then the Micheline roared over a vast bridge and through another tunnel. Higher and higher it went, winding and zigzagging. Below us we could see sections of track we had already covered, while ahead lay the embankment where we would be running in a few minutes' time.

The concept of this acrobatic railway line, 850km in length, goes back to 1871, and is a masterpiece of French engineering skill. You can scarcely count the bridges and tunnels. It took three years just to build a bridge 165 metres long over an inaccessible rocky ravine. Because of the difficulty of transporting them, the individual parts of the bridge could weigh no more than a hundred kilos and be no longer than two and a half metres. Malaria and 'evil spirits' hindered the building and the job of feeding the 48,000 coolies proved almost insuperable. In 1919 the railway finally opened, consigning to oblivion the so-called 'caravan path of a thousand steps' which had previously been the only link with Yunnan-fu.

Now we sat in the comfortable club chairs of the Micheline and were borne in comfort to the high point of those ten thousand steps. The city of Yunnan-fu lay at a height of 2000 metres. The driver had to stop a few times to clear away lumps of rock which had fallen on to the line. Once, a high-pitched piping sounded from the driver's seat. The alarm system connected with each of the wheels was signalling a puncture. The wheel was changed in a quarter of an hour. On the evening of our second day's journey, the Micheline drew into the station at Yunnan-fu. Immediately opposite stood the Hôtel de la Poste, which was a bit of luck as neither of us spoke a word of Chinese.

Until now crossing from one country to another had been effected slowly and gradually, easing the change in customs and traditions and particularly language. After leaving French-influenced Indochina, we were plunged straight into the real China which was completely foreign to us. The men wore long black or dark-blue coats, fastened at the side, and little caps on their heads. The women wore long trousers and short white jackets. Some of them still had bound feet, once the Chinese ideal of beauty. Only the younger women had abandoned this custom. Faced with the dense throng of people with yellow faces, shorn heads and slit eyes, our European perception was incapable of telling one from another. Everywhere there was a constant sound of children crying, as babies were carried around by their mothers all day. If one was hungry, then its mother squatted down on her heels, as everyone does in Asia, and gave it the breast. When it was satisfied, its older brother pushed forward for his turn. At two or even three years old he was still taking his mother's milk. From this nourishment children went straight over to eating rice.

Next morning we travelled by rickshaw to the 'Son of the Great West Gate,' in Chinese 'Sie Men Se,' or simply 'Siemens.' The houses of Yunnan-fu were of one or at the most two stories. They were all overtopped by telegraph poles carrying a fearsome tangle of wires. Surely Herr Kamm could not be blamed for this?

"Oh yes," he laughed, "cables are far too expensive and besides, they are not nearly so fine to see. When somebody has electric light installed, they want everyone to be aware of their new acquisition, even in the daytime."

The engineer soon became a good friend. In his house we met a young German girl who had come out to China as a missionary. Apparently she had not found it to her liking, so she had left her order and come to the Kamms as a housekeeper. Helmuth went on several outings with this high-spirited young creature. They must have enjoyed themselves, although everyone knows there are no two-seater rickshaws. Our stay became extended, partly because of the convivial evenings at the Kamm house, and partly because we were awaiting the first scheduled arrival of a Junkers aircraft. When the shining silver bird finally landed after a couple of laps of honour, three blond pilots emerged, followed by a dozen Chinese VIPs, generals and senior government officials. It was a plane belonging to the Eurasia-Fahrgesellschaft (Eurasia Airline). In the passenger waiting room, in addition to the usual notices, there was one in very small English and very large Chinese characters which read, "Fighting among passengers is forbidden!"

After a few hours the Junkers flew back to Chung-king, and the new line was officially open. I hope the passengers behaved themselves!

A lot of our time in Yunnan-fu was given over to the main object of our journey, which was to research the possibility of travelling right across China. Engineer Kamm could only inform us with certainty on one point, namely, that from Yunnan-fu there was no road link to any other province. We would have had to dismantle the car completely, with no component weighing more than a hundred kilos, the highest permissible weight for transportation by coolies. Kamm was wrestling with the problem on his own account at this time. A power station was due to be built somewhere far away on the Tibetan border. Would Siemens be able to meet the hundred kilo requirement? This meant that the turbines would not be cast but produced as individual pieces of steel plate which could then be welded together when needed. If this was feasible then Siemens would be awarded the contract. Engineer Kamm was in constant contact by telegraph with his head office in Europe.

When we were not sitting down with him and getting the latest information about this exciting project, we were usually visiting the postmaster. He was a very useful acquaintance, and we had already spent many hours in his company. The Chinese postal service is an ancient institution, probably by far the best thing China has to offer. Back in the twelfth century, Genghis Khan already had mounted couriers who provided his headquarters in Karakorum with reliable links to all parts of his enormous empire. His successors further extended the system and there are historical records of news from Hang-chow on the Yellow Sea reaching the River Oder in under two weeks.

In modern times the Chinese postal service possessed maps showing all postal connections, and also the methods of delivery:

1. On footpaths by porters.
2. On muletracks by pack animals.
3. On roads by car or bus.
4. By sampan or by boat.

These maps were invaluable to us, and the more so because in the Papéterie de Paris in Hanoi we had been offered maps of China, and warned in all honesty that they were wrong, intentionally wrong, and in consequence virtually useless. They had been published by the Chiang-Kai-Shek regime with the object of making strategic difficulties for his opponent Mao-Tse-Tung. We were warned that the great struggle for China had already begun.

False maps, signposts turned round – just a few of the tricks used in waging a war!

The Chinese postmaster in Yunnan-fu was adamant in refusing to sell us his good maps, but he allowed us to draw copies of them. This was an exacting task and we were hard at it for days. Of course, the writing on the maps was all in Chinese, but with the help of some students and friendly post office clerks we solved it in the end. It confirmed what Kamm had already told us: there was nothing beyond Yunnan-fu, but going from Hanoi through Kuang-si province looked more hopeful. In Kuang-si itself the post was delivered by motor bus, so no problem there, although in the neighbouring province of Hu-nan porters had to be used and there was a yawning gap. There was no comprehensive motor bus network in Hu-nan, but it looked as if progress could be made somehow. After this on our way to Shanghai we would still have to cross the provinces of Kiang-si, An-hui and Kiang-su. For these, the Yunnan-fu post office had no maps, which was not surprising, since these provinces were many thousands of kilometres away.

Nevertheless, we now had a certain grasp of the situation, and knew that our attempt must begin from Hanoi. It was high time to be getting back there. One of the usual local wars had been raging for some time in the Yunnan mountains, but now the sound of light artillery and machine guns could be heard in the streets of the town. Next came an order from the French and British consulates to evacuate all women and children to Indochina. The men stayed and only we two joined the women. Why stay to play the hero in a civil war in the province of Yunnan? (Before long we were to be mixed up in another one from which there would be no comfortable means of escape by train.) The return journey was not a happy one amid the anxious women and crying children of the European community. On top of this the Michelin-Railcar had broken down, although nobody believed this, convinced that the 'express' was simply being kept back to bring out the VIP's later on. This time the journey to Hanoi took three full days.

We hastened to the garage for a joyous reunion with our travelling companion. To all appearance the car was deeply offended by our long absence, sopping wet as if it had been crying and covered with mould. The hot and humid climate of Indochina was the most unforgiving and the most wearing that we met with on our entire round-the-world trip, and the most germ-laden. The car was an appalling sight. After only two weeks, rust was appearing in places which would normally take years to be affected. The steering wheel was furred all over with grey-green mould, as was the whole car, the cases and the luggage space. A thick musty smell assailed us when we opened the cases. 'Onset of putrefaction' was the only way to describe it. This putrefaction had apparently eaten through the seals in the gearbox. Nothing damages a car more than standing unused for any length of time. Fourteen days would not normally be considered a long time, but in this climate weeks seemed to be as destructive as years.

While Helmuth dismantled the gearbox and repaired the damage, I sat in the Hôtel de l'Alsace and wrote up the report on the latest stage of the journey for the Steyr Works. We often disagreed on how tasks should be shared. Helmuth would have been glad to write the article, rather than lie underneath the car, while I would have liked to mend the car instead of the tiresome business of putting together the account. However, I was obliged to do it by the terms of my contract and in a climate where mould seemed to invade even the brain, this was a painful business.

In Hanoi I had already braced myself for a stern missive from our taskmasters, but there was nothing in the post, although there were no letters of encouragement or recognition either. It was only when we had achieved our objective in reaching Shanghai, conquering Asia by the southerly route for the first time, that telegrams of congratulation poured in. We were naturally delighted by this, but as we had often found ourselves either mentally or literally 'bogged down,' a few cheerful lines would have meant a lot.

Our latest cheque had duly arrived some time back and was waiting for us in the bank in Hanoi. That was a welcome piece of news anyway, but a journey of this sort through Asia takes more than just money.

Before we finally left Hanoi, Consul von Lüneburg provided us with a splendid letter of introduction, this time to Monsieur Simon, the French consul in Lung-Chou, the first city on Chinese soil.

On April 19th we drove out over the enormous railway bridge over the Red River away from Hanoi, after which our way ran through flat country and the tarmac road was lined with paddy fields, bamboo groves and rubber plantations. We found out to our satisfaction that the car could still do 90kph, but we immediately slowed down to a moderate 60kph. It would have been irresponsible to run the engine at high revolutions in that murderous heat. We met not one single car, just a lot of high-wheeled buffalo carts and hand barrows. China was coming closer! It was the last of twelve countries on our journey across Asia, but it was the largest and we would probably find it the greatest challenge.

It was a good thing that there was already a traffic jam (caused by the numerous hand carts) when the car with the Chinese number plate came towards us. We were both travelling slowly and I saw the letters 'CD.' Was it really ... ? Yes, it was. The Hanoi newspapers had already informed Monsieur Simon of our journey. He read the letter of introduction and said,

"With your rather dubious Chinese visa it would be best if we crossed the border together. Wait for me in Langsson, the French frontier town, at the Hôtel des Trois Maréchaux, until I get back from Hanoi. In this hotel you'll even be able to talk Viennese!" And with that he was off.

Talk Viennese? We could scarcely wait to find out.

The 'Three Marshals' was a nice hotel where every evening many officers and officials from the French garrison gathered. Some dressed in uniform and some in white tropical suits. They danced with the few French women and a large number of very elegantly dressed Annamite ladies. The long, close-fitting dresses of the local costume suited the native women just as well as the evening gowns from Paris. Nearly all the Annamite girls wore make-up and perfume and had scarlet finger nails. It soon emerged, however, that these beauties belonged to Langsson high society. Some of them were even married to Frenchmen. We joined in the dancing with enthusiasm, but it was only by chance that Helmuth met up with one Frenchwoman who, as it turned out, was not only the wife of Consul Simon, but also a genuine Viennese. She had come down here with her husband and was now waiting, as we were, for him to return. When the consul got back from Hanoi we covered the last 16km in Indochina together, the consul's car in front while we followed in the shadow of the 'CD.'

A broad, high rampart, on the pattern of the Great Wall of China, ran over hill and dale along the border. Now we were really at the gates of China. The wall was many metres thick and a tall narrow gateway, almost like a tunnel, led through it. The cars stopped. At the end of the long gloomy corridor we could see a tiny snippet of the immense kingdom that lay before us. Consul Simon explained to the soldiers at the frontier post that we were his friends and were travelling with him to Lung-chou, where all necessary formalities would be completed. The sentry allowed both cars to pass. This was simply marvellous, when you consider that motor expeditions were constantly trying to get into China and that only a few of them succeeded. There were the five cars involved in the great Peking to Paris race of 1907, which was won by Prince Scipione Borghese in his Itala. The next after that was the Citroën caterpillar-track expedition of 1932, sponsored by the French state. Then there was Sven Hedin's scientific expedition of 1933 promoted by the Chinese government using Ford vehicles. All these expeditions started from Peking. We were the first to enter overland from the south – we had a lot of luck on our side!

We covered the 70km from the gates of China to Lung-chou in four hours, including a puncture. We drove over numerous small passes cut deep into the mountain and fortified with walls and gates. Between the mountain ridges lay broad fertile areas which were divided up into thousands of glittering lakes – paddy fields. People worked knee-deep in water, pulling a plough through the mud by their own strength. The coolie hitched to the front with ropes would never have been able to move it through the sticky swamp on his own, but a long pole ran from his back to the shoulder of the man behind who was driving the plough and he was thus able to push the 'draught animal' with all his superfluous strength. They smiled as we drove past. All seemed very peaceful in China, in spite of her ill fame. We met riders on little Chinese horses and coolies carrying sedan chairs. We drove through several little towns. These were surrounded by walls with gates that were shut every night. Narrow roads ran through the villages where sometimes great mats on which fruit was drying had been laid across the carriageway. Then we had to stop and there were arguments, but they gave way to the white devils all the same.

In Lung-chou we were the guests of the French consul and his kind lady. The following day Simon contrived to get our Yunnan visa recognised by Kuang-si province as well. This was excellent. Then we were introduced to a little fat Chinese who spoke very good English.

"Thirty-three per cent of the value of the car must be deposited with the customs."

We were silent, but the consul leapt into the breach!

"Look at the vehicle for yourself! It is an expeditionary vehicle with no commercial value!"

The customs chief examined the 'vehicle' and settled on a fee of 500 Shanghai dollars. This was equivalent to 200 Canton dollars, which in turn came to 320 Kuang-si dollars. I asked whether we could pay in the Yunnan dollars we had left over.

"Yunnan dollars?" queried the customs chief apologetically. "No, they are not valid here."

Eventually we were allowed to pay in Indochina piastres. The complicated conversion resulted in 34 piastres. We paid up happily, for this was the cost of the tyres alone.

"Drive on the left in China!" Consul Simon called after us, and on we went towards Nan-ning.

OLD MR LAI SHI

Drive on the left in China! This instruction was somewhat notional, since the road was narrow, and over the whole distance of 270km to Nan-ning we did not meet a single car. It was a military road, a Sleeping Beauty, ready to awake suddenly one day and carry endless columns of lorries towards the border.

After this lonely drive we found the capital of Kuang-Si (Guangxi) all the more astonishing. It had ultramodern government buildings and broad streets of smooth, shiny tarmac teeming with omnibuses. These were army trucks driven by soldiers and hired out by the provincial general in peacetime as a bus service. The vehicles had come into the country via Hong Kong and Canton.

The Chinese are practical people. The government in Yunnan once lent our friend Kamm some soldiers to help with a difficult transport consignment. One of them fell into a raging torrent, and when they retrieved him he was dead. Kamm was extremely worried about how he was going tell the provincial governor, a Chinese general.

"Where is the rifle belonging to the drowned soldier?" was the first question.

"The rifle is here," announced Engineer Kamm.

"Then everything is in order," came the general's reply. "We have plenty of soldiers."

Herr Glathe, a young German businessman, had us to stay with him in Nan-ning. He lived on the third floor of a modern Chinese building, and had several servants and a cook, but the apartment was full of nothing but packing cases, some of which had been roughly nailed together to make 'furniture.' There were also rifles, machine pistols, hand grenades and every calibre of ammunition. These pretty little toys were lying all over the place, and whenever we opened the door, we could expect to slip on a cartridge case or trip over a machine gun. Herr Glathe traded in weapons and horse shoes. He bought up old horse shoes from all over Europe and imported them to China. The sons of the Middle Kingdom were convinced that horse shoes became hard as steel with use and that blacksmiths could turn them into particularly good knives. Vehicle springs were much in demand for the same purpose, and unfortunately this included new ones. This was brought forcibly to our attention when, within hours of our arriving in Nan-ning, the bundle of springs which we had strapped to the front of the car simply disappeared, in broad daylight! The straps had been severed with two sharp cuts, probably with one of Herr Glathe's horse shoe knives. It had been an easy matter with a couple of accomplices, in the crush that usually surrounded the car. We were furious, and mobilised the services of every policeman in Nan-ning.

"That won't get you anywhere," said Glathe. "Come on, let's take a walk round the town. I'll show you enough to take the sting out of it."

The first place he took us to was a curiosity shop where we learned all about Chinese pictures and their remarkable rendering of perspective. Instead of everything receding to a vanishing point as in our method, the foreground is represented at the bottom of the picture and the background at the top, which gives it a long, narrow format. The finer and more detailed paintings are rolled up and you look at them by unrolling the strip from the bottom and working your way up the scroll, gradually winding it in as you go. We didn't have much money to spend but we still bought a number of pretty things in the shop – vases on carved wooden plinths, amber and jade amulets and a bronze sacrificial dish.

Next stop was the street of apothecaries and doctors where I was obliged to submit to an operation which could, alas, no longer be avoided. With the enthusiastic participation of half of Nan-ning, I had a tooth extracted. It caused a veritable sensation, being the first 'white' tooth to which the Chinese dentist had ever applied his pincers. He would take no money for the operation, since he intended to exhibit the tooth in his shop window as an advertising gimmick. He offered to take out a couple more while he was about it, saying that they were also decayed, but I refused. I hoped they might yet be saved when I got to Shanghai.

After this, we decided to buy some painkiller at an apothecary's shop and I was nearly sick at the sight of all the old-fashioned Chinese remedies: snakes and toads preserved in spirit, along with a variety of embryos displayed in the same manner. Behind the counter sat the master apothecary. The thumb nail of his left hand was at least five centimetres long, in token of his leisured status, a particular mark of refinement. In the same matter-of-fact manner in which he would have sold me a powder of ground-up lizard, the apothecary served me with the European preparation I requested.

Now it was time to visit the entertainments district of Nan-ning! In one theatre there was a non-stop performance, of which we naturally understood nothing, but it was worth seeing for all that. All the actors wore masks and long beards. Villains always wore a white mask, while a good man had a green or red face, a fool always had a white nose, and so on. The play, which was given without any scenery, was accompanied by music which, to our ears, sounded quite dreadful. The auditorium and stage were scarcely separated from one another and on a couple of occasions spectators got mixed up with the actors, or a small riot broke out among the audience from sheer excitement. Everyone was nibbling sunflower seeds and spitting out the shells high and wide. Hot towels for wiping off sweat were being skilfully thrown around the room by waiters and caught by both actors and audience. Meanwhile, a death was taking place on stage, and the people were howling with one voice to have it done again. The uproar was indescribable! The way the Chinese abandon themselves totally in the theatre has to be seen to be believed.

My jaw was extremely painful after the tooth-pulling, so Tang, Glathe's secretary, suggested a few glasses of rice wine to bring relief. He said he knew a good bar. I clutched my swollen cheek and let everything wash over me. The rice wine was placed before us in tiny cups. Each of them was only a mouthful, but I forget how many cups we drank. Then the proprietor asked if we would like to see the other rooms.

Yes please, we said. There was a staircase going up and then we were standing in a long corridor with doors at frequent intervals along each side. An old woman came waddling towards us with an enormous bunch of keys and unlocked the first door. We saw a small alcove with nothing in it but a wide bed. A young and (so it seemed to me) very pretty girl stood up and took a step towards us with a mask-like smile. Only the prettiest daughters of peasants have the doubtful privilege of spending a few years here and earning a lot of money for themselves and their poverty-stricken families. The matron unlocked several more doors, re-locking them carefully afterwards, and soon I had the feeling of being in a prison rather than a garden of earthly delights. We went back down into the restaurant and soaked up a lot more rice wine. It was the best I could do for my aching cavity, but being serious China-travellers, we could not have left without seeing the upstairs too.

The police chief of Nan-ning, General Chow, invited us to dine in the officers' club and honoured us with a specially prepared European meal, to be eaten with knife and fork. A few of the other guests made rather a bad job of these, whilst we, on the other hand, were already getting on quite well with chopsticks. Even more delightful than the banquet, however, was the letter of recommendation which the police chief gave us to see us on our way:

"Old Mr Lai Shi," (Lai Shi was the Chinese rendering of the name Reisch and the title 'Old Mr' was a reference to my patriarchal beard, which in China made me an object of the deepest reverence), "accompanied by his young friend [that was the beardless Helmuth!] is making a journey through the Middle Kingdom on hot wheels driven by electric oil. All agencies of peace are directed to lend him every assistance."

We were well aware that this safe-conduct would only be valid for the province of Kuang-si. What awaited us in Hu-nan was still cloaked in obscurity. In every province we were confronted with a completely different set of circumstances. We never knew quite what the score was and the longer we had to do with this curious country, the more confusing it appeared.

In order to counter the constant stream of questions, we engaged a painter to inscribe the visiting card of our expedition in Chinese characters on the front mudguard of the car. The equivalent of 'From Austria to China by car' went something like this:

'With the hot wheels driven by electric oil from the Second Most Fortunate Small Corner to the Middle Kingdom.'

It could scarcely have been more complicated. To call Austria ('au-ga-li-a') the 'Second Most Fortunate Small Corner' was baffling, to say the least, if not flattering. If only we had known where the First Most Fortunate Small Corner was, we might have emigrated!

The text quoted above was not nearly as extensive as you would think. The characters all fitted into a space no larger than the front number plate. It can be seen clearly on various photos.

We also equipped ourselves with our own personal visiting cards, or something similar. It was really a sort of printing set which each of us carried at all times and with which we could produce our own cards. The whole thing consisted of a little hinged box made of bone containing two stamps, one with the text as mentioned and one with Helmuth's name or mine. It also contained an ink pad with red dye. The amazing thing about this printing set was its size. I still have the little box today. Consequently I can give you the exact dimensions of this small miracle of the Chinese craftsman's skill. It is fifty millimetres long, seventeen millimetres wide and nine millimetres deep, and it is worn on a silk cord attached to a small ring. The ink pad is just as fresh and useable today as it was then in Nan-ning when we had the box made in the street of the bone carvers. The larger of the two stamps has a face of thirteen by thirteen millimetres, bearing the entire description of the expedition, as given above. The impression of the smaller stamp, of 13x5mm, reads "Ma Lai Shi" – in German, 'Max Reisch' – which, when transposed into Chinese means 'dependent hope.' This was a most apposite description of our journey. We were always full of hope, but at the same time, how dependent we were in Asia on fate, on chance, on luck and ultimately on the whim of our sponsors back home!

The 'x' of my first name is ignored by a speaker of Chinese, who substitutes an 'L' for the 'R' in my surname. Denizens of the Middle Kingdom always find 'R' heavy going. It is unknown to them and unpronounceable. For instance, a Chinese speaker learning German who was required to say '*Hinter der Brücke die erste Straße rechts*' ('The first street on the right after the bridge') would render it as '*Hintel del Blücke die eiste Stlaße lechts.*' I had already noticed this among Chinese students in Vienna. They would often spend hours practising, trying to learn our 'R.' We used to try and help them. The best results were obtained by taking them out to Salmannsdorf to drink the new wine, and once they'd swallowed enough of it, giving them a hefty thump between the shoulder blades.

With our car bearing its new inscription and our visiting card printing sets in our pockets we drove out of Nan-ning on 4th May 1936. Our main tank and reserve were full to the brim with sixty litres of petrol, besides which we had taken on board three fuel cans of eighteen litres each. The Shell Agency in the Kuang-si capital had petrol in abundance but couldn't tell us where to find any more. This meant taking yet another two cans! In order to make room for them we extracted the two brand-new Semperit tyres from the depths of the luggage space and put them on the rear wheels. We sold the two old tyres to a shoemaker in the bazaar. The Chinese had been putting rubber soles on their shoes ever since the first car appeared in their country, which was long before the white man realised all the possible uses of an old tyre.

The next town of any size was Liu-chou. It lay at a distance of 540 li, approximately 250km. I am bound to say "approximately," since there are many different li in China. A li was originally the distance that a coolie could cover in a precise length of time. In mountainous provinces where the paths are poor and arduous the li is shorter, and in the plains of northern China it is longer. In one of the ministries in Nanking or Peking they actually got around to defining a li as 442 metres, but only on paper. In practice a li is just a li, and it is not defined by any ministry but by the coolie.

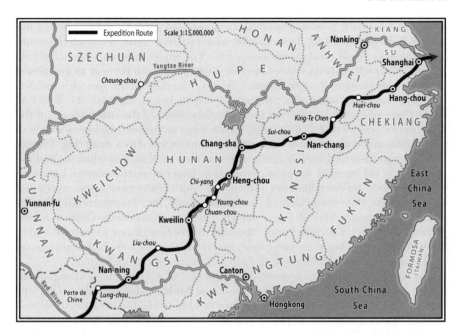

Map 6: The route through China to Shanghai.

The landscape of southern China is a strange one. I had rather expected to find the same conditions as in Southeast Asia. The extent of the country is like that of the Shan States and the influence of the monsoon is similar. Primeval forest, swamp, and jungle should thus have been the norm for south China, so I was amazed to find that most of Kuang-si consisted of open plains. As we went further north the country became well watered, with more and more paddy fields. We had no complaints about the road. The surface did not always have a base but we drove comfortably along over hard clay. In swampy lowlands the road was paved with big flat stones in the old Chinese manner, and was consequently bumpier.

This was the day when we glanced at the odometer more often than we had in the past. It crept slowly on towards the event we had been waiting for all day, with only one kilometre to go. Then suddenly the mechanism clocked up our twenty thousandth kilometre in Asia! I stopped the car and brought out two bottles from the box of supplies. It was sarsaparilla, a slightly alcoholic beverage which the Chinese make from a root and which they consume with enthusiasm. We used it to celebrate the moment in the middle of the lonely steppe and recorded it on film. Taken with the delayed-action shutter, it is the only shot in which we both appear.

After a 12-hour journey with our 'hot wheels' we reached Liu-chou. We could see the masts of the radio station and the hangars of the aircraft factory long before we got there. There was indeed an aircraft factory and a flying school in south China. Mr Stevens, an Englishman, was the factory manager, and we had an introduction to him. He soon came out to see us through the one heavily fortified door in the fenced perimeter of the compound. It was guarded by the Kuang-si military, and Mr Stevens apologised for being unable to admit us because of recent incidents of espionage. He advised us to spend the night at the French mission. Like all mission stations in inland China, it offered the only opportunity of decent overnight accommodation for white travellers.

The French father had gone on a journey by litter, but a Chinese priest allowed us in. He went to a lot of trouble for us, evidently proud to be giving shelter to white men. He even invited quite a number of friends round in the evening to show us off, thereby gaining much 'face.' He spoke not a word of either French or English. We had almost no Chinese, and communication was thus somewhat difficult. It occurred to us, however, that this pious man must surely know some Latin. Of course, he did. And of course his Latin was far better than ours! As we hunted for words, Caesar and Ovid emerged from dusty recesses of our memory, and when the priest enquired, "Café post?" we did not immediately grasp his meaning, until finally it dawned on us. Ante Christum natum ... post Christum natum ... Before the birth of Christ ... after ...

"Yes please! Coffee afterwards!"

The landscape around Liu-chou, just like everywhere in the north of Kuang-si province where our route lay, had an aspect quite unlike any other. The area was in many respects a normal plain, criss-crossed by many rivers and dotted with swamps and paddy fields. Yet right in the middle of this flat landscape, without any transition, appeared pointed spires, needles and spheres of rock. It looked for all the world as if somebody had sawn off the jagged peaks of the Dolomites and planted them all jumbled up in the middle of an empty plain. And yet it was not just a dozen or so of these peaks but hundreds, even thousands, of fantastically shaped rocks, whose bizarre forms seemed to have been conjured up by the hand of a god. We drove many hundreds of kilometres through this odd landscape which defied any description or explanation other than magical. These versions of the Sugar Loaf, the Vajolet Towers, the Fünffingerspitzen or the Santner Needles were on average two hundred metres high. Each rock had its own Chinese name and was home to a good or a bad spirit. Perhaps some of our geologists may one day explain how and when the Almighty created this landscape. Geologists I have asked up till now have told me all sorts of things, drawing various comparisons, but I am none the wiser for all that. So the magical landscape of Kuang-si may just have to remain unexplained, beautiful and mysterious like no other.

25

MOTOR CAR VERSUS EVIL SPIRITS

The going was still good and the thrill of the journey had us in its grip – only a few thousand kilometres to Shanghai! We covered the five hundred li from Liu-chou to Kuei-lin in two days in spite of two rivers with no bridges, which we crossed by ferry. All the same, these rivers were perilous. Although mostly small, they were deeply gouged into the countryside. Without any obvious warning the road would drop vertically thirty or fifty metres to the river. It was so steep that the brakes alone were not equal to the task. We would be trundling happily along without a care in the world, dozing in the south China sunshine, when a void would suddenly loom before us, the road having come to an end, and the car would be hurtling over stones and mud down the side of the gorge to the river far below. On one occasion it was a very close call and I only just managed to bring the car to a stop on the edge of the murky rushing torrent. Happily the Steyr was an open car and at the worst we could always have survived by swimming. An American missionary had fared badly, though. He had brought over a brand new eight-cylinder car from the States in which he had plunged at full tilt to a watery grave.

Of all the ways of joining your ancestors ante diem, drowning seems the most natural to the Chinese. Maybe it is because of the massive floods that occur nearly every year, or maybe they are particularly fond of water, but whatever the reason, rescuing a Chinese from drowning has curious consequences, especially if the rescuer is a 'white devil.'

"Once was enough," asserted Engineer Kamm in Yunnan-fu. "I pulled one of these fellows out of the water and the next day he turned up in my office. I suppose you think he wanted to thank me. Not a bit of it! He declared to me in no uncertain terms that I had kept him from the halls of his ancestors where he would have been happy and not had to work any more. Because of my intervention he was still alive and maybe I would be kind enough to provide him with a pension!"

Perhaps one should not draw any general conclusions from this incident, but it still says a lot about the oriental mindset.

It was the porters, gasping for breath, who were a constant reminder of the low value set on human life. These fellows ran literally on compressed air. It was strange to see how, after a short rest, they would pump themselves full of air and hurry on with short rapid steps for a few hundred metres. By then they would be so blue and purple in the face that they would have to rest again. You could hear them letting

Where is the Missionary Station?

Can you guide us to the...

Catholic :   Protestant:

益群社 你往何處   徑呢能否指示我们的路 何處走天主教堂 耶穌教堂

A sample page from our improvised English-Chinese vocabulary.

out the air as they used it, just like opening the valve in a bicycle tyre. It went on whistling for a while till the pressure ceased and they would breathe normally for a bit. Then they would pump themselves up again and carry on. By doing this, each coolie could transport a hundred kilos or more at a time. It was no way to make old bones, as they all fell victim to the evil of tuberculosis.

We often met with litters occupied by elderly Chinese. Pigs, too, were being carried along the road, although not in litters, of course. Bamboo wickerwork was woven around the hog's body, like a sort of made-to-measure litter through which the legs hung down in a comical fashion. This meant that, if necessary, the porker could run along under its own steam whenever the coolies (out of sight of their overseer) took the bamboo poles off their shoulders and settled them on their hips. Then the animal's legs just reached the ground!

Employing two human beings to transport an ordinary pig seems like an expensive luxury. This was not so in China, if you did the arithmetic. Supposing the animal had to walk 30km, then a man would have to be hired to drive it and the pig would lose a kilo in weight by the exertion. The drover would cost forty cents a day and the lost kilo of fat another eighty cents, making a dollar twenty altogether. If you had the pig carried by two coolies, then it would lose no weight and the two porters together would cost only eighty cents. The pig's owner would therefore be richer by forty cents, which was a lot of money in China.

In Kuei-lin we put together an English-Chinese dictionary because, as experience had already shown us, it was not possible in China to get by with English alone. We pronounced Chinese words badly but almost all Chinese could read everyday characters if they had to.

We wrote down the most important questions: "Where is the nearest mission? Where can we put the car? How many li is it to ...?" and so on, each question on a separate card. We had the Chinese translation painted underneath and could then show it whenever we needed.

Some expressions were not so easy to render. The question "May we garage our car here?" had to be given in the following courteous manner, as required in China:

"Most highly honourable elder born, we younger born citizens of the Second Most Fortunate Small Corner Au Ga Li A (Austria) travelling through the venerable Middle Kingdom beg that you would manifest your boundless generosity by allowing us to shelter our hot wheels driven by electric oil in your most estimable house."

Old age has always been highly respected in China and with my splendid beard I counted as aged and was consequently worthy of respect. Certain concessions I got from authorities and law enforcement agencies would never have been obtained so promptly without a beard.

Quite frequently I was also taken for a priest, since the majority of missionaries in China sported flowing beards, and there were some embarrassing incidents when I was out walking when Chinese suddenly came and knelt down before me, asking for a blessing. My knowledge of the language made it impossible to explain their error, and the poor Christians were most perplexed when I would not comply with their request. I fear they must have immediately begun to doubt their newly acquired faith. One little boy begged so piteously that my feelings were overcome and I gave in to his wishes. He went away beaming with happiness, but the next day I had a new card added to the dictionary which read, "I am not a priest! Please apply to the nearest missionary station."

Driving the car in Chinese cities was not easy. In the first place, the narrow alleyways were almost impassable. Streets were deliberately built so as not to run in a straight line but to have as many corners as possible. The point was that evil spirits could only run in a straight line but good spirits could dart from side to side. Thus evil spirits got confused in narrow alleys and were always bumping into the walls. Good spirits liked living there, and this was the object of the exercise. It was only gradually that we learned how our good little Steyr might also be used as a weapon in the fight against evil spirits.

We soon noticed that the Chinese never moved out of the way, on principle. Why should they? It was for the electric chariot, that infernal machine, to get out of the way. Even when we sounded the horn repeatedly, it was very rare for anyone to move over. A better course with the Chinese was to give them a gentle nudge, and then they would jump aside. To begin with, we also found the rest of their behaviour extremely weird. If a Chinese was running down the right-hand side of the street and heard the car coming he would suddenly dash over to the left-hand side at the last moment, just like a chicken. They would rush past us at such close quarters that we were constantly in fear of running them over. And had one of these yellow coolies been determined enough, then we would undoubtedly have been saddled with providing for his family for the rest of our lives. Court cases about such accidents could get very awkward for the driver, even if he were totally innocent according to western concepts of law.

We remained in ignorance for some time as to why the Chinese behaved so oddly in the countryside as well as in the town. Were they as nervous as all that? Later on it was explained to us that every Chinese is being pursued by evil spirits. He does all he can to get rid of them. A really good ploy is to leap across the road in front of a car, because it's certain that the evil spirit will get run over!

26
IN CHINA IT'S DIFFERENT

We scarcely noticed when we crossed from the province of Kuang-si into the province of Hu-nan. There was no barrier, no customs or passport check. The only differences were the soldiers' uniforms and the currency. Father Lacroix, the American missionary from Kue-lin came with us. He had business in Hu-nan and his help was a great asset. He served as guide and negotiator, money-changer and interpreter and solved all the difficulties we encountered when hiring coolies. We now had to use big money, meaning Shanghai dollars, although in the Chinese interior people were not keen on accepting paper. Here people still reckoned in tiau, cho, tungotse and sapecke. The smallest coin was the 10 sapecke piece, called tungotse. One Shanghai dollar was equivalent to 6000 tungotse which meant that 20 Shanghai dollars worth of this metal coinage had a weight of around 40kg. This currency had survived among country people from the time when the only form of transport was a man's back. Consequently a robber would never steal more money than he was capable of carrying.

Sixty li from the city of Yaung-chou, our next destination, our way was blocked by a small torrent. There was no bridge, no ferry, not even a pair of boats that we could have used in the absence of anything better. I would gladly have given a whole sack of tungotse to find a solution. Helmuth went off on foot to reconnoitre and found a small village downstream with a stone foot bridge. It was three metres high with steps leading up to it and it was also provided with gates of good fortune so that evil spirits could wreak no damage on it. With some trepidation, Helmuth checked its width with the bamboo staff on which the exact dimensions of the car were recorded. Thank goodness, at least the width seemed sufficient. However, the steps remained. And how were we going to drive through the gates of good fortune with their thresholds 30cm high?

It was worth a try, in any case, and our first task was to drive the car up to the bridge. Even that was not so simple, as the way led for several hundred metres through paddy fields with standing water, and it was so narrow that only one pair of wheels would fit on to it. Father Lacroix negotiated with a group of coolies working nearby and as soon as they agreed to help us, things got going. We drove with two wheels on the path and the other two on three strong planks, which the coolies kept taking up from behind and laying down in front over the mud. Half a dozen of them dragged the planks and six others pushed the car. Little by little we moved forwards, although the car kept threatening to slip and capsize going round bends. At such moments, all twelve men hung on to it and for the umpteenth time we thanked our stars that we hadn't been landed with some costly exploration vehicle.

At last we came to a stop below the bridge. After thorough consideration, we decided to take a run at it, with the coolies pushing as hard as they could. This actually seemed to work. After a series of spring-shattering jolts we found ourselves half way up, but the coolies' strength gave out and we slipped back a few steps. The bridge had no parapet and the car hung there perilously with its wheels on the outer edges above the rushing water. We urged the coolies on again, they heaved and pushed at the car, the engine raced, the wheels spun round, and a great cry went up. The brave little Steyr had reached the top!

But we hadn't won yet. We still had to get over the thresholds of good fortune. Helmuth took a quick decision, grabbed a hammer and chisel from the tool box and began to chip away at bricks and door hinges. Father Lacroix got very agitated but it was too late. As for the Chinese, their laughter died away. They didn't seem to approve of what we were doing and began to rush about in all directions. As the second threshold of fortune fell to pieces under the blows of the hammer, there arose a loud wail of dismay. We were too busy getting down the other side to worry about it. The car bumped downwards step by step while the coolies held it back with ropes. Some wedged themselves against the mudguards which were already flapping about like broken wings, since they had been used as handles to pull the car on the way up. Finally we came to rest on the opposite bank. It was already long after midday and we'd had no time to eat. We were wet through and covered with mud.

Meanwhile, the commotion in the village was getting worse all the time. Father Lacroix explained that destroying the thresholds of good fortune had opened the way for evil spirits to cross the bridge and hordes of them were now storming the village. Speedy action was necessary to repel them, and so the people rushed into the houses and reappeared with rockets and small cannons. There were great bangs and crackles as a battle against the evil spirits got going. Everybody streamed up the steps on to the bridge, in tightly serried ranks one behind the other, in order to force the spirits back. While some people fired rockets, others quickly rebuilt the wall forming the threshold. The battle was won and no more wicked devils crossed the bridge.

Even the village street was so narrow that it looked several times as if we would have to resort again to the hammer and chisel. We managed to get up more steps which led from the lower to the upper stretch of the main street. Another wall had to be removed, whose beaming owner we rewarded with six dollars compensation. At the end of the village we came upon the foundations of a road which had been begun for military reasons, and which for different military reasons had never been finished. Here we said goodbye to Lacroix with many heartfelt thanks. Without his help we could scarcely have 'driven' so far. He was now having a far more comfortable journey back to his mission station by sedan chair.

That same day we came to another river, where, on the far bank, we had our first sight of the large city of Yaung-chou, but it was already getting late and the ferrymen refused to row the car over, so I decided to go over in a small boat and look for the Italian mission.

Helmuth looked after the car and waited. Nobody came. Today of all days, and quite unusually, we had nothing to eat on board, apart from the iron rations that were at the very bottom of the luggage compartment. Helmuth got hungry, smoked a lot of cigarettes, and whiled away the time by making entries in the log.

By dusk I had not returned. Night fell, and I still did not appear. Helmuth was gradually becoming more alarmed and he began to wonder what could have become of me. Chinese bandits? Sudden illness? An accident? What should he do? After six hours I eventually turned up at dead of night with a Chinese from the mission.

Helmuth was understandably a bit short with me.

I took the basket the Chinese was carrying and produced from it, as if by magic, a chunk of smoked meat, bread, cheese and a couple of bottles of beer. "You'll never believe it! They're not Italians over there, they're Franciscans from the South Tyrol!"

"You're the first Tyrolean visitors I've had in all the 28 years I've lived in China," said Monsignor Jessacher next morning. He still could not quite grasp the fact that we had come directly all the way from home by car. Then he had another thought. "You are not only the first Austrians, you are also the first non-missionaries to come through here, apart from a few Russian refugees."

We were very impressed by the trouble the fathers took to entertain us, and we were delighted to accept their invitation to visit two mission stations and thus to learn something of country life in the outlying villages. A four-hour journey on the river brought us to the 'village on the cold water,' and then a walk of over 20 li to the station called 'Home of Happiness.' Alas, it did not live up to its name, since the missionary Othmar Stimpfl from Bolzano had been murdered there by robbers. The mission house with its little church lay a short way off the track in a gloomy pine forest. It was a sinister place. We stood aghast in the dead man's room where the bullet holes in the wall were still visible. Father Kleinhappel from Styria now worked here on his own.

In the courtyard of the mission a number of dogs were enjoying a rough-and-tumble, young ones and old ones. One afternoon I was sitting on the steps of the veranda, playing with a half-grown dog. One of the mission servants who spoke a little German, came up to me.

"You like him?"

"Sure! He's the best of the bunch!"

The servant nodded, looking pleased, and gave the jolly little chow a firm pat on its sturdy rump.

The servants had announced that there would be a special celebration that evening. The priest informed us that jumping jacks would be let off, paper lanterns would provide the illumination and a Chinese meal would be served. Were we interested in the real food of the countryside?

We were full of enthusiasm and the meal exceeded our expectations. There was a wonderful soup with chicken and noodles, then an array of vegetables, with salads garnished with 'thousand year eggs,' and the main course resembled our

Kasseler Rippchen (spiced pork loin) with rice. I would never have believed that simple Chinese cooking could be so tasty. The only sort we had experienced up to then had been the city variety, which was as different from country food as hotel meals back home would be from food on a Tyrolean farmstead.

The next day I went out into the yard again to play with the dogs. "Where's the young one from yesterday?" I asked the servant. "But, sir, you liked him so much!" "Yes, I did. So what?" The servant seemed offended. "Last night you asked for a second helping of him. Was something wrong?"

Young dogs and rats are considered a delicacy in China, and so are new-born mice, which are plunged into boiling water and eaten whole. They are very popular. People do not actually eat earthworms, and the so-called 'thousand year eggs' are not really as old as that. They are buried in clay for a few weeks, during which time the inside of the egg ripens in a similar way to cheese. The smell is not putrid, but rather like a good camembert, with much the same taste. But pork roasted with honey and eaten between two flat cakes of sweet dough is truly wonderful.

Whenever we stopped at a small inn we would make a bee-line for the kitchen, because we could only order a menu by pointing at the various dishes. All over inland China we could get fish soup, rice noodles with soy beans, chicken with vegetables, and thousand year eggs. There was plenty to enjoy and some of it was absolutely delicious. What we never got was bread, and on such a long journey we really missed it.

From Yaung-chou we got a telephone message to Father Reiter, a missionary from Karneid (Cornedo all'Isarco) near Bolzano, who was living in Chi-yang. He came out to meet us and we drove into Chi-yang together. Our grand entrance defies description, for we were the first car ever seen in the town. People lined the narrow streets. We got some idea of the sensation caused by our arrival when we learned that the first motorcycle had reached the town only a few months before. A Chinese had brought it in from Chang-sha. He had ridden his amazing machine round and round an enclosed space outside the town and charged an entry fee for the performance.

We could not garage our car at the mission, but several Chinese offered to have it in one of their shops. A fight nearly broke out over which business would be allowed to shelter the car! We identified a suitable shop and the Chinese owner worked hard to clear a space for it. He had to clear out massive sheaves of rice and stack them somewhere else, but everyone envied this shopkeeper. The crush of customers all wanting to see the hot wheels was alarming.

No charge was made for the garage, quite the opposite. We were rewarded by being solemnly presented with models of two mythical Chinese beasts. I've looked all over Europe for a garage like that!

The mission also dealt with things that were usually of little concern to a priest. For instance there were the foster-mothers to be paid. These had taken on the care of young children, for which they received a certain sum. One of the missionaries kept a very careful set of accounts, because women were constantly attempting to claim the money twice over. Not only did this offend Christian morality but it doubled the manual labour, as was obvious from the enormous baskets filled with copper coins that stood ready for the payments.

Attached to the mission there was also a school for brides run by highly skilled old Chinese Christian women. Here the girls learned cooking and sewing, and made their own outfits. They were much in demand by men in search of a wife. The mission demanded a payment from every suitor, a sort of transfer fee for the bride, and this was willingly given, since everyone was sure of getting a good and capable wife. The money was used by the mission (which was completely self-financing) to pay the foster-mothers, thus benefiting the many children who in China were casually abandoned by their parents.

Overpopulated China was cruel, unsentimental – and practical. One could not fail to notice the many 'public conveniences.' These consisted of an enormous barrel with a little house built over it, reached by climbing up a ladder. They were found in great numbers along the country roads, often several within a short distance, or one on either side of the road. The peasants invited the traveller in with friendly words. "Come to my little house!" At the same time you might hear the neighbour calling, "No, come to mine!"

None of the precious product was wasted. It was all collected and used as top dressing to manure the fields. Actually it was not the fields themselves which were sprayed by the so-called honey coolies, but rather the half-ripe fruit, thus creating a fertile breeding-ground for all kinds of bacteria. This was why prudence demanded that anything destined for European stomachs should be washed with potassium permanganate or cooked. The Chinese were not so fastidious, and their stomachs seemed to tolerate considerably more cholera germs than ours. Avoiding contact with evil spirits is far more important to them than avoiding contact with germs, although both are equally invisible.

Chi-yang had its tower which rose high over the town and we found similar six or eight storey structures in many other places. In the top storey dwelt the town's tutelary spirits, but getting up there was an art in itself. Arriving at the top, you would suddenly realise that you should have taken Ariadne's advice and laid a clue of thread through the labyrinth of dead end staircases and corridors. Access was made deliberately difficult with the object of keeping the evil spirits away from the good ones.

Our departure from Chi-yang caused almost as much of a sensation as our arrival. The son of the shopkeeper who had garaged our car appeared in ceremonial costume and asked if he might ride with us as far as the city gates. We were glad to oblige him and he did a great job of piloting us through the maze of narrow streets. We could not get round the numerous corners without a great deal of manoeuvring back and forth, and yet again the many raised thresholds of good fortune proved the greatest obstacles.

In the next town, all we had to do once again was to show our card with the question, "Where is the Catholic mission?" and we were sure of being taken somewhere that would give us a warm welcome. We got the impression wherever we went that the fathers enjoyed taking us around to all sorts of places, thereby demonstrating that they were getting 'reinforcements.'

This was also the case in Hêng-chou. It was evident that the fathers were particularly keen to show us Buddhist and Taoist temples, where they were on extraordinarily good terms with the priests and monks.

On the square before the temple several hundred priests were gathering for prayers. They were all dressed in black with yellow wraps. Their heads were shaved and branded on the scalp with the six dots that are the sign of a consecrated priest.

In a small stone shelter a dying priest had just been laid out on his bier. The community had waited until he was in his death throes before gathering to pray. Then, before life was quite extinct, the pyre of wood was lit beneath the dying man, and by being burned alive he immediately attained nirvana.

27
A WAR ZONE

Before we got to Changsha, the huge capital of Hunan province, we had to cross the Hsiang Kiang. There was a motor ferry running, but the official would not allow us over the river. It appeared that we had no visa for Hunan. It mattered nothing to him that we had been travelling through the province for weeks already, nor that we had come nearly half way across it. He simply refused us entry. Only very lengthy negotiations, coupled with the fact that my beard conferred on me the dignity of old age, finally persuaded him to change his mind and let us on to the ferry.

The Hsiang Kiang at Changsha was at least twice the width of the Danube at Vienna and teeming with junks, steam launches, ships and motor boats. Packed rows of junks were anchored along the river bank and there was a hum of activity like the sound of a beehive. Washing fluttered in the wind, a thousand different smells wafted up. Children played on the boats, jumping from one to the other, while the parents showed a complete lack of concern. In fact, if a child fell in the water, no one was going to make a fuss about it.

In Changsha, city of over a million inhabitants, we found excellent accommodation at the private hospice run by a German medical man, Dr. Eitel. Of course, we paid for this, just as at the Catholic missions. It's true that money was often refused, but we managed it one way or another.

A number of Germans lived in Changsha and one of them introduced us to Engineer Tso, a Chinese who had studied in Germany and who was the top man in charge of road-building here in Hunan province. As an important public figure, he made every effort to help us with the rest of our journey. He got us information on the state of the roads by telegram and by telephone, but above all he invited us to give a lecture in Changsa. He promised us projectors so that we could show as many photographs as possible of our trip and said he would invite his engineers and also various members of the provincial government. In this way he would have no difficulty in procuring us Chinese permits for other provinces and a string of letters of safe conduct. When Dr. Eitel heard of this plan he gave me a lot of valuable advice. I should make no disparaging remarks about any Asian country. For example, I should show the pictures of the Padauung women without any comments. At the very most, I might allude to the difference in customs, since the Chinese were very sensitive and quick on the uptake. They would be justified in assuming that if I made fun of Southeast Asia in their company, I might take the mickey out of China when I was back in Europe. So I took care when preparing my lecture to keep it as diplomatic as possible. Engineer Tso translated, Hermann showed the pictures and the large audience responded with enthusiasm. On the very next day, the bonus we had earned appeared in the form of a stack of letters of recommendation.

Now we could set about planning our route and sorting out the confusion surrounding our mail. On setting out for China we had had only a vague notion of where our post from home should be sent. On the whole, as it turned out, we had been nowhere near the towns we had given as postal addresses. We had scarcely got this straight in our minds when we tried to change the arrangements and then the difficulties set in. Alas, countless letters never reached us. They were eventually returned to the senders, who handed them over to us personally in Vienna, months later, insisting, "Just so you know I honestly did write to you!"

This time we had got the last delivery to Shanghai sent to Han-kou, and were in hopes of being able to pick it up in person quite soon, as the captain of the Scarab had promised to take us down the Hsiang-kiang by ship to Han-kou and back again. The Scarab was a splendid English ship which had been sent out to Changsha to protect the Europeans. It was armed with guns and carried a store of automatic rifles. When we turned up on the quay with the necessary luggage, news came at the last moment that the captain had been ordered to carry out firing practice and consequently no civilians were allowed on board. We turned back disappointed, unaware that this cancellation was really a piece of good luck.

Meanwhile, we were inundated with news of military activity. Troops from the two south western states of Kuang-tung and Kuang-si had crossed the border of the province almost overnight and occupied Yaung-chou, Chi-yang and Heng-chou. The news made us very anxious for the good friends we had left behind in those places only a few days before and who were now in danger. On May 30th we decided that we too must get out of Changsha. The German Ford representative provided us with another generous supply of petrol. It was streaming down with rain as we made our way through the outskirts of the city, past the poor little wooden houses on to the open plains. Gloom descended on my spirits. The water was lashing into the car because the two side flaps had broken. Only a pathetic remnant of the celluloid window panels hung in the canvas surrounds. As for repairing them, what hope was there? There was no celluloid here in the middle of China. It would have to wait until Shanghai. The heavy rain put us in a foul mood. We would have been just the same if the sun had been shining. People who have been battling their way through Asia for a whole year are hard to please. Either it's too hot for them or it's too cold, either they're in high spirits or they're down in the dumps. It's what you call 'nerves.' Nerves need a rest now and then, and so you dream of mountains and alpine meadows, and lots of milk and butter. Or maybe just a place with no mosquitoes and a bath without Lysol soap. Or a fresh bubbling spring instead of the filthy water that has to be cleared of germs with a special mixture which turns it purple before you can drink it.

Swathed in blankets and mackintoshes we drove slowly across the bleak Chinese landscape. It was an open steppe with no buildings, only an occasional village with paddy fields and then steppe once more. Sometimes a sedan chair went swinging by. On a rainy day like this, China seemed huge and boundless, even larger than it actually was. There were still 1600km to go to Shanghai, the last leg in Asia. We had already put 21,500km behind us, so we would manage the rest. A mere nothing, we told ourselves, hands gripping the steering wheel more tightly ...

The rain continued, the road was muddy and progress was slow, mostly in second gear. Then came a river. A river meant a ferry, so we struggled out of our waterproof coverings and hunted for the card with "Where are the ferry men?" The boat was rocking all alone on the waves and there was nobody in sight. A peasant came by and we thrust the card under his nose, but he grinned helplessly. It was obvious that he couldn't read. "*Maskee* – it doesn't matter!" We patted him on the shoulder and resigned ourselves. Maskee is a marvellous word, and using it makes you feel quite good for a while, but eventually maskee begins to take over and sap your will, till you come to a sad end. People out east call it 'going to the dogs.' The climate positively encourages you to let yourself go..

Every time we crossed a river, I made a mark on the side of the car. It was already peppered with them – once we notched up eight ferries in half a day! It was nearly always the same procedure. First the ferry men had to be fetched from wherever they were, then there were a few anxious moments as the car wobbled across the creaking planks between the bank and the boat. Then we would stand on the ferry smoking a cigarette and listening to the coolies whining "*Kumscha!*" (begging for a tip). Today it proved even more awkward. The little peasant was cunning and made signs that he would fetch someone from the nearby village who spoke English, and indeed, after a while, a more prepossessing gentleman appeared who had the air of a schoolmaster. We put the matter to him.

He answered, "Yes."

"Will it take long?"

"Yes," he agreed.

"Where are the boatmen?"

"Yes."

It was the same answer and we soon realised that our friend's knowledge of the language stopped there. This was not going to be much help. We were inwardly annoyed but outwardly bound not to show it. We offered him a cigarette (but not the same way as in Europe, for that would have been most impolite – you must first take the cigarette out of the packet yourself and offer it with both hands).

Then the man dragged me off to the nearby village. I followed him willingly, assuming that he would take me to the ferry men. However, we ended up at the school, where a song was sung in my honour. This was the schoolmaster's way of showing gratitude for the cigarette, after which he carried on with his teaching as if nothing had happened.

I was feeling like a schoolboy myself as I trotted back to the car all alone. Meanwhile Helmuth had got hold of another Chinese and gone to work again with the card dictionary. His efforts bore fruit and soon the ferry men were taking us over the river.

Now we turned east in the direction of Hangchow, capital of the province of Che-kiang. Everywhere things were coming to life and the Chinese had apparently been shocked out of their lethargy. We kept meeting troop transports – American trucks

Above: Roads in South China were built for strategic reasons, but the surface shows that traffic consisted mainly of pedestrians and wheelbarrows.

Below: A dirt track carrying very little traffic ran for 270km from Lung-Chow to Nan-ning. We met no other car. In China one drives on the left (in theory, at least!).

Above: The fairytale landscape of Kuansi. Every rock is home to a spirit that no Chinese would dream of disturbing. None of the peaks has been climbed.

Right: Coolies bringing planks from behind and laying them in front. The car moves forward bit by bit. The man on the right with a stick was our interpreter.

Left: An ingenious method for using the entire strength of two men to plough a paddy field: the father steers the plough and the son draws it. The father's remaining strength is transmitted via a pole from his own shoulder to that of his son.

packed full of soldiers – and we even saw a few of the very latest Mercedes diesel models go rolling past. There could be no doubt that we had landed in the middle of a civil war, but was it the big one between Chiang Kai Shek and Mao Zedong, or just a squabble between two provincial generals? We were only to learn this later, but the situation was becoming critical. The troops kept threatening to block our route and we were particularly anxious lest some lesser general should confiscate our car, which he could certainly turn to good use. Alarmed by the general haste and made uneasy by the panic among the local people, we began to increase our speed. However, we were soon seeing nothing but trenches and dugouts and all branches of the military, and it seemed impossible to go further. We saw infantry walking with mules bearing loads of heavy weapons. We saw mountain artillery and machine gun units. Soldiers on the march waded for the most part barefoot through the mud. Sometimes a troop of ten or so would come by, then a few stragglers, then a couple of men with mules, followed by a larger troop. It was total confusion with no sense of order and not an officer in sight to lead the horde. Hanging on the mules alongside the weapons there were actually little cages with songbirds, but for all that, it was a grim rabble and we began to realise that in China not much distinction is made between soldiers and bandits. There is a Chinese proverb that says, 'You don't make nails from good iron and you don't make soldiers from good people.' Poverty drove most young Chinese to take up soldiering. They were very badly paid. Sometimes they got no pay at all, and then they would desert, form themselves into bands – armed, of course – and go on the rampage. They tyrannised whole provinces and with the plunder acquired on their raids they enlisted other soldiers. One of them usually set himself up as the leader. Big concessions often had to be made to these robber chiefs and if they could not be brought to heel they were taken into the Chinese army with the rank of general. Many Chinese generals were said to have such careers behind them.

Understandably, this region was beginning to make us feel very uncomfortable. Oddly enough, none of the soldiers showed any hostility towards us. As we approached Ping-siang, the road was blocked with barbed wire barriers. Helmuth got out, I sounded the horn and several Chinese soldiers with machine pistols emerged from a tent. Just for fun, Helmuth raised his hand to his pith helmet in a military salute and said in German, "*Guten Tag, meine Herren!* Would you please open up for us and let us pass? We are completely harmless and only want to drive on to Shanghai, so just move these barriers, all right?"

To our complete astonishment, the soldiers removed the road block, saluted in a friendly manner and let us through. We thought we'd better step on it before they changed their minds! The engine roared and we sped over the border into Kiang-si province. The next day we came up against a similar obstacle, but in the meantime, Helmuth had been refining his act. He made me sound the horn while we were still some way off, while he stood upright in the car, saluting and haranguing them in typical Viennese fashion.

"Pleased to see you, gentlemen! Now then, what's all this? Why aren't all these barriers out of the way to let the Austrian Trans-Asia Expedition through? We should have lovely lasses lining the road and waving, not all this rubbish clogging the carriageway! Look lively, you bunch of toffs, *ein bissl dalli, gemma, gemma!*"

I was often reminded of the motorcycle trip to India a year or so before. Everything was much more difficult with the car, as was I was frequently bound to admit.

Right: Distances in China were enormous and the ferry always seemed to be on the other side of the river. You soon learn to wait and be patient when you drive through Asia.

Below: Working the bellows of a small blacksmith's hearth on the river bank.

And it worked! A couple of squads of guards shot out of a tent, got into line and presented arms while others removed the obstacles. We acknowledged them with great condescension and drove through.

We were puzzled by the friendliness of these people. Had we really such a military air in our khaki shirts and pith helmets? It was not until we reached the next town, Nan-chang, that the mission doctor, Dr Petersen, was able to give us some explanation for the civil war and the behaviour of the soldiers.

The real reason for the civil war was not political. Yet again, it was all about opium! Kuang-si and Kuang-tung were progressive and had forbidden the cultivation of opium. (In any case, the poppy did not flourish in the flat marshy land of these two provinces.) But they also controlled the ports, and the province of Kuang-si alone took twenty million dollars a year in transit duty for opium. This was a nice little earner and not nearly so much trouble as growing it themselves.

However, the governors of the neighbouring provinces to the north had suddenly decided to go progressive too, and to outlaw the poppy in their territories likewise. This was an outrage. What would become of the customs duty? Something had to be done. Now, these sleepy, nay, opium-befuddled provinces had long been suspected of doing far too little in the way of arming themselves against possible invasion by a foreign power, be it the Russians or the Japanese. This was surely the case, and if so, then this presented a danger for one's own province, did it not? There was nothing for it but to rush to the aid of one's weaker neighbour, now under threat, and place his country under 'protection.' It was a selfless and noble impulse (and of course the poor peasants were so keen to re-plant their poppy fields).

So these were the real reasons why the Kuang-si military was streaming northwards and why the Hunan troops were on the move. We could thank our proverbial lucky star yet again. We had been driving northwards just ahead of the Kuang-si troops and straight through the mobilisation of the opposing Hunan army. Had we stayed longer in Changsha, had we taken up the invitation from the captain of the Scarab and accompanied him on the excursion to Han-kou, we would have ended up in the thick of it. The loss of our car would have been the least of our problems, for, as we heard later, all whites had fled from Changsha by way of the river.

When Dr. Petersen learned how we had been treated in the deployment zone, he gave it as his opinion that either we had been taken for German training officers conducting trials of a new vehicle, or for staff officers involved in the deployment of the Chinese armies.

So, we had enjoyed a double dose of good fortune on this dangerous stretch of the journey. St Christopher, whose medal we carried in the car, had certainly been keeping a watch over us and the plucky little Steyr!

Above: The tracks between marshes and paddy fields near Yaung-Chou were only a metre wide, enough for sedan chairs and wheelbarrows but too narrow for a car. The Trans-Asia Expedition certainly exercised our patience. We were 17 months getting to Shanghai – 510 days, to be precise.

Below: Should we take a run at it? The flight of steps was not steep, but near the top it was no wider than the wheels of the car. Slipping off the edge would have damaged the sump. A slow approach helped by coolies with ropes was the better option.

Steps and 'good luck thresholds' in the cities of central China posed problems for the expedition.

Above: There were so many 'spirit walls' sticking right out into the road that they had to be removed. This caused a considerable outcry, perhaps for the loss of protection from evil spirits, perhaps for the rebuilding it demanded.

Above: The 'honey coolie,' carrying liquid muck from houses out to the fields. He would push his way unceremoniously through bustling crowds in the narrow streets, knowing that all would give way to him.

Above: The Widows' Arch in Chi-Yang. Our expedition was the first motorcar ever to drive through Chi-Yang. Only a few months previously, a resourceful Chinese had brought a motorcycle from Shanghai (2000km away) and charged fees to show it.

Opposite: The village schoolteacher has the children sing a song in honour of the 'long-noses' (Europeans).

An Incredible Journey

Right: The Catholic mission in Kyiang certified that we were the first car to appear in the town. The Chinese name for motor car was 'hot wheels' (locomotive) driven by 'electric oil' (petrol).

Below: China experts in Europe whom I asked for advice insisted that I was too young to command respect in the land where age is honoured, and that no help would be forthcoming. "Do like the missionaries – grow a beard, and you'll be amazed at the effect." It was true. Shopkeepers vied for the honour of garaging our "hot wheels driven by electric oil" and the following day we were given presents. Even with a beard, such a garage would be hard to find in Europe!

216

Above: Funeral of a Chinese Nationalist general, killed fighting the Red Army of Mao-Zedong. The portrait of the dead general was carried at the head of the procession ...

... followed by his sedan chair and bodyguard.

Above: Distinguished mourners, including the mayor of Yunnan-fu, dressed in white.

Above: Entrances to the temples of Chinese gods are guarded by doorkeepers with terrifying expressions.

Above: Official banknote of the province of Hunan. Each Chinese province had a different government, different regulations and different money.

Above: A leper. He was carried in his little hut, as in a sedan chair, and set down every day outside a different house where he would be fed and cared for.

Below: Did the Chinese gods anticipate space travel? This splendid group of figures in the Temple of a Thousand Genies bore the suggestive title 'Reaching for the moon.'

Above: To step into the temple precincts through the Gate of Happiness is to experience a timeless atmosphere of peace and beauty.

Below: We were reluctant to use female coolies for carrying our luggage, but missionaries told us that they needed the work more than men did.

Above: The expedition car attracted a lot of attention even in big cities like Chang-sha with over a million inhabitants. The flags are advertisements put up by Chinese shopkeepers. The flags were usually made with oblong holes in them to allow the wind to blow through.

Above: Rotten eggs on sale in the market. They are actually a delicacy. Hard-boiled eggs are packed in clay and buried in the earth for several weeks. The white turns gelatinous and yellow, while the yolk becomes olive-green and rather like cheese. Missionaries used to claim that the Chinese also ate earthworms, but in fact they were confusing them with brown soybean noodles.

Left: Thousands of rice bowls for thousands of Chinese. The best kaolin is found near King-Te-Chen, and the whole town depends on porcelain for a living.

Above: Following local custom, two ladies travel cross-country by wheelbarrow – a rather bumpy ride over paving stones.

Above: In central China petrol was sent out by porters to each stopping-point on our journey. Preparations made well in advance were essential to the success of the expedition.

Right: Running through bamboo groves, a typical Chinese paved road, used by pedestrians, litter-bearers and wheelbarrow passengers.

Above: Although roads were good as we neared Shanghai, the sedan chair was still common. This old Chinese peers out suspiciously at the 'white foreign devils,' also known as 'long-noses.'

Above: Road building in China. Machines were a rare sight, but there was never any shortage of manpower.

Above: Not only humans rode in sedan chairs, but pigs too! Specially made 'chairs' were woven from bamboo. Walking the pig to market meant that it lost more value in weight than the cost of hiring coolies.

Above: Bus stop and police station on the approach to Shanghai. The gate was kept closed. Even the few government or private cars had to stop here.

Above: China's millions await their destiny.

Above: Ancient and modern architecture in Shanghai, which had a population of three million. Journey's end: we had travelled 25,700km from the Mediterranean to the Yellow Sea.

Above: Leader of the Nationalist Chinese troops, General Chiang-Kai-Shek. As the Trans-Asia Expedition crossed China, the civil war between Chiang-Kai-Shek and Mao-Zedong had already begun. A lot of luck and a certain amount of bare-faced cheek enabled us to slip through between the advancing armies. The main danger was always that our car might be confiscated.

Above: Woman with bound feet. The toes were bound under the ball of the foot and the points of the shoes were just for show. Bound feet were seen only among the 'better' classes of society. Their original purpose was to stop women running away.

Left: Bilingual notice on a public lavatory in the British Concession of the Shanghai International Settlement.

20

WHAT MARCO POLO SAW

If you are not familiar with Chinese geography, then many provinces seem to have similar names. This can be thoroughly confusing for Westerners like us whose language is not tonal. There are a Kuang-si, a Kiang-si and a Kiang-su, likewise a Hu-nan and a Ho-nan, a Ho-pai and a Hu-peh, a Kuang-tung, Shang-tung, Shan-si and Shen-si, and with the towns it's much the same story.

To our eyes, Nan-chang was a particularly ugly city, since all the beautiful old Chinese stuff had been torn down and replaced with wide streets, modern skyscrapers and traffic control posts. Our 'hot wheels driven by electric oil' seemed to have aroused the suspicions of the last-mentioned, for one day we were summoned by the police (alias 'peace officials') to show our driving licence. We were accused of having no driving licence for the province of Kiang-si, and none of my letters of recommendation from the neighbouring province would save the situation. It was quite true that I had no licence for Kiang-si, but where could I have got it from? In some village we drove through, maybe?

"Things are different here in the provincial capital," the police official explained through his interpreter, politely but coldly. "This is not just anywhere, you know. In Nan-chang we abide by the rules!" I produced my international driving licence but it carried no Chinese text. Just because it was international did not mean it was valid all over the world.

"You must take a driving test," declared the official.

I explained via the interpreter that we had already crossed a dozen Asian countries and all the Chinese provinces between Hanoi and Nan-chang.

"So you actually know how to drive?" he asked suspiciously.

We nodded as gravely as possible.

"Truly?" He did not seem convinced.

"Yes, really!"

Our repeated solemn declarations finally seemed to satisfy the bureaucratic conscience. We received a driving licence to cover our journey through Kiang-si but limited to a maximum of 14 days. This cost us two Kiang-si dollars, after which they let us go and wished us well.

The porcelain capital of China, King-te-chen, was about 800km from Shanghai. Now that we were nearing our destination we were getting nervous, but we were determined to make time to see this town, which was rarely visited by Europeans.

After all that we had been through, 800km was a mere nothing. For Europeans living in Shanghai, going this far inland was almost an expedition in itself. The vehicle depot at King-te-chen lay on a hill some way out of town. Here we parked the car, and hired a woman to carry our luggage and camp beds into town. As well as the heavy load, she carried her baby on her back. Female coolies are not unusual in China, and I soon got over the habit of refusing them out of pity. Their need for work was probably greater than that of their male colleagues.

China clay (kaolin) is found in an unusually pure form near to King-te-chen. The town is very ancient, and because of its export of porcelain, it is one of the richest in this enormous country. The same stamp which was used on famous old vases of the Ming dynasty is still impressed on King-te-chen's wares to this day. Even the greatest experts are said to have difficulty in distinguishing a modern reproduction from an original.

King-te-chen was run by gangsters, like Chicago used to be. A local band of ne'er-do-wells exacted protection money, and the rich porcelain makers gave in to their demands, knowing that if they did not pay, they would soon find their entire stock smashed to pieces. Broken china seemed to typify the porcelain city, as we noticed immediately. It was everywhere underfoot, the streets were strewn with it. Then there were coolies all over the place carrying pots, kaolin or firewood. Stacks of cheap household china towered in the shops, while in high-class establishments there stood figures and gorgeous vases of every size, ornamented and painted with dragons, trees and flowers, an almost inconceivable variety of shapes and motifs.

We left King-te-chen with two little crates full of porcelain. Now we were on our way through the provinces of An-hui and Che-kiang to China's most beautiful city, Hangchow. It certainly lived up to its reputation. This was where the Tsien-tang river flowed into the sea, its waters feeding the numerous artificial canals that branched off it, criss-crossing the city, spanned by stone bridges. Small junks and rowing boats floated alongside the streets. Pagodas and towers smiled down from every hilltop around the city, but the most beautiful of them and the most delightful stood on the islands of the West Lake in the centre of Hangchow. Along the causeway linking the shore to the islands was an avenue of scented acacias. As we passed all the pavilions with their curved roofs, and the little temples and summer houses, we seemed to be heading straight for Paradise.

In the evening, the lake came to life. In the 13th century, Marco Polo noted in the account of his travels that it was the custom to go rowing on the lake in the evening with beautiful women. The province of Che-kiang had a lively tourist office, which had seized upon this for publicity purposes, and the practice was encouraged, as the following extract shows: "Six hundred years ago Marco Polo went for boat trips on the West Lake and appreciated the beautiful women. Why not try a trip for yourself? Maybe you will sit in the same boat that Marco Polo used and enjoy yourself as much as he did!"

The famous traveller had not only extolled the beauty of Hangchow's women, but also that of the wonderful Ling-yin pagoda. These days one can drive straight into the city of temples past the larger than life-size figures of sentinels and dragons, but the impression of the age, holiness and sheer sublimity of the site is so overwhelming that you suddenly feel bound to get out and continue reverently on foot. There were formal gardens of indescribable beauty, by which we came to a dragon spouting water, over red-lacquered bridges and past smoking sacrificial bowls to the temple itself. The doorway was small, which made the space we entered beyond it seem larger and more mysterious in the semi-darkness. Three gigantic golden Buddhas, each on a high plinth, wore curious distant smiles. Behind them towered a sort of rock wall, like a mountain, representing the world striving to reach heaven. It was magnificent, and yet we were only half aware of it. Our minds were set on the vision of a modern city by the Yellow Sea. Nothing could stop us now – Shanghai was calling – but on rocks, on stone pinnacles and in caverns we could see carved figures, Buddhist saints and hundreds upon hundreds of human figures, whole families with children, old men, women, coolies, peasants, all kneeling with folded hands and praying to the Enlightened One in search of his Four Noble Truths. The Buddhist community of the whole world made obeisance to its holy Gautama, while he sat enthroned above them, smiling down with compassion on their sufferings, aware of it all. The golden figure stood tall and bright in the gloom, illuminated by light falling from a cunningly set window in the roof, a radiant symbol of purity and the greatness of heaven.

We stood for a long time absorbed by this spectacle, and were still walking in a dream as we returned to the city. You would have thought that our brush with the supernatural would have put us into a peaceful and contemplative mood, and yet the Ling-ying pagoda only served to stretch our nerves nearer to breaking point.

However, on the same afternoon we had an invitation to visit some Belgian nuns who were running a hospital, and a prettier and cleaner place you could not have asked for. We liked the kindergarten even better. The whole design was so delightful, but it was the Chinese children romping amongst the little tables, chairs and beds that were quite the sweetest thing. We had never seen such adorable doll-like faces on any children in Europe.

29
ʃHANGHAI

We kept looking at the tachometer. We had never checked it so often as during these last few days. Only a few kilometres now lay between us and Shanghai. In only a few hours we would be able to say that we had done it, that we had crossed Asia by motor car!

We found the going slow, although the ferries were powered by motor boats and more rapid that anywhere else in China and the roads were very good, thus allowing us a higher speed. Nothing could satisfy us. We were more jittery than at almost any other time on the whole journey.

June 19th 1936 brought us in sight of our destination. After a quick dip in the Yellow Sea, we dressed in our city clothes – long white trousers, white shirt and pith helmet – and so we were ready for Shanghai.

The traffic was building up all the way in. Factories lined our route. We passed the Eurasia Airfield, and before we knew it we found ourselves in the French settlement of the Chinese metropolis. From here we found our way by broad tarmac avenues to the Bund, the magnificent waterfront in the British district. We had completely forgotten what it was like to drive in this sort of traffic, and also the sight of such huge buildings. There were the Bank of England, the Bank of China, the banks of India and Australia, hotels and company offices. Lines of buses, trolley-buses, private cars and rickshaws pressed forward together and the harbour was tightly packed with an amazing variety of shipping.

We wondered where to go first. In the end we drove straight to the Automobile Club of China. As our car drew up outside the building, the gentlemen of the club crowded round it. It looked very small and insignificant. Dented and rusted as it was on the outside, albeit young and sprightly within, our noble Steyr had to submit to yet another detailed examination. 23,200km in Asia? Had we crossed the whole of China? Completely by land? All we could do was to show our passports with entries by the various provincial authorities, also our letters of recommendation and the declarations by the missionaries confirming that our car had been the first to visit their stations. Our documentary proof overcame all suspicions at the Automobile Club. Telegrams were dispatched to Vienna to the Automobil und Touring Club (ÖTC/ÖAMTC), to the Sport-und Turnfront, to the Geographical Institute, to the Steyr Works and the other concerns who had sponsored our trip. We were eager for the reply, as we were dying to go on to

Japan and home via the USA. What news would they send us? Money was what we needed in any case.

The first and most pressing problem was accommodation. Of course, there were fabulous hotels along the Bund, but with the money we had left, we could barely have stayed a couple of days there. The Austrian consul, a kind old gentleman by the name of Ockermüller, had the answer and recommended the 'Pension Paschen.' Since Consul Ockermüller had put in a good word for us with the landlady, we were able to start living on credit straight away, which seemed to be the practice of every European in Shanghai. Nothing was paid for in cash any more. Instead, you signed a chit. It was a simple process and signing was easy. The bills were then sent to your home at the end of the month by your creditors (the bar, the shopkeeper, the tailor, and so on), to be paid on the first of the following. Of course, this meant that you started out broke and had to begin signing chits all over again. It was a dangerous way to live and many people came to grief. For the moment we were obliged to live on chits too, although we resolved to be extremely careful. Even so, we had to pay a considerable sum at the end and it was impossible to deny any of it because every chit had our own signature. We signed for absolutely everything – cigarettes, food, drinks, even laundry and a Palm Beach tropical suit. We were evidently trustworthy.

Within the first few days, Consul Ockermüller had notified the press and we gave an interview in the Austrian consulate. A lot of correspondents turned up and all the resulting articles celebrated the first crossing of China by motor car as a great achievement. It gave us particular satisfaction to read this in the Shanghai papers because it represented the judgment of people who knew China. That was the big difference. If you tell a European journalist that you have just crossed some wildly inhospitable country for the first time, you can make all your difficulties and adventures sound as exciting as you like. The European reporter, who has never set foot in the country, will faithfully serve it all up to his readers as a sensation, with maybe a slight dramatisation here and there. By contrast, the press conference in Shanghai was rather the reverse. The reporters – Chinese, British and American – had motored around China a bit for themselves. They knew what could be done, and also what exceeded the bounds of possibility. In their various accounts they declared that we had gone beyond these bounds, albeit with a hefty dose of good luck. It may have stuck in the craw of more than one Anglo-Saxon journalist to report that two Austrian students had succeeded in making this pioneering journey, but they did so with admirable objectivity and sportsmanship.

Following the articles in the international press in this city of three million inhabitants, we received many private invitations. We bought flowers for our hostess with chits, like we bought our new tropical suits, but we now knew that money from home was on its way to us. The only question was how much. Enough for Shanghai and the journey home, or enough to take us round the world, which would require quite a considerable sum? For the time being we had nothing but debts, but our credit was good in Shanghai and Frau Paschen had even given us the best boy in her establishment as our personal servant. This lad never failed to astound us with his love of order, his efficiency and his omniscience. Without our saying a word, he knew exactly when and where we had been invited every evening and the elegant tropical suits and all the accessories would be laid out waiting for us.

中 國 汽 車 借 行 社

The Automobile Club of China.

(Members Alliance Internationale de Tourisme, Brussels).
(Affiliated to the Royal Automobile Club of Great Britain and Ireland,
the Automobile Association of Great Britain, the Automobile Association of America,
the Singapore Automobile Club, and the Royal Java Motor Club).

TELEGRAPHIC ADDRESS
"MOOROB"
SHANGHAI

CODES:
BENTLEY'S 1ST EDITION
BENTLEY'S 2ND EDITION

TELEPHONE 10704.

P. O. BOX NO. 1049

SECRETARIES: BECK & SWANN.

17 THE BUND.

SHANGHAI.

3rd July, 1936.

Secretary,
Austrian Touring Club,
Schubertring 7,
WIEN 1.

Dear Sir,

We have pleasure in certifying that on 19th June, 1936,
Messrs. Max Reisch and Helmuth Hahmann of the Austrian Trans
Asia Motor Car Expedition arrived in Shanghai after travelling
through the interior of China via Kwangsi from Indo-China,
and that these gentlemen were the first motorists to pass
through Kwangsi Province by motor car into Hunan Province.
Many portions of the roads traversed by them on this journey
were in an unfinished condition, but with the assistance of
the Kwangsi highway officials they found it possible to
overcome the various difficulties and complete their journey.

Messrs. Reisch and Hahmann are undoubtedly the first
motorists to have travelled from Indo-China to Shanghai via
Kwangsi by motor car.

Whilst the construction of roads in China is proceeding
rapidly, it should be realised that what are known as first
class roads here can only be considered as second class in
Europe, and many of the roads which these gentlemen travelled
on were second and third class roads for China, the latter
being practically unusable except in favourable weather.

We are, dear Sir,
Yours faithfully,

Secretaries.

The Automobile Club of China confirms that Helmuth and I were undoubtedly the first
motorists to come via Kuang-si (ie solely by land) from Indochina to Shanghai.

"To Mr and Mrs Jensen's this evening, master."

"How do you know that?"

The boy grinned from ear to ear and never betrayed the source of his information.
However, we learned from Shanghai veterans that the boys were always telephoning
each other, even if they were not personally acquainted, and sharing any important
knowledge that would facilitate their services to their 'master' or 'missis.' There

were several thousand boys employed by whites and they had to work hard in the knowledge that millions of intelligent Chinese were queuing up for jobs like theirs.

"Eight o'clock at the Jensens, then. With the motor car it will take you about 20 minutes. Take the Bubbling Well Road going east, then the Bund northwards and after the bridge, the first road to the north, number 34. Oh, and Mrs Jensen is especially fond of tea roses. Here are the flowers. Here is the chit. Sign please ..."

It was quite amazing!

There was plenty of opportunity for fun, for drinking and dancing and wild parties in Shanghai, and who would begrudge it us? We had 14 months of abstinence behind us, we were young, and we had some catching up to do! While Fasching was on in Vienna, we had spent the whole time in the swamps of Southeast Asia. We had missed lots of glasses of Heuriger and lots of parties and swapped all that carefree enjoyment for the crushing burden of responsibility and endurance. Now we were introduced to Shanghai's answer to the Prater. It was a four-storied house of entertainment with fourteen stages where performances went on without interruption around the clock, where almost as many cinemas ran a continuous programme and where you could dance without stopping all day and all night. This is to say nothing of all the acrobats, conjurors, fire-eaters, fakirs, wrestlers, beer halls and restaurants that could also be found under the very same roof. We ate Wiener Schnitzel at the 'Blue Danube,' a delightfully furnished restaurant with pictures of Vienna round the walls and when our Shanghai guide, kind Herr Waldbauer, saw how much we loved it, he said, "I must take you straight on to the next Viennese establishment!"

"Two lots of Vienna in Shanghai?" we exclaimed in amazement.

"Shanghai is a completely international city," he explained, "where all nationalities are at home. You'll find a Munich beer hall, a Black Forest snug, a Dutch inn and a lot of English pubs. If you go to the Caucasian restaurant you can eat better than in Russia before the revolution, and get the best varieties of vodka. If you prefer champagne, there are plenty of French restaurants, but you can also have rice wine if you for Chinese or Japanese meals. And that's not all. You can dance and flirt with Chinese girls, Japanese girls, Korean girls, Indians, Malays, Filipinos, Manchu, Russians. In Shanghai you can have just about anything!"

To show us what he meant he took us to a Chinese dance hall which was full of pleasant surprises. The dance music was excellent and the decor was stylish. The dance floor was floodlit from below with different colours. What really appealed to us were the great blocks of ice standing all round the walls into which were frozen the most wonderful flowers – orchids, roses and all sorts of gorgeously coloured tropical varieties completely unknown to me. These blocks stood in big copper dishes which caught the melting water and they had fans installed behind them so that pleasantly cool air was blown through the room.

We met some charming young ladies in Shanghai high society, who extended a very proper invitation to tea. Of course, we wanted to dance too, but there were no suitable records available. "Never mind," said one of the girls and went to the telephone. In Shanghai there were about a dozen privately-owned radio stations, continuously broadcasting music and advertisements, and they provided a brilliantly original service to the public: a telephone call would get the record of your choice played as the next number, or maybe the one after that. You could make up a complete programme in this way, and we made full use of the opportunity it offered.

One day, one of the charming young ladies, on whom I was rather keen, dropped me a hint.

"Well, maybe ... but not with that beard."

That same evening I handed Helmuth the scissors and said, "Take it off! It's the only way!"

Helmuth set about it, but we were both very sad to see it go. The rejuvenation seemed of such historical significance that Helmuth gathered the results of his labours (measuring over ten centimetres) into a thick envelope and wrote upon it, "Max's missionary-style beard. Begun in Afghanistan, cut off in its prime at Shanghai."

Then I shaved, whereupon the skin of my cheeks and chin came up looking like a guinea pig, white as alabaster, while the rest of my face was tanned like leather and dark brown. I looked frightful. I felt naked and it was draughty in the bits where the beard had been. I was so miserable that my courage failed me and I never claimed the reward for my beardless condition! It was a sad admission, and I realised that, at 22, it was better to sport an impressive beard than to be clean-shaven and demoralised.

The money from home arrived. It exceeded our expectations and ensured that we could travel on to Japan and the USA. We booked a passage on the Nagasaki Maru and the time was fast approaching when we would say farewell to Shanghai. We invited all our friends to a party at a Chinese restaurant, because that meant eating with chopsticks and drinking plenty of rice wine. Both these activities livened things up so much that a very merry time was had by all. At six o'clock in the morning everyone helped us pack up the car because we had to be at the Nagasaki Maru by seven, and it all went swimmingly, even though none of our entourage was exactly sober.

Soon our friends were standing on the pier and we were on board, letting fly paper streamers. The passengers held on to their ends. while the other ends were caught by all the family members, friends and sweethearts who had come to wave a last goodbye. In this way our bonds lasted a few moments longer. We exchanged sad glances as the last ties with the Chinese mainland and with all the kind people we had met were broken, the ship's engines began to turn, and the Nagasaki Maru set sail for Japan.

30

PROBLEMS FOR THE FOREIGN VISITOR

Crossing the China Sea from Shanghai to Nagasaki did not take long and we were due to set foot on Japanese soil in the afternoon of the following day. We took lunch while still on board and by each place lay a map of the southern part of the island of Kyushu. A thick red circle had been drawn around the city of Nagasaki.

The passengers sat in the restaurant, intently studying this unusual map with the words:

> *Notice: Passengers are hereby respectfully informed that any photography, sketching, etc in Nagasaki and its environs is forbidden by law.*

This warning was our first experience of Japan. However, it scarcely prepared us for the countless interrogations we were to experience from the immigration police, or for the close watch kept on us by officials of both sexes, or for the colossal questionnaire awaiting us in the country. Even before we arrived there seemed to be an exceptional number of friendly Japanese on board who were keen on conversing with the passengers. All conversations turned on the three topics of where we had come from, where we were going to, and why. Sensible travellers gave detailed and patient answers, because the more you tried to resist, the more unpleasant the process was liable to become. Japan already had a reputation for being particularly thorough in the way it kept tabs on foreign visitors.

The Nagasaki Maru berthed at the quay, and the passengers crowded down the gangway. Most of them were women of every nationality, escaping from the heat of China to recuperate in the spas and mountain resorts of Japan. Meanwhile, their noble husbands continued to sweat it out in the offices of Shanghai.

How delightful it is to watch the bustle and excitement that goes on just after a steamer has docked when you are not involved! We had no qualms about waiting until last to leave the ship. The Steyr was still roped down on the forward deck, shrouded with tarpaulins, and until customs officials had given it the once-over, we couldn't touch it anyway. They were more thorough than their colleagues in any other Asian country. Both the car and every separate piece of luggage were checked – they were extremely polite but also meticulous. Once a piece had been cleared it received a blue-and-white label with a red spot. There was no room for this label on a small, squashed cigarette packet still containing four cigarettes, but it still had to be marked with a rubber-stamp 'Nagasaki Customs.'

After two hours we were at last ready to go and were just about to move off when a customs official remarked, "But you have no Japanese registration plates!" We admitted rather sheepishly that we had not, but pointed out that we were provided with international documentation for the car.

"International? That may well be the case, but it is certainly not Japanese!"

A long telephone call was made to the police. Eventually we were instructed to present ourselves at once. An official took us there while the car remained in the hands of the customs. At the police station it was explained to us that Japanese number plates were absolutely necessary, but today, Saturday, was too late to get them. The next day, Sunday, was also the Lord's day in Japan and a day of rest. We could discuss it again on Monday.

We were thus denied the opportunity of spending the weekend in the lovely mountain resort of Unzen as we had originally planned, so off we went to find a hotel in Nagasaki. The owner came out to meet us in the doorway, bowing deeply, while behind him stood a line of girls, smiling and inspecting us with great curiosity. As in every Japanese home, the rule here was to take your shoes off at the door and exchange them for a pair of light house shoes provided by the hotel. With our house shoes on, we were led up to the guest rooms on the first floor, where numerous pairs of dainty slippers lay in the corridor. The geisha restrained us gently and pointed to our feet. We took off our house shoes and put on the room slippers. We were then allowed to choose a bedroom. This was a very strange business to our way of thinking, since bedrooms in the European sense did not exist. The floor of the big upstairs area was covered with straw mats of a standard size (about one by two metres). Between every two mats there was a wooden runner, with another on the ceiling above, so that screens could be slid along them. These consisted of a wooden frame on to which painted paper had been glued and tastefully decorated with monochrome brush drawings of trees, flowers or animals. Using these screens, a room was now constructed for us of exactly the size we wanted. The room was then 'furnished' with equal rapidity, although there was not much in the way of furniture: a low table barely a foot high, cushions to be used as armchairs, a small dressing-table, a couple of vases with flowers, and the thing was complete. Unfortunately, this was a very uncomfortable set-up for Europeans. Not only was one obliged to sit on the floor, but everything had to be left lying around there. This has led more than one white guest to assert that when you stay in a Japanese guest-house, you feel like a monkey, crawling constantly on all fours. The outer walls actually had little alcoves and at first we thought we might use these for keeping watches or other small articles. However, the official travellers' guide warned against this: "The alcoves are the room's places of honour and decorated with carved and polished wood or some other ornamentation. Needless to say, they are not intended for the traveller's personal effects. The alcoves should be treated with respect." So we had to go on crawling around amongst our 'personal effects' in the middle of the floor. How and where we were going to sleep that night was still a mystery. We had seen no sign of anything resembling beds in our room. It would have to a surprise. Maybe secret pleasures were included ...

In their language, the Japanese often refer to us as monkeys, but that has nothing to do with the gait one is obliged to adopt in the guest-houses, but rather with our

Above: Travelling by car allows one to appreciate romantic landscapes to the full.

Above: We flew the Japanese flag on our car. Japan was a peaceful country and the villagers were friendly, so camping was a pleasure.

Above: We came round the bend in the Steyr 100 just after this accident had happened. Another lucky escape! Luck smiled on us for all the 40,000km of our round-the-world trip, and only deserted us right at the end, 300km from home.

Below: Japan had a highly-developed newspaper industry, almost like America's. The day after this was taken, the landlord in the little village near Fujiyama brought us the afternoon edition of the Yokohama nichi nichi shimbun complete with photograph of foreign visitors at the foot of Mount Fuji. Helmuth Hahmann is sitting in the centre, with Max in Samurai dress to his left.

236

hairiness, which appears even more accentuated once you have observed their yellow skins, smooth as an eel, next to you in the bath. We were to have plenty of opportunity for this on our first evening at the hotel. One of the friendly girls came in and gave us to understand in very broken English that the bath was ready. She brought the kimonos that the hotel provided for its guests and seemed quite unable to understand why we were so reluctant to get undressed. Hadn't she come on purpose to help us? Geishas have no notion of shame as we understand it. The sight of a naked white man is for them at most slightly interesting, and certainly very ugly, so we allowed her to lead us down to the bathroom. This in itself was no simple matter. First we left off our room slippers and put on the corridor shoes. Outside the bathroom we had to leave the corridor shoes behind and were presented with bath sandals. In a Japanese hotel you have to be constantly changing between three different sorts of footwear, and if you go out on the street, your own shoes make a fourth.

Many other guests were already gathered in the bathroom. We glanced round surreptitiously, in order not to offend too much against Japanese etiquette. We noticed that, to begin with, you scrubbed yourself with soap, then you took a shower and finally, in your purified state, you climbed into the big tub of hot water which was meant for all the guests together. The travellers' guidebook commented, "Foreign visitors who are averse to bathing in water that has already been used may avoid this by being first into the bath." This advice was brilliant in its simplicity. However, although the Japanese usually bathe in the late afternoon, in our experience the 'foreign visitor' will never manage to be first. On sliding aside the unlocked door of the bathroom, he can be sure to find other guests already happily ensconced and conversing within.

So, we soaped ourselves all over and then attempted to use the shower, which required some acrobatic contortions, since it was little over a foot above floor level. Helmuth was an unforgettable sight as he crouched on all fours like a salamander and crawled back and forth under the shower head, once on his belly and once on his back in order to wash all the soap off his body. He then vaulted elegantly over the side of the tub, but he was out again as fast as he had gone in, and as red as a lobster! The Japanese all laughed, and so did I, but that was before I had tried it myself. The water was nearly boiling. For our untrained bodies, it was impossible to stand it for longer than a few seconds. It was only some time later that we managed it for a minute or two, but we never succeeded in wallowing in it in comfort as the Japanese did. We soon learned how to wrap ourselves in the kimono after bathing and also that it had to be used for drying. If you asked for a taoru or hand towel, it would be brought to you so wet that it was about as much use as a sponge.

Back in our room we found a Japanese meal laid out on the low table, which was a great disappointment after Chinese cooking. The best thing about it was the saké or hot rice wine. The serving girl kept refilling the tiny bowls that scarcely held as much as a thimble. She would hand them to us, saying softly the long drawn out syllables "Doooshoooo ..." meaning "If you please."

Then we gave her to understand that we wanted to sleep. We were curious to know how this would be done. "Doooshoooo ..." said the geisha and brought two rolls of bedding. This was all spread out on the floor, and "doooshoooo ..." the beds were ready. The kind girl helped us once more to get undressed, covered us up neatly and tidily and then, with another "Doooshoooo ..." and something that probably meant 'goodnight' we heard the soft sliding of the screen behind us and then we were alone. When it comes to geishas, people have obviously got the wrong idea.

Early on Monday morning we went straight to the police station. The interpreter thought it would take a few hours. In the meantime they had plenty to keep us occupied: I had to take a driving test and the car was to be given a mechanical check in order to determine whether we were actually suitable for 'Japanese traffic conditions.' The Japanese were under the impression that they had invented the motor car – a somewhat arguable point of view, although it was in all the school textbooks – but there was no doubt that they had invented the toughest driving test in the world. Some time later, I saw a driving school in Osaka. It was housed in a whole building complex and the level of activity resembled a European high school. Dressed in their best, the Japanese sat at school desks, each with his collection of books and jotters. Drawings were made and coloured pencils were used to show red oil, yellow sparks and blue cooling water in a way that would have gladdened the heart of any kindergarten teacher. The school yard was divided up into lots of streets with sharp bends and dangerous blind corners and the students drove around this course in Japanese Datsun cars of diminutive proportions.

The police official in Nagasaki directed me to a government garage workshop where, to my amazement, there was a modern unit for checking the roadworthiness of vehicles, impeccably run by the Sons of Heaven themselves, which astounded me. The Steyr's lights were checked by means of a complicated American apparatus which measured power of radiance and range of beam. We passed with top marks. Checking the brakes was to prove more embarrassing.

I was instructed to drive at about 20kph up on to a platform and then to brake suddenly. The platform was divided into four sections through which the effectiveness of braking on all four wheels was transmitted. The result was shattering – total failure. The brakes had to be corrected. We were given another appointment for the following afternoon. Meanwhile, Helmuth bled the brake fluid and put everything back. We made test runs and everything seemed to be in order, with all four brakes pulling equally. In the meantime we had learned that the Japanese require the handbrake to be separate from the footbrake, that is, with its own brake block. The Steyr did not have this, and we were afraid this would make problems. We learned later that the owner of the only Steyr then on the road in Japan had been obliged to have this feature specially built in, apparently using a Japanese-produced cardan brake.

We mounted the braking platform again and this time everything was in order. When asked where the handbrake engaged, Helmuth replied that the rear brake drums were twice the width of the front ones and contained separate brake shoes. Thank goodness the official did not look underneath the car, and so we were sent on our way.

After testing the car, it was the driver's turn. Driving tests at home were always conducted in heavy traffic. Not so in the land of the Rising Sun. The official test area was closed to all traffic. Some of the indicated streets were scarcely wider than the car. It was really more of a test of skill which depended on your knowing to the last centimetre what the back wheel did when you turned the front one. You had to manœuvre yourself through the narrow streets marked out with stakes, strings and paper screens, and to drive at the right speed between two parallel stretched lines.

Above: Bad weather kept us from climbing Mount Fuji and we were held up in the pilgrim village of Umangaeshi. A Japanese film company had time on their hands like ourselves, and the director Kinugasa had them take a few shots of me in samurai costume, striking a suitable attitude!

Below: In spite of the bad roads (used in the main by local people who knew where they were going) there were lots of signposts.

Particular value was laid on the hill-start. In short, you had to be totally familiar with your car. I am quite sure I should have failed the test if I had been made to take it in any other car but my own.

The Japanese driving licence that I eventually acquired was an extensive document. My father and mother and my four grandparents were cited by name. Subjoined was a detailed description of me, which resembled a 'wanted' poster. Not much faith seemed to be placed either in me or in our car, since the licence also contained the following specifications:

> Speed on streets up to 3 metres wide 12kph
> Speed on streets over 3 metres wide 25kph
> Highest speed on country roads 40kph

This was not very generous, but we were only too glad to be allowed to drive ourselves rather than to have the car hauled across Japan by a team of oxen.

It was all sorted out by three o'clock in the afternoon. The Japanese were quite charming, and kindly inquired what number we would like. Since our Austrian number 2020 was not available, we settled for Nagasaki 2396. We had to pay for the number plate and the screws to fix it, but that was all.

So could we start now? Alas, no, not yet. We still had no travel permit. First, we must wait for a reply from Tokyo. Further information was required – in other words, we had the driving licence, we had the number plate, but as yet no authorisation for our journey. Another day went by in Nagasaki, and a second and a third. We had already visited the British and French consuls and Mr Otsuka, the Secretary for Foreign Affairs. All we could extract from him, in spite of his kindness, was the promise that "We are doing all we can. We are awaiting telegrams from the provinces through which you will be travelling."

At last an idea occurred to us. The official Japanese Tourist Board must be able to help us. We applied to the director, Mr Imanaga. "Japan is advertising itself all over the world for tourism. What's the point of posters saying 'Come and see beautiful Japan!' if you end up stuck in Nagasaki?" Mr Imanaga sucked in air with a hiss through his teeth before answering us. "I will do all I can to help you, but the police are a stubborn lot. They would much prefer it if no foreigners ever entered the country." He agreed with us that one of those two institutions, the Tourist Office and the Tourist Police, was certainly superfluous. We knew anyway that foreigners using the railways were very well cared for by the Office, and it was only our coming by private car that made such difficulties. However, it was not our friendly interview with Mr Imanaga that did the trick, but a visit to the police chief in Nagasaki. We managed to touch the right chord for his sporting instincts by showing him photographs, and more photographs. We showed him many of the articles we had written, which made an impression in Japan where they were obsessed with newspapers and the circulation ran into millions. He finally announced that the conditions for our round-the-world trip were favourable, and when, after a stop of six days in Nagasaki, we actually got all the documents in our hands, the British consul declared: "Well, you've set a new record for getting permission to travel in your own car. It usually takes many weeks and plenty of travellers have waited in vain."

Typical street scene in a small Japanese town. The rapid, almost frantic development of an agricultural country into an industrialised state brought with it unlovely forests of telegraph poles and wires for electric light, like those seen here. Living standards among the general population remained modest, however, and low wages offered a growing challenge to the higher demands of American and European industrial workers.

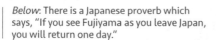

Above: My Japanese driving licence, acquired after days of patient exertion. A foreigner driving his own car through the country was regarded with the deepest suspicion.

Above: Japan has a dense railway network and excellent inland waterway transport. Roads were consequently neglected on some islands. Since vehicles were getting heavier, the old embankments frequently gave way.

Below: There is a Japanese proverb which says, "If you see Fujiyama as you leave Japan, you will return one day."

31

'YUKU MICHI' IN THE LAND OF DELIGHTS

The word for landscape in Japanese translates as 'mountain water,' and this certainly characterises the impressions we received on our travels in the island empire. Wherever we went, we encountered the perfect harmony of mountains and waters. Wonderful views opened before us from high above the many long inlets on the ocean or on the Inland Sea. This is bounded by the two islands of Kyushu and Shikoku and the main island of Hondo. The road we followed in Hondo clung to the rocks with an almost perpendicular drop to one side, just like on Lake Garda. The deep blue waters swarmed with the white sails of junks. Islands appeared on the horizon, little wooded rocks with a few fishermen's houses. Sometimes the mountains receded and a glorious beach would stretch before us with old fishermen sitting in the sun mending their nets, children playing on the sand, bathing and hunting for shells, a small paradise of peace. If this part of the coast was reminiscent of the Mediterranean, other places recalled Scandinavia. We drove through forests just like in our own country, and through meadows full of flowers and majestic mountain valleys. It was all Japan, but a Japan where any European would feel at home, and on top of that were all the details that gave the country its special charm: the houses, so tidy, so spick and span in even the tiniest hamlet, women like butterflies, children like dolls, gardens, always gardens, and temples in beautiful well-kept grounds.

The loveliest holy place we visited was the island of Itsukushima in the Inland Sea, famed as the 'island of temples.' Its Shinto temples, known as shrines, are built out on stilts over the water. At low tide the buildings and roofed-in pillared galleries which connect them stand far above the waves, but at high tide they appear to be rocking gently upon them. The temple island can be recognised from a distance by the gigantic gate of camphor wood which stands in the sea half way to the opposite coast. This torji, painted a light red colour, seems like an invitation to the pilgrim to embark for the holy island. We looked around for a motor boat and soon found ourselves amongst a milling throng of devotees and sightseers, all with the same end in view. There were women with babies on their backs, brightly-dressed young girls gracefully wielding their sunshades, men clad in kimonos and straw hats or European travelling suits, old Japanese in dignified black, and amongst them the fishermen who provided the boats and made their living from the pilgrims and the tourists.

When we landed at the little harbour, no sooner had our feet touched dry land than we were greeted by herds of white-spotted deer. They came up and nuzzled at us, looking for titbits and pushing their rose-pink noses into our trouser pockets. There were stalls where you could buy food for them and groups of deer crowded round dear little doll-like Japanese girls, pushing their rivals out of the way with their antlers, but so carefully that the children came to no harm.

Hordes of pilgrims wandered around the site. Many had come a long way to pay their respects to the eight million Shinto gods. We followed them, carrying our shoes in our hands. We passed halls for music, halls for prayer, terraces hung with bells, the treasury and the temple of morning prayers, until we approached the holiest shrine. Here a priest ordered us to stop. As foreigners, only the lesser halls were open to us. From here we watched a Japanese woman perform a rite of honour. From the roof of the holy shrine hung a thick rope connected to bell. The woman shook the rope to set the bell in motion and to beg for attention. Then she bowed her head and clapped her hands sharply. That was all, but it was fascinating to see the depth of feeling expressed by this simple procedure.

It was pleasant to wander in the shade of the pillared galleries. Everything was of wood with not a single iron peg or bracket to hold the structure together, a masterpiece of ancient Japanese architecture. The main shrine was established in 811 AD (CE) and its hall and several smaller buildings are preserved in their original state. Everything we saw was painted in bright soft colours. The railings had almost the same effect as modern architectural features, for the carving had no figurative designs, only decorative patterns. As we wandered about, the outlook between the pillars was constantly changing. The park landscape around the shrine was particularly lovely: huge trees, exotic plants, paths strewn with fine gravel, benches in the shade of ancient pine trees and long rows of stone lanterns. Through it all were views of the shimmering blue sea, the sacred red torji in the foreground, and in the distance the coast of the main island of Hondo, with its scattering of houses.

Suddenly, amongst all the Japanese we caught sight of a white woman, a fat old lady making straight for us. In the broadest American accent she declared, "I had them arrange me an outing from the hotel in Kobe, and they brought me here! Can you maybe tell me where I am and what all this means?"

She was a typical case and it was quite hopeless: a 60-day round the world trip with all comforts thrown in. It was Helmuth, the camera man, who found the right answer.

"You just take a lot of nice shots of the place with your movie camera. When you get home, have a film show and engage a Japanologist to explain it to you!"

He sounded so serious and convincing that the dear old lady exclaimed with gratitude, "Oh yes, what a good idea!"

The Japanese are highly skilled in the art of garden design. Their parks, even those not belonging to a temple, are quite miraculous, especially the parts where entire landscapes are represented in miniature. There are specially grown stunted trees which appear to be tiny pines, and others little deciduous trees. A variety of moss has been transformed into miniature grass, and with the aid of these plants, together with watercourses, tiny temples, houses, bridges and delicate figurines, charming scaled-down versions of Japanese landscape are created. This is to say nothing of the fish ponds! They were swarming with goldfish of all colours, right down to dark red, some with veil tails and some with protruding telescope eyes.

The cultivation of these plants and creatures and the way the gardens fit so perfectly into their surroundings are clear evidence of how intimately Japanese thinking is connected to nature. A centuries-old tradition of sensitivity to its myriad beauties has fixed it in their blood. Thus, Japanese families will have certain nights dedicated to admiring the moon, when the overpowering sight of the peaceful landscape bathed in bright moonlight inspires the Japanese soul to solemn veneration. The Japanese habitually seek beauty in the smallest, most insignificant things. We brush away a buzzing mosquito with an irritated hand-movement but in summer the Japanese hold a festival for listening to insects, appreciating the delicate unceasing tune of their flight. Tiny cages of woven bamboo are on sale everywhere, containing giant crickets. These are placed on the balcony in the evening so that their chirping can give pleasure.

There is an even more pronounced love of flowers. While we reckon the year in months, the Japanese count their days according to blossom times. The cycle begins with plum blossom, symbol of youth and maidenly purity, followed by peach blossom, the emblem of married bliss. In April the pale drifts of pink cherry blossom herald the beginning of rapturous celebrations throughout the country – peonies, wistaria and azaleas are succeeded by irises, the boys' flower. The lotos blooms in all its glory in August, followed in autumn by the chrysanthemum, the Japanese imperial flower. As the world of colour slowly fades, there is one more flash of brightness before winter sets in, when brilliant maple leaves signal the close of the flowering year.

Fashion follows this year of flowers. Particular kimonos are worn at particular seasons, with the pattern always chosen to reflect the flower or tree of the moment. At the very least, colours are determined by the predominant natural hues. The obi, the broad sash, the sunshade, the bag, the silk handkerchief, absolutely everything has to be right, and this profound sympathy with the manifold glories of the natural world means that women in Japan dress more charmingly, more stylishly and more colourfully than anywhere else on earth.

A whirlwind tour through Japan, land of delights, was an attractive idea. Alas, the inhabitants' sense of beauty had not, to date, extended to the motor road system. To be sure, modern roads had recently been built in the environs of the cities of Kobe, Osaka, Yokohama and Tokyo, but these represented only a small percentage of the total. When it came to built roads, those in the south of Japan were the worst of our whole journey. It is scarcely possible to give a European any idea of their condition, because by that date we had literally nothing resembling it at home. Imagine a track across the fields, so narrow that there was almost nowhere for two vehicles to pass each other. Along this track, in its original state, heavy motor traffic had been passing for a number of years without any improvements worth mentioning. Driving on these roads with their deep potholes and ruts took a toll on our nerves as much as on the vehicle. Mostly we had to use second or third gear, with a speed, if you could call it that, of 15 to 25kph. We never spotted any road-menders, heaps of road-stone or any other sign that repairs were being considered. Of course, there were no private cars either, but on the other hand we came across plenty of omnibuses and lorries, which gave the lie to the assertion that transport in Japan was so well served by railways and sea routes that roads needed no special attention. The omnibuses were all brand new and very splendid, and no wonder, since they must have got shaken to pieces on those roads in a very short time and needed replacing pretty often. It was impossible for the drivers to act as ticket-sellers, since they had to keep their attention focused on the road. This function was performed by pretty young girls who exercised the most tender care over the passengers' well-being. Not only did they sell them the tickets, but also helped them in and out of the vehicle, obtained fruit or drinking water for them at the bus stations and kept the whole bus in the best of spirits with their kind and pleasant manners. On Japanese country roads the prevailing atmosphere was charged with a spirit of comradeship, politeness and mutual consideration. Drivers waved and laughed and competed to give way to one another. This was dictated not only by the national character, but by the condition of the roads, which were so dangerous that every driver had to rely on his colleagues to help him. It was not only the neglect in maintaining the carriageway that made them so hard to drive on, but also the natural terrain. On a Japanese road one could never be sure that the full width as it appeared to the eye was safe to drive on. On the edge of a precipice, lorry and bus drivers always knew that the ground over which their front wheel ran safely might collapse under the heavier weight of the back wheel. There were never any safety barriers, railings or kerbstones. We saw several cases of accidents to lorries which were no fault of the drivers. It was simply that the ground on the outside edge of the road had given way and the lorry had plunged down with the avalanche of stones and earth.

Because of this, lorry drivers in Japan were constantly dicing with death, but for this very reason they were always ready to help. We would frequently come round a bend and find ourselves face to face with a lorry. One of us would have to reverse. Who would it be? In Europe this would lead to a heated argument. In Japan each considered it his duty to help the other one out of trouble, and without a second thought they would both reverse. When the passing place had been reached and nothing had been seen for a while, one would sound the horn. Meanwhile the other one would also have found a passing place and he would sound his horn likewise. One would wait for the other, but out of sheer politeness he wouldn't come. In the end one of them would set off again and meet the other in exactly the same place as before. Everyone would laugh and joke about the ridiculous situation, and so the game could begin all over again. We had many conversations with Japanese drivers, even though we knew nothing of the language, simply by pointing and laughing and facial expressions.

Finding our way was sometimes a perplexing business. We frequently drove through heavily built-up areas with many side roads. How could we find the right way? The signposts were in Japanese, of course, and we had to compare them laboriously with the signs on the map. It was a railway map, the only one we could get hold of. No motoring atlas was available anywhere in Japan. There were scarcely any private cars and bus drivers did not need a map. We covered all 2700km of this journey with only a railway map, and of course by constantly asking the way. The first thing we learnt to say was "*Yuku michi ...?* Where is the road to ...?" So it was yuku michi here and yuku michi there all day long, and of course we often got lost.

Unfortunately, the names the Japanese see fit to bestow on their towns and villages are ferocious tongue-twisters. For example:

Mimasakaowake
Chugokukatsuyama
Bingotokamachi
Higashikakatsu

The smaller the place, the grander the name. On to this assemblage we then had to tack 'yuku michi.' We were rarely given wrong directions, although the road often turned out to be a cul-de-sac because it had subsided or been buried in mud.

Once, a friendly lorry driver offered to show us the way to the next town by driving ahead of us at a suitable distance (so we shouldn't have to breathe in all his dust) and waiting for us at each crossroads. This was really the height of generosity, and we gratefully accepted his offer.

For a while this worked splendidly, and then suddenly the lorry disappeared. Half the road ahead of us had slipped away! We braked sharply and leapt out of the car. In a paddy field, five metres below the level of the road, the lorry lay on its back and we could just see one of its front wheels still turning in the air. As it finally came to rest, a window was smashed and our kind lorry driver crawled out of the front seat. He lay face down in the paddy field, carefully extricating his feet through the splintered window. We hurried down to him, but he was already standing, up to his calves in the squelching mud. Then his co-driver emerged on all fours. They were both unscathed. They exchanged glances and then burst out laughing. Their facial expressions were unforgettable. Relieved, they climbed back up on to the road and surveyed the disaster. They examined the landslip and, as one could read from their faces, established that the back wheel had caused the verge to cave in and the lorry had then tipped over and gone down the slope. It was simple ... Nothing to get excited about. Then they tried to explain to us how to find our way, now that they could no longer help us.

Knowing how to stay calm was also a good thing on city streets, less so in the daytime, when the sight of tramlines that were not embedded in the ground was merely a bit alarming. We often pitied the poor cyclists who had to ride them like a sort of obstacle course, but it was the nights that really strained the nerves of a European motorist. Even great cities of three million inhabitants like Osaka with its elegant residential quarters would take on the aspect of a medieval settlement. There was no street lighting at night, not even in Kobe or Tokyo. The only light to reach the street came from the shop windows of department stores, and from tiny lanterns along the pavements. It was almost like driving blind. On the other hand, all cars without exception had their headlights on full. Anyone knows that the effect of this is to dazzle and make it harder to pick out pedestrians. Either Japanese drivers had got used to these conditions, or perhaps their narrow eyes gave better protection against the harsh glare.

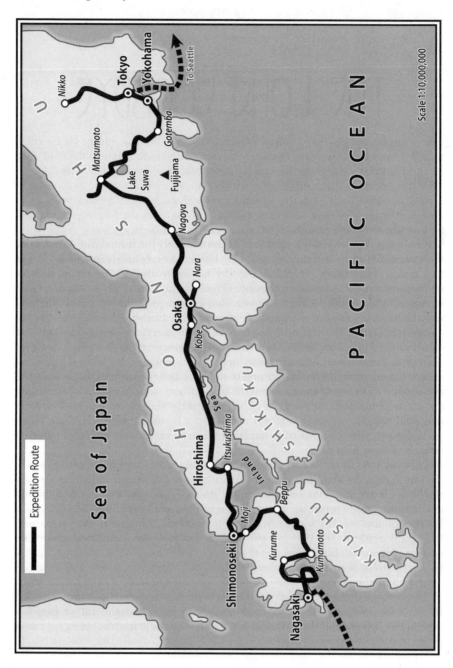

Map 7: Through Japan.

32
THE LONG GOODBYE

Our first experience of mountains in Japan was Aso-san, in some respects the largest active volcano on earth. It could be reached from the town of Kumamoto on Kyushu Island by a road that we were obliged to take in second or even first gear, since it bore more resemblance to the bed of a stream. The mountain was approached through a wild rocky ravine with roaring waters tumbling down on our left and the glittering track of the railway line on the right. Massive pipes from two power stations nearly made us forget we were in Asia. High-tension wires on pylons crossed the valley. Only the little houses with their pretty doors and windows and deep thatched roofs, clinging bravely to the steep slopes, reminded us where we were.

The way closed in on us as the little Steyr climbed higher and higher. Ahead of us and to either side, there was nothing but rock. The bends in the road continued. Then suddenly we broke through into the open. There were blue sky, clouds, smoke and green countryside. From the dark and dismal gorge we had emerged straight into paradise.

There was a wide circle of mountains enclosing an enormous caldera, the largest crater in the world, with a circumference of 61km. In the centre was the magnificent spectacle of the eternal fire of Aso-san with clouds of smoke spewing out of the mountain. All around it, the cooled material ejected from the volcano had evolved into highly fertile soil. Golden fields rippled in the light wind, cows grazed in lush meadows and in the orchards, trees bent low under their heavy crop. The last great eruption of this volcano had been in 1904, but sixty thousand people had since returned to settle in the crater, hard-working farmers who never knew one day whether they would still be alive the next.

We crossed the flourishing farmland of the outer crater and soon found ourselves at the foot of the central massif consisting of five volcanoes, of which Nakadake was the only one presently active. There was a turning to this holy mountain in the village of Uchinomachi. It was a private road and well worth the toll we paid for its width and good condition. We covered a difference in altitude of eight hundred metres in an hour on splendid zig-zags and came to a stop outside the modern hotel, twenty minutes below the mountain top. Dozens of motor buses were parked around the place, with a corresponding number of tourists crowding around the souvenir stalls, which were selling exactly the same sort of rubbish as back home. Only the tradition of walking stick badges was missing, but they had another custom instead.

Every Japanese carried around a little book which looked rather like a mouth-organ made of absorbent paper. At tourist destinations you could have it stamped with a jolly little coloured print, for example 'Souvenir of Aso-san' in Japanese characters. Autographs seemed to be very popular too, because people were holding out their books to us and we wrote in them, "Von Österreich zum Aso-san." Nobody could read it, but they all loved it.

We trooped up to the summit with everybody and strolled the 3km around the open crater. The inner sides fell almost vertically into the crater mouth from which white smoke billowed. Aso-san is one of those famous volcanoes into which lovers threw themselves, locked in a tight embrace and dressed in wedding kimonos, if for some reason they were prevented from marrying.

The next mountain we wanted to climb was Fujiyama, the emblem of Japan, but we were still hundreds of kilometres away from its beautiful snow-covered peak. First we crossed the island of Kyushu on a switchback road through delightful countryside, which was constantly changing. We bathed in the hot sulphur springs of Beppu which every year bring two million visitors to the 200 hotels of the resort. We intended to cross from Moji to the main island of Hondo, but long before we reached the town, we packed away all our photographic and ciné equipment, since we were approaching another of those strategic zones where photography was a serious crime. In Moji we drove straight to the police station, which is the wisest thing to do as a foreign motorist in Japan. We knew that we were expected. News of our arrival had been signalled from Beppu – this was done ostensibly to 'help with our journey' – and then, as in all other cases, we had expressed our gratitude by bowing deeply many times. We provided the Moji police with the necessary information, replying to all their questions, although they must have known most of the answers already. Then a policeman accompanied us to the ferry along the famous Shimonoseki road.

We had scarcely stepped ashore in Shimonoseki when another friendly gentleman greeted us. It was no surprise. This time it was the gendarmerie who put us through the mill.

Only a greenhorn would count on getting through by pointing out that the harbour police already had all the information. We tried it, but we were immediately informed that whatever the harbour police knew was not nearly enough to satisfy the gendarmerie. Furthermore, why should they be expected to fetch that information from their colleague at the harbour office? Hadn't the representative of the gendarmerie the right to hear it first hand for himself? We began to see the way of things. So began the fourth interrogation of the day. Here is a summary of this psychological torture:

1. Interrogation by the Moji gendarmerie.

2. Conversation concerning sport in Japan punctuated by numerous short questions in the office of the harbour police at Shimonoseki.

3. Nice chat with an interesting lady on board the ferry, starting with the privileged position of the Land of the Rising Sun in the general scheme of things and ending with my grandparents' dates of birth.

4. Discussion with a smiling gentleman of the gendarmerie in Shimonoseki on the subject of which hotel we intended to stay the night in. Further discourse

concerning the purpose of a journey by motor car in Japan, complemented by the completion of a four-page questionnaire.

Total duration, some five hours!

On 21st August, Helmuth wrote in his diary, "Mount Fuji lies before us in all its glory!" Out of the mist rose that sublime and timeless shape, with its softly sweeping outline. The summit was clear, whilst at a lower level the tops of the surrounding hills were veiled in delicate drifts of half-transparent mist. Beyond the peak lay the void and a flurry of clouds with the merest inkling of the sea. The summit was pale with a covering of fine ash which fluttered like a banner in the wind. Further down, the holy mountain darkened where the lava fields began, while its foot was ringed with sombre forests of evergreen.

We stood for a long time in silence, drinking in the beauty of this classic Japanese landscape. Then the mist thickened and rolled up the lava slopes until Mount Fuji was completely hidden. However, we had hopes that the mountain would show us more favour on the following day and we made an effort to reach the little town of Umangaeshi before nightfall, as this was the place from which people set out to climb the mountain. Such climbs have a purely religious significance for the Japanese, and Umangaeshi is a place of pilgrimage with many temples and temple guesthouses. Here was where the pilgrim expeditions began, and we wanted to share the experience. We had been advised to wear rubber shoes for the ascent, because these were more suitable for walking in the deep lava ash. Since we also needed a rucksack, we went into the nearest Japanese sports shop. The dear little sales girl spoke no English at all except for 'Yes' and 'No,' and we had no Japanese except for 'Please, thank you, which is the road to? ...' We exchanged silly jokes with her, and Helmuth remarked, by the way, "Little girl, do give me a rucksack, and some woolly socks and some shoes, my darling butterfly!" She gave us a charming smile like all Japanese girls, and said in her little piping voice, "Rucksacku, rucksacku, o yes, yes, yes." Imagine our astonishment when a rucksack was exactly what she brought us!

Our English-speaking landlord explained this remarkable phenomenon.

"As Austrians you are surely aware that your famous Hannes Schneider visited Japan and introduced skiing here. Before this, we in Japan did not ski or climb mountains, and consequently nearly all mountaineering terms have been taken from the German and slightly adapted to our language."

Thus a walking pole was a Bergstock, and an avalanche was a Lawine, and a ski-slope had the same name in Japanese. Only the word Langriemenbindung (long strap binding) gave rise to certain pronunciation problems. The Japanese must have tied themselves in the same sort of knots over it as we did with the word gaikokudschni, as applied to ourselves (it means 'foreigner').

The evening in the guest-house was spent, inevitably, crawling around on the floor. We had ourselves woken early next morning in order to make the best of the day. But alas, it was pouring with rain. The mountain had completely disappeared, but we were willing to wait a day longer. There was a young American in the hotel with whom we had intended to make the ascent, and now we were all of us staring out at the rain while he told us all about the States and gave us a few letters of introduction. In return, we wrote some letters to friends in China for Huycke, as this was where he was going next.

We were interrupted by one of the chamber maids, who knelt down and drew out a piece of paper all scribbled over with Japanese characters, from which she began to read. We couldn't believe our ears when what she read out from the paper was the following sentence in totally distorted German: "Director Kinugasa would be very pleased to greet his German friends if they would join him."

We followed her in amazement as she led us to another room in the guest-house. A Japanese rose as we entered and spoke to us in quite good German.

"I am the film director Kinugasa, and I am very pleased to meet you!"

We introduced ourselves likewise and sat down. Over a few dishes of green tea, all was explained. Mr Kinugasa had spent a year in Neu-Babelsberg where he had studied film-making and learned German. At the moment he was shooting an historical film in the Fuji area. There was a white paper doll hanging in the window of his room with a paper covered in Japanese characters pinned to it.

"What's this?" we asked.

"Oh," the Japanese laughed, "this is our weather god! The letters on the paper say 'Please send good weather for filming!'"

Mr Kinugasa showed us rushes he had taken and introduced his colleagues: Mr Matsushita his assistant, Mr Suhiyama the cameraman and Mr Kong the sound engineer.

Today the actors had returned early to Kyoto on account of the bad weather. It was a pity that we could not see a shoot.

"How will the weather be tomorrow?" we asked nervously.

Kinugasa cast a despairing glance at the doll on the window and shook his head gloomily. "A poor prospect," he admitted.

Suddenly he came to life and jumped up. "Would you like us to take a few photos of you in Japanese costume?"

Wouldn't we just! The director gave orders to bring a heavy suit of samurai armour and two squires' outfits. It took half an hour to get the armour to fit properly. It weighed on the shoulders like lead. It was almost impossible to move in it and one felt as helpless as a baby.

Kinugasa took all kinds of shots, grouping us next to the car in the courtyard of the guest-house. It was tremendous fun, especially for the spectators who had gathered. As for ourselves, we photographed all the groups around us and acquired a set of pictures such as few travellers to Japan manage to bring back with them.

Of course, members of the press soon turned up and they wanted to take pictures and have interviews too. We invited them to the saké party afterwards and everyone had a good time.

Next morning, the owner of the guest-house brought us the newspaper, the *Yokohama nichi nichi shimbun*. I rubbed my eyes – on the front page was a huge photograph of two samurai sitting on a Steyr! The article, which our host translated for us, was in a humorous vein, and included our various pronouncements in praise of Japan, recognition of our achievement on the journey, and ended by describing our appreciation of the Japanese rice wine saké. Apparently we were so fond of it that we always kept a bottle of it in the car next to the gear stick, and had thus made the discovery that saké should be kept warm when driving. This was without doubt the most hilarious article written about us during the whole of our round-the-world trip.

Unfortunately, the prospects for climbing Fujiyama were no better than on the previous day, so we decided to return to Yokohama.

From here to Tokyo with its five million inhabitants was a distance of 30km on which not a single green spot was to be seen. It was just a mass of houses and factories. Three high-speed electric railways linked Yokohama and Tokyo, and it already seemed probable that in the future the two cities would merge and together form the largest city on earth. The traffic was incredibly dense. Motor vehicles drove in four lanes on a newly-built road, which was already proving much too narrow. The traffic was also much impeded by cyclists with trailers or sidecars.

We thought it better to use the railway for a short excursion, and found that travelling on a Japanese train was most entertaining. Children were the main attraction, as they were allowed complete freedom. Adults gave up seats for them, mothers breast-fed their babies without inhibition. Men took off their kimonos and sat there in their underpants, and this gave offence to no one. An army officer calmly divested himself of his uniform and put on a kimono, with no embarrassment to himself or other passengers. At the stations all sorts of food for the journey was on sale, hygienically packed. Wood chip boxes held sweet rice, fish, candied fruits, confectionery, chopsticks and two toothpicks. The whole packet cost just a few sen. When you had eaten the contents, you got rid of the box through a trapdoor in the floor. Every compartment had one. Even babies were held out over the trap. For ten sen you could also buy tea at every station, in a rather stylish and dainty little pot with an equally delightful cup to match. Only ten sen! Both objects were far too pretty to even think of throwing them away as the other passengers did.

In Yokohama, there was a stack of paperwork to be got over before we could be on our way to the United States, but on September 5th 1936 we saw the car safely on board the President Jefferson, and at twenty minutes to midnight we boarded too.

When we had set foot in Asia the previous year in Palestine, we had hoped to cover the ground in about nine months. Many obstacles had cropped up along the way which had slowed our progress. Nevertheless, some of it had been more successful than we had dared hope: the first part of the journey to India, most of which I knew already from the motorcycle trip, went quickly and according to schedule. We covered the 13,000km to Calcutta in only four months.

Then came new territory, not only for me, but for any sort of powered vehicle. The challenge this represented can be told from the time it took : the next 5000km took us six months, but we did complete the first ever crossing of Southeast Asia by car. In China our progress was just as slow, with three months needed for the 5000km journey from Hanoi to Shanghai. In Japan it was quite another story, where we did 2700km in three weeks.

Now our ship was edging its way out of the harbour, bound for America.

There is a Japanese proverb that says, 'If you see Fujiyama as you leave Japan, you will return one day.' We stayed on deck for hours, hoping for one last glimpse of Mount Fuji, even its silhouette, but it never deigned to appear.

The last lights of the Japanese coastline sank in the west, and the wake of the ship showed as a green ribbon of phosphorescence.

We were leaving Asia behind.

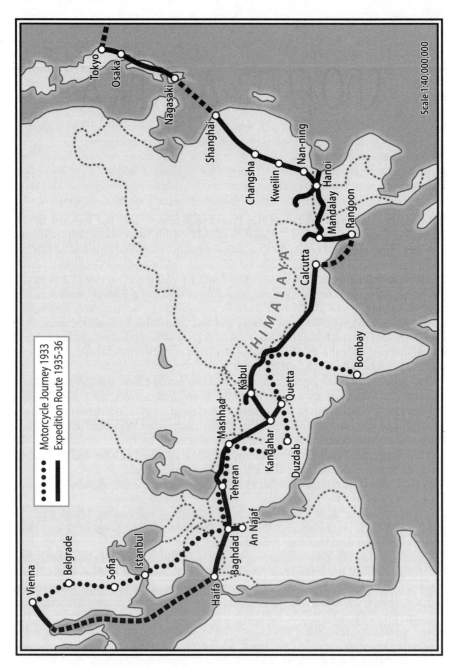

Map 8: General view of the Asian journey, comprising 25,700km from Haifa to Tokyo.

33

CROSSING AMERICA

Every day the clock on board the President Jefferson was put forward by 42 minutes, so that we went through September 10th twice, once as a perfectly ordinary Thursday and once when we crossed the international date line at 180° as an interpolated 'meridian day.' This day was much celebrated as a God-given bonus for those travelling from west to east. But could we really add an extra 24 hours to our lives? Alas no! When we set out round the world in an easterly direction, we were losing minutes or maybe only seconds with every day we travelled, depending on our rate of progress. Between Vienna and Yokohama this had already amounted to eight hours, to which another sixteen would have to be added to account for our return journey, over the Pacific, crossing America and then the Atlantic. This time was made up by the meridian day.

The daily ship's newspaper explained all about it and I kept the 'Meridian Day, September 10th' issue as a souvenir. The *Daily Jeffersonian*, as it called itself, published a profuse array of news items culled from wireless transmissions, which seemed to be of absorbing interest to the American reader. We would scarcely have clogged the air-waves back home with bits of news such as:

"Cincinnati: Mr Frank Houston claims that his goose died of a broken heart after losing its favorite playmate, the dog Phipps, in a road accident."

News flashes of similar world-shattering import were to be found every day in the *Daily Jeffersonian*. One report in particular attracted our attention:

"Vienna, Austria: Karl Lutz, husband of the sports personality Maria Lutz, is seeking a divorce on the grounds that he is obliged to do the housework and look after the children while his wife plays football."

There was only one German among the 300 passengers, a planter from Java with his Dutch wife. All the others were American and British, not forgetting Reverend Schlosser, the missionary. Although he spoke no German, he laid great stress on his German ancestry, and explained to everyone that his surname derived from Schloss, the word for castle, which must indicate his descent from the landed aristocracy. He was very proud of this. Since a Schlosser is a locksmith, we thought we would leave it to Saint Peter to enlighten the good missionary when he arrived at the pearly gates, but it would be a mean trick if he set him to grinding the keys of the kingdom!

The first thing we saw as we docked in Seattle on America's west coast on September 16th 1936 was a huge signboard on the quay, which read, "This is the biggest dock in the world!" There could be no doubt, if we ever had any, that this was America! Car and luggage soon got through customs, with only the Japanese oranges giving cause for concern. You were not allowed to bring any fruit into the United States for fear of introducing plant pests. Then it took only three minutes, without any formalities, to provide us with an American driving licence. Filling out the American questionnaire was more difficult and proved to be an exact science. One had to declare whether one was an atheist, a bigamist or had some other abnormal tendency; whether one was in possession of money, where and how much; what one was now, what one had been, what one intended to do in America; whether one had relatives in the States; which childhood diseases one had had – the details continued one after another and the question sheet was well over a metre long, resembling a small banner!

But, at last, that too was completed. Scarcely were we out on the street when we were surrounded by a swarm of reporters and photographers. We were snapped from every angle and interviewed with great thoroughness. In the hotel that evening we ran into a fellow traveller, a young American student who had been visiting relatives in Japan. His collection of Japanese fabrics and curiosities had excited our admiration while on board ship. It must have been worth several hundred dollars and we had secretly envied the affluence that had allowed him to make such lavish purchases. Now he confessed quite openly that he had only eight dollars left in the world to get him home. We asked where he lived. "In Latrobe, out Pittsburg way," was the answer. I should explain that it's as far from Seattle to Pittsburg as it is from Vienna to Afghanistan.

"With eight dollars?" we exclaimed in disbelief.

"Yes!" he replied. He was going to hitch-hike. Free transportation by this means was quite usual in America. Either you rode on a freight train (and most of the rail companies seemed to raise no objection to this) or you stopped vehicles on the roadside. It was a sport usually indulged in by students on the way to a football match, or by people looking for work. We asked Charlie Keener whether he'd like to go with us to California.

"Okay!" he said, and so the next morning the three of us set off towards Mount Rainier. We drove south through dense pine forests. After a year and a half in Asia, I can't tell you how wonderful it felt to be gliding with no apparent effort along macadamized roads. We were close to Canada, and although it was only autumn, we could tell that the winter must be bitterly cold. There seemed to be a lot of fog too, because the kerbstones, the barriers and the line down the centre of the road were painted yellow, a colour which shows up best in those conditions. Along the road we saw little boxes on poles, each with a name attached. These were the mailboxes of farmers who lived either side of the main road. When we looked more closely, we were intrigued to see that the boxes were all different shapes, cobbled together out of tin in a primitive way, and had no locks! Nobody would touch another person's mail. We also found stray milk cans and sacks of corn on the roadside, with nothing but a label to identify them.

We revelled in the glorious cool air of the forest and wherever the trees cleared we had glimpses of the snowy peak of Mount Rainier. We came to a halt at a heavy wooden gateway with a sign reading "Mt Rainier National Park" – some park! It extended over 250km². A friendly official took our one dollar entrance fee and provided us with a brochure all about the mountain which had apparently been worshipped as a god when Indians still dwelt in its ravines. We were now climbing steadily up the Paradise Valley to 1800 metres, having left the ocean at Seattle that very morning. The mighty volcano, extinct since ancient times, seemed to grow more and more majestic. It was 4800 metres high.

Now we were passing by glaciers and there was new-fallen snow melting under the wheels of the car.

Here is the history of Mount Rainier according to the brochure:

1782 First sighting of the mountain by a white man
1833 Dr William Fraser Tolmie reached the foot of the mountain after fighting the Indians
1870 The mountain was climbed for the first time by Lieutenant Kautz, the son of German immigrants
1905 Building of the Paradise Valley road
1916 Permission given for women to drive automobiles along the road

It was already getting dark as we came to the end of the road. Here on the breezy heights a camp had been established, one of the thirty thousand overnight stopping places in the USA created especially for motorists. For a dollar twenty we were allocated a hut where we could set ourselves up any way we liked, with no restrictions. You simply had to bring your own bedding. In the 'cabin,' as these huts are called, we found a bath, running water (from the mountain), a stove, firewood, and in the grocery store we could buy what we needed for supper. In America you do not have to be an expert in order to cook for yourself. Everything came ready-made in tin cans and was heated up in a few minutes. The following afternoon, however, we invented a process that saved us the trouble of heating. On leaving Mount Rainier Park, we secured two cans of beans-and-bacon under the bonnet with wire to the exhaust manifold and after driving for a couple of hours, we had a hot meal ready.

On the road people would call out, "Hallo, what's that?" And quite a few would laugh at our 'home-made body.' Policemen, roaring up in front of us on their heavy 'Indian' motorcycles, would stop us and ask "Hello, where do you come from? What a funny car! You came all over Asia? Wait a minute and have a cigarette!" We smoked many a friendly cigarette with policemen on our way through the United States.

Even American superlatives aren't sufficient to describe the sequoia forests through which we had now been driving for several hours. It is simply impossible to comprehend the size, age and splendour of these gigantic trees. The 'Father of the Forest' has a circumference at the base of its trunk of thirty-five metres. It is one hundred and forty four metres tall and its smallest inner growth ring dates from the time of the Great Pyramid of Cheops. In between the columns of tree trunks you would think you were in some enormous cathedral rather than a forest. In the camp where we spent the night, one group of people had brought along a record player. Bach's organ music swelled and echoed through the mighty forest, and then the trunks really seemed to close in, forming the aisles of a vast natural church. We sat in silence around the fire, amidst all that solemnity and beauty.

The sequoia forests are of inestimable value, and the state of Oregon reserves the severest penalties for lack of care concerning fire. A driver throwing down a cigarette end has often found that it burned a hole in his wallet. Pretty lady drivers are reduced to tears, with no quarter given to the fair sex. Our friend Charlie was keen to explain. "Oh yes, we have to obey the rules here. Of course, forest fires still do happen, quite often actually," and he suddenly pulled over and began to sniff the air. We had noticed the smell of smoke too, but we had to drive quite a few kilometres further before we established that it really was a forest fire. The focus must have been some distance off, but Charlie was apologetic, saying this would mean we'd be hard at work for the next few days.

"How's that?" we asked

"It's the law in many states that if there's a forest fire, everybody has to help."

We came gradually closer. Now we could see cars queuing on the road ahead, and Charlie ducked down between us in the middle of the car and said, "I don't speak English!"

We got his message. To our left we could see the forest in flames, with columns of smoke rising skywards. There was only a narrow lane ahead between the parked cars but we worked our way carefully through it. When a forest official signalled us to stop, we reacted by asking in broken English, "Which is the way to New York?"

The man was taken aback. He looked first at us and then at the vehicle which was so strange to American eyes. Then he barked an order, "Get on there! Don't block the road!" We were delighted, because we had done quite enough shovelling in the jungles and deserts of Asia.

So, to the border with California. Even though USA stands for United States of America, crossing the borders is not always as simple as you would imagine. Sometimes, you are completely unaware of the change from one state to another, but another time you might be subject to a very stiff inspection. Here, as in Seattle, it was merely a check to see whether we were bringing any forbidden potatoes, seeds or fruits into California. Thanks to these very strict measures, the rich fruit-growing country had thus far succeeded in remaining free of citrus canker disease, which had wrought havoc with fruit crops in other parts of America. They had likewise avoided the boll weevil, an insect that threatens the cotton plant.

The officials were courteous in the extreme, and explained most politely the reasons for the whole procedure, after which we were cleared of suspicion regarding potato worms, seed worms, lemon worms etc. and sent on our way. Soon we were speeding towards San Francisco, where we hoped to find the first news from home since reaching America. The letters were waiting for us at the consulate, as well as the necessary funds with which to continue our journey. We took leave of Charlie who was hoping to get home more quickly by hitch-hiking, and after only a few hours stop we were on our way once more, heading for Yosemite National Park. It wasn't just the natural beauty we were out to see. We were keen to follow up the rumour that the Austrian ski racer Schroll was staying there. When we asked the official at the entrance to the park, he said,

"You mean Hannes? Sure, I'll just put a call through to him!" He rang up the Yosemite Hotel, and we hadn't long to wait before a car came roaring up and out leapt Hannes, giving a joyful yodel.

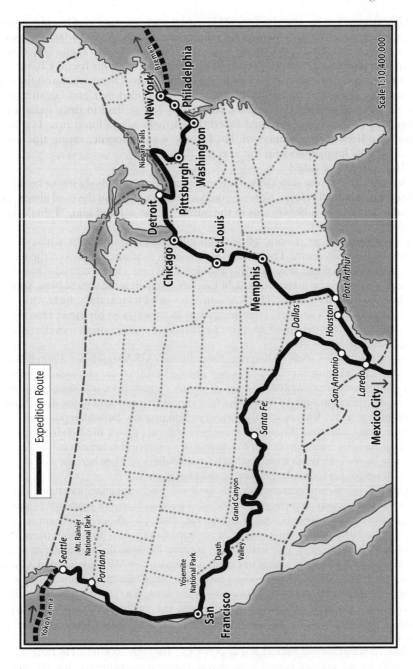

Map 9: Our crossing of North America, with the ill-fated excursion into Mexico.

"Get in your jalopy, and follow me!" cried Hannes and we soon realised that he was far and away the most popular man in Yosemite National Park. He seemed to be leading an enviable existence there as a ski instructor in winter and a sport and tennis coach in summer, with all the Hollywood film actors (and better still, actresses) for his pupils. They loved him. He had the knack of communicating his natural enthusiasm in English and always made an unforgettable impression. For his skiing lessons he had invented a series of intriguing new words, which had the Americans in stitches. In referring to the rear end of the human body, Hannes would use the German euphemism 'Apparat' (thingummyjig) with English pronunciation. The film divas from Hollywood would laugh themselves silly when Hannes instructed them on the proper position for the 'apparate' when skiing.

"Now look here," he said, appealing to us in his Austrian brogue, "why don't you stay on in America? I'll take you on as assistant ski pros. You can drive, eh? You can sing and yodel too, enough to turn the heads of all the screen goddesses." (He called them 'film divans.') "What more do you need? You'll earn enough to put something by, and if you don't like it after all, you can go home with a fistful of dollars!"

It was a tempting proposition, but the homeward urge was strong, quite apart from having to bring back the expedition car.

So we left Hannes to manage by himself, flirting and joking with Hollywood beauties, designing the ski huts and resort hotels, which were all being built according to his designs and specifications. He was a really capable type, with a lot more to him than just yodelling. He took us in his beautiful automobile to see all the glorious views in which Yosemite abounds, and then we drove on in our own car over the Sierra Nevada.

There was an extraordinary change of climate when we reached Route 395 and turned south on it. We entered a zone which was markedly desert-like in character, and with a hot, dry climate. It became so uncomfortably hot that we were forcibly reminded of Persia. The area became more and more deserted with only occasional clumps of organ pipe cactus and the ruins of what had once been the dwellings of gold prospectors. Instead of gold, the inhabitants found only worthless rock seams. We were nearing Death Valley. When, after a descent of 2000 metres from the glory of Yosemite, you arrive in this valley, far below sea-level, bare of vegetation and baking in the sun, it seems to live up to its name. Lack of water in the valley of death did indeed claim the lives of many pioneers who migrated to California during the gold rush. Today the valley has lost its terrors, but the heat is every bit as intolerable. Even so, colours in the landscape give it a vivid, exotic beauty. The mountains are yellow, brown, red and purple. The valley between them is filled with sand-dunes, fields of salt that glitter in the sun like ice, craters with soda and borax springs appearing in their depths, the edges also shimmering like ice. Through the middle of this totally barren landscape the grey ribbon of the road runs in a dead straight line. Deathly silence reigns, with scarcely a breath of wind. The heat is stifling. To the south is the so-called Devil's Golf Course, a salt field extending over many kilometres, and containing a spring with the name 'Bad Water.'

We took a day to drive through Death Valley. Four days later we experienced the deepest and most abiding impression that the natural world in America has to offer. We stood on the southern slope, the 'rim' as they say, of the Grand Canyon. We had heard about its incomparable beauty when we were still in school. Hundreds of writers have attempted to describe it, and I do not intend to join their ranks. I was struck dumb, and so I still am, whenever the Grand Canyon comes to mind.

Above: One of the USA's thousands of tourist camps. For a dollar a night you could occupy one of these comfortable little huts.

Right: 'El Capitan' in the Yosemite National Park. Hannes Schroll, the Austrian ski-pro and climber, whose eccentricities made him a favourite in the park for many years, was filmed climbing it on several occasions.

Above: Indian reservations are announced by roadside signs.

Above: Giant sequoias. These swamp cypresses grow to over a hundred metres and can be several thousand years old.

Below: Wares on offer to American tourists in the numerous tourist shops: Indian craftwork, including rugs and pottery – sometimes very artistic – and primitive agricultural machinery from past centuries.

The famous Greyhound buses are double-deckers, comfortably fitted out with washroom, WC and reclining seats. They provide speedy transport all over the continent, and are cheaper than the railways.

Descending into the Death Valley depression.

Above: Gas station in New Mexico in the shape of an Indian tepee. We were happy to trust the world-wide Shell brand, since it had already organised petrol dumps for us throughout China.

Below: Death Valley, hottest spot in the USA. Engines get thirstier here too.

Above: Ancient steam traction engine with trailers, seen at the potash works on the edge of Death Valley. Having such a short history, the Americans have preserved a lot of the sort of stuff that we left to fall apart.

Below: In Salzburg, the car collided with a foreigner driving on the wrong side of the road. The damage was soon repaired, and the Steyr is still roadworthy to this day. It is registered as a historic vehicle, and its licence is regularly updated.

Poster advertising an evening lecture by Max Reisch on the Asia Expedition. Before the advent of television, these lectures were always sold out. The entrance fee of 50 groschen represents less than five eurocents – those were the days!

Max Reisch was one of the first collectors of veteran vehicles in Austria. He preserved all the cars and motor cycles from his travels and expeditions. These can be viewed as part of the Max Reisch Collection by anyone who is interested. (These photographs of the expedition vehicles were taken by the Innsbruck photographer Gerda Eichholzer)

Right: 1930 Puch 175, known as the 'Stilfser-Joch Puch,' which Reisch used for his early long-distance trips. On one of these, he crossed 12 Alpine passes.

Below: 1931 Puch 175, the 'Gardasee-Puch,' was taken around north Italy when Reisch was compiling a travel guide to the Lake Garda region.

Above: 1932 Puch 250, the 'Sahara Puch.' Reisch rode this through the northern Sahara. His account covers Spain, Morocco, Algeria, Tunisia, Libya and Italy.

Left: 1933 Puch 250, the 'India Puch,' the first motorcycle to reach India by the overland route. This feat gave a decisive impulse to the development of road transport in Asia. (See *India – The Shimmering Dream*, Panther Publishing Ltd 2010. ISBN978-0-9556595-9-1)

Above: The 1935 Steyr 100, known as the 'Asien-Steyr,' the first motor car to traverse Southeast Asia and China as described in this book.

Above: 1952 Jenbacher GUTBROD Atlas 800, 'Sadigi.' Europe's first camping car, taken to the Arctic Circle (1951), and on desert trips to Saudi Arabia (1952) and north Africa (1953).

Above: 1956 OPEL Olympia 'Moses.' Trips to the three deserts of Egypt and the Sinai Peninsula (1956), and an expedition to Afghanistan (1958).

34

THE COLLECTOR

We hurried on, driving day and night, gripped by the American tempo. As we went, we frequently encountered the Greyhound Line buses. They were outsize vehicles which could cross the continent at high speed in a few days. They did not offer such a comfortable ride as the railway, but they were far cheaper, and you could enjoy all the magic of the American landscape and the romance of the road. The old mail coach man had become the modern bus driver, enthroned in his cabin over the first deck, far above the rest of the traffic, a sort of captain of the highways. The sound of his horn was much feared. It was loud and had several notes, forcing all other drivers to get out of the way as fast as they could. The Greyhound would plough a furrow through the traffic and overtake ruthlessly, which was unavoidable if one wanted to cover the distance from Los Angeles to Chicago in 36 hours. We too would pull over on to the roadside as fast as possible when we heard the blast of the horn, and almost in the same moment the streamlined double-decker car in its blue and grey livery would go sweeping by. It was recognisable at night, too, by its special array of lights. It had four headlamps in front and two green sidelights on top, with an illuminated panel between them showing the destination. There were green lights on the sides too, with some red lights at the back, also a sign operated from the driver's seat which would light up with the words 'Wait' or 'Ahead' to tell cars coming up behind whether the way was clear or not.

Once in the night, I can't now remember where, the road had become very bad – which was unusual, but maybe it was storm damage. We didn't have much trouble getting through on our high wheelbase, but then we came upon a Greyhound stuck fast in a rut, with passengers and driver standing around wondering what to do. This gave us the opportunity to get a closer look at the vehicle. It was a bus with sleeping compartments, with the words 'Nite Coach' on it. The beds were built one above the other and the upper ones could be folded back. There was a small wash-room for the passengers and of course a lavatory. There was a special compartment where the luggage was stowed.

Once we also saw a bus station. One of the overland buses was just pulling in, and a swarm of coloured men leapt into action, one with a fuel line to fill the tanks, another with a hose to put water in the radiator, a third with an air line to pump up the tyres. Two mechanics opened the bonnet to check something over, and various personnel got vacuum cleaners and cleaned out the sleeping compartments. Yet more of them washed the windows and scrubbed down the chassis. Meanwhile the driver sat in the bar having his meal and drinking a bottle of Coca-Cola. The stop lasted 20 minutes, by which time everything was done and the bus went on its way into the night.

It was daytime when we came to Santa Fe and the Indian reservations of the Navajos and the Apaches. The remnants of these proud tribes are sad to see – a few fat old women selling primitive pots at the roadside, and a few young Apache men in boiler suits at a petrol pump, and that was all.

The Rocky Mountain landscape was clothed in winter white, stretching out peacefully before us into the far distance, and overhung with heavy snow clouds of inky blue. We were still completely absorbed in the contrast this view presented, when we noticed something come out and scuttle across the road. The car gave a slight lurch, and a skunk perished beneath our wheels. Holding our noses, we cut off his splendid tail and tied it on to the back of the car. When we looked round, we could see it fluttering in the wind like a flag.

In Raton, New Mexico, we stopped to fill up with fuel, intending to drive on northeast up to Chicago via Denver. However, when we got into conversation with the pump attendant, he thought it would be far more interesting to stay on the road to Texas and go as far as Dallas, where a great exhibition was taking place.

For Texas and its capital Dallas it was the 100th anniversary of their breakaway from Mexico, and this event was being celebrated with the 'Centennial Exposition.' The manager, Mr Olmstedt, gave us a free entry pass to everything in the form of press cards, with the simple request that we would allow our car to be exhibited. He thought it would be a special attraction for visitors.

So for the full duration of our stay in Dallas, our car became one of the exhibits, with the loudspeakers regularly advertising the first automobile to drive across Asia, to be viewed in Pavilion 16 on Avenue 8. "And the two Asia Expedition pioneer drivers are at present in the Old Texas Restaurant!" How on earth the announcer knew this, we could not imagine. There were always lots of autograph hunters at our heels, and we found this quite amusing, because we didn't feel we were famous, nor were we sufficiently Americanised to behave like stars. Instead, we were deeply impressed by the exhibition that a small place like Dallas had been able to mount.

Among the hundreds of people we talked to, there was a pleasant old gentleman, one Mr Norman.

"Well, boys, this is a right shaky old heap you've got here. What do you say to finding yourselves a nice new eight-cylinder model at the Exposition? It shall be yours and you can take it back to Austria, if you just give me your old vehicle in exchange."

"???"

"Why, yes! Just think how amazed your friends will be!"

"But we can't!"

"Why not? Here in the USA you can do anything!"

"But what do you want to do with our dear old Steyr?"

"Nothing. I collect automobiles the way you people in Europe collect stamps. Lots of people here collect cars. Old cars from the turn of the century, cars that heads of state have ridden in, successful racing cars and even funny little cars like yours!"

We both scratched ourselves behind the ear and said nothing. Eventually Helmuth heaved a deep sigh. Mr Norman turned to him and said, "Very well, my young friend, you too shall have a car."

I was on the point of saying something, but the automobile fanatic was not taking no for an answer.

"Come now, we'll go right over to the Dodge Palace, the Chevrolet Palace, the Chrysler Palace, wherever you like, and pick you out two brand new cars."

This was certainly a tempting offer, but alas ... At last I managed to get a word in edgeways.

"The car has to return to Europe. I have a contract with the Steyr Works."

"That's no matter, I'll cable them and get it all fixed up."

"You can try, but I can tell you right now, it'll be no use."

"Why not? With a cable from Harry Norman?"

"You'll have to approach the Technical Museum in Vienna. That's where the car is due to be exhibited."

"Ow, dammit! I can never get anything out of museums, it's a waste of a telegram! These museum directors never let you have a thing, I know that from experience. Well, boys, good luck on your journey back to the museum with the old heap. Goodbye!"

35

MEXICO TO SALZBURG: DISASTER STRIKES!

The beautiful weather in Dallas inspired us to new feats. Lots of people had recommended that we go to Mexico, following the Pan-American Highway down to Mexico City.

In spite of the Mexican visas we had acquired in Dallas, there was some confusion at the border, including the approval for our re-entry to the USA, which of course we were going to need. We therefore spent the night at a very nice auto camp where we met 'Mister Jo,' the owner of 'Jo's Money Exchange.' He had emigrated from Vienna 14 years before, and was now running an exchange booth. We spent an evening together that was both pleasant and interesting.

Next day, the problems with the border were all resolved and we made our getaway. Four kilometres outside Nuevo Laredo we negotiated two enormous horse-shoe bends, and after that the road lay ahead of us, shimmering in the hot Mexican sun, looking as if it ran dead straight to infinity. After 10km a customs official stopped the car, just to double-check our papers. The man seemed quite civilised, but he had scarcely completed the check when he said, "Give me a cigarette!" We had already heard this ritual expression in the customs office in Nuevo Laredo. Everyone asked for cigarettes – it seemed to be the done thing here. After another 10km, there was another customs check. "All in order. A couple of cigarettes, please!"

We had now come 45km in a straight line over the plain without a single bend. When the road curved slightly for the first time at 61km, we realised that this was probably the longest straight stretch in the world. Surely there would be a notice-board somewhere, confirming it as a record?

But there wasn't, because we were no longer in the United States!

It was strange country we were in: a sort of prairie with thorn bushes, cactus plants as tall as trees, yellow earth, with the straight asphalt road running through it and the burning blue sky above. The villages were tumbledown and dirty, the people were poorly dressed and the children terribly neglected, in stark contrast to the USA. Towards evening by the light of the headlamps everything took on a ghostly look. A feeling of uncertainty had begun to dog us. There was no particular reason for it and we couldn't say why, but it was always there. We drove on late into the night, and at last found a suitable place to camp, setting up our beds between tall cactus. All around it was pitch-dark with not a glimmer of light, no houses and certainly no people for miles around. I began to make Helmuth quite nervous because I kept on saying, "I hope it will be all right." I couldn't understand what was making me so apprehensive and depressed. There was no water to be found near our camp site, so the next morning we packed up quickly, intending to go on until we could find somewhere to wash, and then relax over breakfast.

We were driving along as the day dawned when suddenly there was a bang that went right through us. It came from the back axle and sounded like cogwheels seizing up. "The differential!" shouted Helmuth, and I groaned, "I knew it! Mexico was a bad idea!"

It didn't take Helmuth long to get the screws undone and he soon came upon thick oil and the wreckage of the planetary gearbox. One thing was clear immediately – we would have to return to the States! We stood out on the road, stopped all the trucks and at last found one to tow us with a rope to the nearest town. It was a sad business. In Monterrey the whole expedition had to be loaded on to an articulated lorry (semitrailer). We rode all the way sitting in the car high up on the top of the truck and had plenty of time for bitter self-reproach. We had been given money to take us across the American continent from west to east. Had it also been part of our brief to venture into Central America? No. We had been trying to fit it in on the side, so to speak, and now the car was seriously damaged, we would be pinned down for weeks and the money might run out. To be honest, wasn't it youthful irresponsibility that had taken us to Mexico? We were even seriously considering sending a wire to Mr Norman. "Asia car ready for pick-up in Mexico. Send Buick eight-cylinder and value of second car in ready cash." After drafting this imaginary telegram between us, we cursed each other thoroughly for entertaining such a shabby idea, and after this we felt better.

The Mexican customs people looked surprised, deplored our bad luck, and stamped our passports.

On the American side another truck took over and towed us to the tourist camp. It had been a deliberate decision to bring the Steyr 450km back to the USA, because it was perfectly certain that nobody in Mexico would be able to help us, and our chances were better in the States. But was that really the case? Maybe in Chicago or some big city with modern workshops, but not in a godforsaken border town like Laredo. These were our thoughts, and we had just decided to put the car on a train to Houston when Jo, the Viennese moneychanger, came up with an idea.

"Why not go to Mr Blair? He's got a workshop at the end of the village. He'll help you." His tone was one of utter conviction. Full of doubts, we approached Mr Blair and showed him the broken differential cage. Then something happened which I will never forget as long as I live. Old Blair took us out on to the edge of the prairie which began just behind his shack. There, overgrown with grass, lay a scattered assortment of old engine parts. Mr Blair wandered about for a while amongst his treasures. At last he picked up a heavy lump of iron, pock-marked with rust – it was the shaft of an ancient steam traction engine – and said, "I'll make you a new differential cage from that!"

We said nothing but the look on our faces caused him to declare further, "You just wait! Old Blair's gonna show you he's worth more than all them motor factories put together!"

In four days the cage was ready. It would take a full knowledge of the complexity of a casing like that, holding four cogwheels on the inside and the crown wheel on its circumference, to appreciate the skill of that mechanic down on the Mexican border. The man deserves a place in engineering history, so let me record here and now that his differential never broke down. Later on, Steyr also began to make reliable differentials. Whether the crucial improvement was purely an invention of the Steyr works or whether Mr Blair's version played any part in it, we need not discuss here. As far as we were concerned, the old man was a technical genius, and we were back on the road!

The route we had chosen to take with the car after its overhaul was the one to bring us to Chicago by the shortest way. We knew that the landscape had nothing special to offer on the next stage, so we decided to drive by night as well as day in order to eat up the kilometres. We were way behind schedule because of the Mexican excursion, and it occurred to me that we might at the same time discover how long it was possible to stay at the wheel.

We set out on 21st October at eight in the morning from Rosenberg, a town in southern Texas, 40km from Houston. The only interruptions in the 12-hour journey until eight that night were stops for oil and petrol. At the same time we could eat fast food American-style, which was usually to be found at or near the gas station. We had to cross two rivers by ferry. For the night-time, we provided ourselves with plenty of fruit and cigarettes and made desperate attempts to keep a conversation going, which we managed until two o'clock in the morning. However, after sitting side by side in a car for a year and a half, each of you knows all about the other, and it gets harder and harder to find something to talk about. At three o'clock Helmuth nodded off, and the next three hours until daybreak were the hardest. I alternately smoked and ate oranges – the tricky business of peeling them while going along was the best way of keeping awake – or I would grip the steering wheel hard, change gear when it wasn't necessary, and try by every means possible to resist the overwhelming desire to sleep. Next day, the sun brought me back to life somewhat, but by eleven o'clock it was beating down (we were still some way south) and sleep threatened to overcome me once more. We decided to take a 15-minute midday break, and at two in the afternoon we arrived in Memphis and found the post office where we were expecting to pick up letters. That revived us too, but we set off again immediately, straight into a thunderstorm. Our windscreen wiper was broken, which in this instance was a good thing. The loss of vision meant I had to strain all my senses and also the heavy traffic kept me busy right into the night. Then fog came down, and I gave up. There was no point in tempting fate. If our great journey had come to a sudden end in America it would have been unbearable. We fell into bed at Chenoa auto camp, dog-tired. I had been at the wheel for 40 hours, during which time we had covered 2100km, representing an average speed of 52.4kph in a car that had already crossed Asia, with 26,000km to its credit over a period of 16 months.

In Detroit, at Ford's gigantic factory, the River Rouge Plant, we saw how cars are turned out like hot cakes, and we were introduced to American advertising psychology. True, we didn't get to meet Henry II, but otherwise they treated us as if we'd just gone round the world in a Ford. We were given princely accommodation, taken all round the factories, involved in conversations on motor car engineering and asked for opinions, nay even advice, on one thing and another. At dinners and suppers we always found ourselves at the centre of an attentive audience.

It was only a few days later that we realised that all this was not so much a personal honour, but a precisely designed programme for 'distinguished visitors' which had been trotted out a thousand times already. One was very cunningly and unobtrusively stuffed full of goodwill propaganda, so that afterwards one would sing the praises of Henry Ford in the most glowing terms.

Whatever the ulterior motives, we thoroughly enjoyed our days in Detroit. On a round-the-world trip for Steyr, in spite of being one of Ford's special guests (or maybe because of that), we had to admire these advertising psychologists. I believe that Chevrolet, Chrysler, Packard or any of them would have given us the same treatment. The few dozen dollars it cost them were well spent, in the sense of the American slogan, 'It's all in the name.'

So now we were in the eastern states, the industrial and cultural centre of God's Own Country, in Washington, seat of the government and of all foreign embassies.

The Austrian ambassador was not only a diplomat, he was a human being. He greeted us warmly without ceremony and admitted apologetically, "I've got to report to Vienna, to tell them when you'll be back."

They seemed to be getting up a reception committee back home. Well, it was the first time anyone had been right round the world by motor car. Other countries had tried it, but the Austrian Trans-Asia Expedition had closed the last gap in the land route with our pioneering journey through Southeast Asia and China. Dimly, we began to realise that we had achieved something special. After all, the ambassador had said so at a large press conference.

New York was big, beautiful and massive, but what interested us most was the harbour. It made us feel nearer to home, and a sort of happy anxiety took hold of us. Various ships were sailing in the next few days, but then the Bremen came in. That was our ship! Hundreds of people were busying themselves on our account. It was all out of our hands now. We were not travelling, so much as being transported. Telegrams were sent to Bremerhaven and the Deutsche Automobil-Club in Munich, with lots of telegrams to Vienna.

The Statue of Liberty glided past and the Bremen reached the open sea. I'd been through plenty of violent storms in much smaller ships, never stopped smiling and never lost my appetite, and yet here on this ocean giant, with a very slight swell, my chicken vol-au-vent was refusing to stay down. Something was not quite right.

The doctor made me look in the mirror. "See your yellow eyes, and yellow face? A clear case of acute jaundice."

So I was put on a strict diet, which was especially hard when the Bremen offered such a lavish menu. Helmuth proved what a true friend he was by finding that he couldn't enjoy the food without me. Our friendship had been sealed by all we had been through together and both of us, as friends at home soon realised, seemed to have aged by many years.

Europe came into sight through a December fog. The jaundice was forgotten. "Tanned by tropical suns," was how a journalist in Bremerhaven put it. We were taken to Bremen in a parade of cars from the Deutsche Automobil-Club, where there was a long evening reception and a short night. On we went to Munich, and another banquet of many courses at the Preysing Palace, headquarters of the ADAC. Getting through all that without disgracing myself (it wasn't jaundice, it was a 'leathery tan') was quite an achievement.

"Don't you like the food?" – "Of course, but after thousand-year eggs in China, European cooking takes some getting used to!"

A call was put through to Vienna, "In about eight hours time ..." Some preparations were certainly afoot. Perhaps a minister might come out to welcome us, and the newsreel would certainly be there.

We were nearly there, but as for our faithful Steyr which had been through so much, it had certainly earned its place of honour in the Technical Museum, that is, it would have earned it, but alas ...

Near Salzburg we crossed on to home ground, which meant we had to drive on the left. We had to keep a lookout, as this changeover between Germany and Austria had already been responsible for hundreds of accidents. We kept scrupulously to the left-hand side of the road. It would be too silly if anything happened now, after going 40,000km round the globe.

It was inconceivable!

A car came tearing round the bend. I swung further over to the left, but the other man, a foreigner, had a shock reaction and steered to the right. The idiot was on the wrong side!

Could I brake? Too late!

There was an almighty crash, splintering glass, blood ... and that was it!

Postscript

The accident as described here did not in fact take place until February 6th 1937, but Max Reisch chose to use it as a dramatic ending to the account of his travels.

– Reisch-Orient-Archiv

36

EPILOGUE: THE STORY CONTINUES

So, what happened to the famous motor car that had gone round the world and conquered Southeast Asia and China for the first time?

The car was completely repaired at the Steyr Works, but only spent a short time in the Technical Museum in Vienna. The factory exhibited it with great success at various trade fairs and exhibitions at home and abroad.

The outbreak of war in 1939 found the car back home on the Steyr premises in the Laxenburgerstraße in Vienna. Here, it managed to survive the first part of the war in spite of a few knocks, and then, as the Red Army advanced on Vienna, it was transferred to the factory at Steyr. Here it sustained some (thankfully very slight) damage from air raids, and was repaired in 1950.

Max Reisch brought his beloved expedition car back to the garage at his home in the Tyrol. In the 1980s it was still running successfully in all sorts of rallies. In its old age, the famous car was still a sensation at any event.

The vehicle is still kept in good order, taken on test runs and declared officially roadworthy every year, so that Max Reisch or his son Peter Reisch (Dipl.-Ing.) have it ready for the off whenever they want. Maybe for another trip round the world ...

Max Reisch, 1984

My father died in 1985, since which time I have continued to manage his legacy in the same spirit, together with my son, Peter A Reisch. The Asia Steyr, together with Max Reisch's other expedition vehicles, is the great attraction of the Reisch-Orient-Archiv, and is still kept in full running order.

We are always pleased to show the Max Reisch Collection to anyone who is interested. It contains many historic motor cycles and cars together with their equipment, Orientalia, films, photographs and travel memoirs.

The revised German edition of this book, with additional material from the Archive, was timed to coincide with the 100th anniversary of Max Reisch's birth.

Peter H Reisch, 2012

For more information about the author and the collection, visit www.maxreisch.at

APPENDIX

Notes on the Steyr Type 100 car used by Max Reisch on the expedition

Although forgotten today, the Austrian firm Steyr-Daimler-Puch AG once built cars with a worldwide reputation.

In the 1930s Steyr was an innovative manufacturer which grew stronger through mergers, although it was also hard hit by the worldwide economic depression. In 1934 the Austro-Daimler factory amalgamated with the Austrian company Puch (which produced bicycles, cars and motorcycles) to form the large-scale enterprise known as Steyr-Daimler-Puch AG.

Between the two world wars Austrian-built vehicles were able to enhance their international reputation, both on European race tracks and through the long-distance Austrian motor expeditions which attracted much attention in those days. Popular motor shows were used to gain recognition: in 1929 the legendary Steyr 'Austria' aroused much interest in France and at the International Motor Exhibition in the New Hall at Olympia, England. The designer of this prestigious model was no less a personage than Ferdinand Porsche.

Back in 1933, Steyr was not unknown in England: it had agents such as KMW Ltd in Tamworth, Staffordshire and AS Forsyth in London.

In the 1980s, Steyr-Daimler-Puch disappeared almost completely from the scene as different production divisions were sold off. Little Austria felt the impact of globalisation at an early stage. Puch motorcycle production was swallowed up by the Italian group Piaggio, road-trucks by MAN of Germany and buses by the Swedish Volvo Group. Today, Steyr and Puch as brands exist only as memories.

One car bearing the historic Steyr name is the Max Reisch expedition car, a Steyr 100. This particular vehicle has come unscathed through various upheavals, so that today it often the focus of attention as a unique contemporary example of Austrian motor production.

The Steyr 100 was introduced in 1934, a conspicuous feature being the so-called 'streamlining.' It was the first streamlined car to be mass-produced and was a great commercial success. Streamlining at that time was still something special on which many European and American designers were working. Streamlining diminishes wind resistance, thereby lowering fuel consumption as well as increasing speed. This was an important selling point, which the comparatively small Austrian car manufacturer was able to exploit.

At the same time, great American factories, such as Chrysler, were producing the revolutionary 'Airflow' shape. However, because of the conservative tastes of the American public, this never caught on. The Rover Company also followed this trend, but even so, between 1934 and 1936 it only built 380 examples of the 'Streamline Coupé,' while over the same period Steyr put 3000 of the Type 100 on the road.

The Austrian Steyr 100 design can be seen as a distinct success, since it combined modern streamlining with customers' traditional ideas of what a car should be.

Steyr-Daimler-Puch was always open to technical innovation, especially where this helped to reduce the weight of the vehicle. Particular mention should be made here of the thermo-siphon engine cooling system. In the Steyr 100 it was possible to do without the water pump that had previously been the norm. Hubert Schier writes as follows (*Die Steyrer Automobilgeschichte* – Ennsthaler Verlag 2015): "To avoid using a water pump, they went back to the principle of thermo-siphon cooling. This cooling system was highly favoured by British motorists at the time and was praised in specialist magazines for being exceptionally simple and technically advanced."

http://what-when-how.com/automobile/thermo-syphon-water-cooling-system-automobile/

Max Reisch refers to this in Chapter 3. He would have been glad to have a water pump nevertheless, since this version of thermo-siphon cooling only works well if a certain speed can be attained. This was impossible given the difficult road conditions and the heavy load the car was carrying. "The overloaded springs were groaning on the bumpy road … The radiator boiled and whistled."

However, Reisch had taken on the task of driving the car across Asia in order to prove the reliability of Austrian engineering, and the car did indeed survive this test of endurance.

Another technical innovation embraced by Steyr was the 'dynastarter.' Two separate components already being used in car construction were melded into a single unit: the starter motor and the current-producing dynamo were combined in a starter-generator, meaning that one component was responsible for both functions.

This innovation had welcome side effects: weight was saved, and less servicing was needed. It was first used in vehicle construction by the firm of Robert Bosch AG in 1933.

www.energie-lexikon.info/startergenerator.html

Max Reisch also describes the problems he had with the differential gearbox which broke down several times. However, it was later acknowledged that the car had the 'wrong' differential, which could not cope with the resistance of sand or thick mud. There was in fact also a 'short transmission' differential for the Steyr 100 which could take greater strain, but by mistake Max Reisch was sent off on the expedition with a 'long transmission' differential designed to facilitate higher speeds. Max Reisch describes in detail these alarming breakdowns, which on three occasions threatened the success of the expedition.

After 19 months, the Steyr 100 finally made it back to Europe, where Max Reisch managed to keep it going through all the upheavals of the war and the postwar period, just as he had driven it triumphantly over the rough roads of Asia.

The round-the-world car built in 1934 still goes on exhibition, and is a favourite with the media on the subject of historic vintage cars.

Peter Reisch
February 2017
tr. AF

Also from Veloce Publishing –

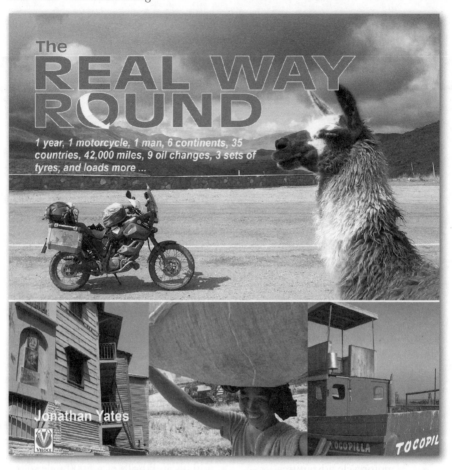

A pictorial diary of a once-in-a-lifetime motorcycle trip across 35 countries on a
Yamaha Ténéré XT660, and a modern practical guide to motorcycling round the
world – what to do first, what to plan for, and how to cope with the unexpected.
Features stunning photography, details of bike modifications, route maps, points of
interest, and practical guidance on freighting a bike.

ISBN: 978-1-845842-94-9
Hardback • 25x25cm • 224 pages • 692 colour pictures

For more information and price details, visit our website at www.veloce.co.uk
• email: info@veloce.co.uk • Tel: +44(0)1305 260068

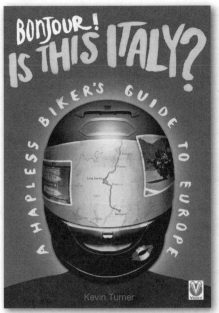

Following his dismissal from a job he never should have had, the author packs a tent, some snacks, and a suit, and sets out on a two-wheeled adventure across Europe. With no idea where he's going, and only two very large and confusing maps to rely on, he heads out to prove that planning and forethought are the very antithesis of a motorcycle adventure.

ISBN: 978-1-845843-99-1
Paperback • 21x14.8cm • 144 pages
129 colour and b&w pictures

Critically acclaimed author Kevin Turner heads off on another ill-thought out adventure, this time aiming his heavily laden Kawasaki north towards the towering waterfalls of Norway, before heading east on a long and treacherous journey to Moscow. This fascinating adventure – part sprint, part marathon – charts the perils, pitfalls and thrills of a 6000-mile solo motorcycle journey across Europe, Scandinavia and into Asia. The author's observations and anecdotes transform this motorcycle guidebook into a laugh-a-minute page turner, which inspires and entertains in equal measure.

ISBN: 978-1-845846-22-0
Paperback • 21x14.8cm • 160 pages
134 colour pictures

A Life Awheel

—— The 'auto' biography of W de Forte ——

Wilberforce de Forte

A veteran motoring journalist's extraordinary life, told through delightfully eccentric stories and charming diary extract. This unique book is packed with fascinating stories about classic cars and motorcycles, set in a bygone world, and properly fixed in time.

(*Fiction*)

ISBN: 978-1-845848-44-6
Paperback • 21x14.8cm • 288 pages • 5 b&w pictures

For more information and price details, visit our website at www.veloce.co.uk
• email: info@veloce.co.uk • Tel: +44(0)1305 260068

INDEX

Air France 154
Alexander the Great 9, 81
Allenby, General 25
Amanullah, King of Afghanistan 73
Anglo-Indians 91, 93, 106
Anglo-Iranian Oil Company 39, 43,
    47
Automobile Association (Britain) 100
Automobile Club of China 228, 230
Automobile Club of Palestine 23

Bamiyan monastery 76, 77
Borghese, Prince Scipione 186
British Petroleum 39
Burmah Oil Company 107, 110, 111

Chiang Kai Shek 208, 224
Croisière jaune, La (Citroën
    expedition) 55, 180, 186

Deutsche Automobil-Club 275
Dietrich, Bruno 9, 10, 17, 100
Differential gearbox 15, 97
    breaks in Mexico 273
    breaks in Thailand 151
    Mr Blair's version 273, 274
    photo 171
    replaced in Luang Prabang 167
'Dutch woman' 91

Eurasia-Fahrgesellschaft 182

Firdowsi 45

Ford Motor Company 204, 274, 275

General Motors 58
Genghis Khan 38, 183
Götzl, Paul 17
Greyhound buses 261, 269
Gurkhas 77, 78

Hahmann, Helmuth 15, 16, 23
    advises tourist 244
    diary of stay at monastery 138-140
    fever 130, 136
    girls 91,121, 182
    jailed 48
    shoots lizard 32
Hedin, Sven 17, 186
Hejaz railway 26

Ibn Saud 27
Iraq Petroleum Company 24, 26-28

Jentschke, Karl 14
Johannsen family 88, 91
Junkers aircraft 182, 183

Khayyam, Omar 41
Kinugasa, Teinosuke 252

Lawrence, TE 64
Letters of recommendation 17, 24, 38,
    40, 75, 165, 170, 181, 185, 189, 191

Mao Zedong 208, 217

287

Marco Polo 226
May, Karl 56
Mercedes 208
Micheline, rail car 179, 184
Missionaries 106, 121, 123, 128, 141
   with beards 192, 193, 195, 197,
    199-201, 203, 216
Mix, Tom 107
Monsoon 86, 110, 191

Nairn Transport Company 23,
Niedermayer, Oskar von 64

ÖAMTC (Austrian Automobile Club)
   16, 100, 228
Opium 117, 125, 133, 136-138, 143,
   211

Porsche, Ferdinand 14, 278
Puch motorcycle ('India-Puch') 10, 12,
   13, 31, 38, photo 267

Quetta earthquake 38, 89

Reisch, Max
   beard 72, 189, 195, 203, 216, 232
   death and centenary 277
   design for car 14
   flies over Kolkata 97
   forty hours at the wheel 274
   has tooth extracted 188
   injury 20, 37, 38
   Japanese driving licence 242
   jaundice 275
   malaria 112, 115
   motorcycle trips 9, 161
   smokes opium 136, 137
   University of Lucknow 93, 96
Royal Geographic Society 180

Sao Kaung Tai (Sawbwa of Keng-Tung)
   119, 132-135
Schneider, Hannes 251
Schroll, Hannes 258, 260

Semperit tyres 190
Shah Abbas 39
Shah of Persia 10, 49
Shell Oil 190, 221
Siemens 182, 183
Siemens-Schuckert 68
Silk Road 13, 38
Sondhi, Professor 84, 85
Sport- und Turnfront (Austrian Sports
   Authority) 101, 128
Steyr 100 car 8, 11, 12
   autographed 96, 132
   breakdown in Mexico 273
   breakdown in Thailand 151
   conversion 14
   crash photo 265
   crashes 276
   damaged by mould 184
   design history 278-282
   dismantled, shipped on Mekong river
    164, 173
   exhibited in Dallas 270
   faults 97
   ground clearance 86,124
   in sand 33
   later history 277
   puncture 43
   on mountain path in India 83
   serviced in Burma 111
   stuck in water 127, 128
   resized in Baghdad 31
   shipped to Japan 233
   tested in Japan 238
   thermosyphon cooling 25
Steyr-Daimler-Puch AG 7, 12, 228,
   271, 278-281
Stratil-Sauer, Gustav 75

Tichy, Herbert 23, 31, 39
The Lives of a Bengal Lancer (film) 79
Tung oil 134

Zoroastrians 53